The Accountant's Guide
to Corporation, Partnership,
and Agency Law

Recent Titles from Quorum Books

Managing Employee Rights and Responsibilities
Chimezie A. B. Osigweh, Yg., editor

The Coming Crisis in Accounting
Ahmed Belkaoui

Managing Human Service Organizations
Lynn E. Miller, editor

Behavioral Accounting: The Research and Practical Issues
Ahmed Belkaoui

Personnel Policies and Procedures for Health Care Facilities: A Manager's Manual and Guide
Eugene P. Buccini and Charles P. Mullaney

Designing the Cost-Effective Office: A Guide for Facilities Planners and Managers
Jack M. Fredrickson

The Employment Contract: Rights and Duties of Employers and Employees
Warren Freedman

Lobbying and Government Relations: A Guide for Executives
Charles S. Mack

U.S. Protectionism and the World Debt Crisis
Edward John Ray

The Social and Economic Consequences of Deregulation: The Transportation Industry in Transition
Paul Stephen Dempsey

The Accountant's Guide to Corporation, Partnership, and Agency Law

SIDNEY M. WOLF

QUORUM BOOKS

New York
Westport, Connecticut
London

Library of Congress Cataloging-in-Publication Data

Wolf, Sidney M.
   The accountant's guide to corporation, partnership, and agency law
/ Sidney M. Wolf.
      p.   cm.
   Includes index.
   ISBN 0–89930–281–5 (lib. bdg. : alk. paper)
      1. Corporation law—United States.   2. Partnership—United States.
   3. Agency (Law)—United States.   I. Title.
   KF1355.W587   1989
   346.73'066—dc19   89–3784
   [347.30666]

British Library Cataloguing in Publication Data is available.

Library of Congress Catalog Card Number: 89–3784
ISBN: 0–89930–281–5

First published in 1989 by Quorum Books

Greenwood Press, Inc.
88 Post Road West, Westport, Connecticut 06881

Printed in the United States of America

The paper used in this book complies with the
Permanent Paper Standard issued by the National
Information Standards Organization (Z39.48–1984).

10 9 8 7 6 5 4 3 2 1

To my sister Maureen,
whose friendship has meant a great deal to me in recent years.

Contents

Part III: Agency

Introduction

Often when a person associates an accountant with a legal subject, that subject is federal tax law because of the major role accountants play in preparing income tax returns. But many accountants experience the law well beyond the Federal Tax Code, and this encounter is chiefly in the area of business law. Business law is important enough to the accounting profession to be part of the Uniform CPA Examination, the passage of which is a precondition to becoming a Certified Public Accountant. Among the most important facets of business law with which accountants must have a significant understanding is the law of business associations. The three major forms of business associations are corporations, partnerships, and agency. This book is about the law as it concerns these three forms of business associations.

There are many books available to the accounting profession on tax law. There are few books for accountants concerned with business associations. This book attempts to fill that void.

The author of this book is not an accountant, but rather an attorney. During part of the time this book was being written, the author was engaged in a law practice heavily concerned with business law matters and, as a result, dealt frequently with the accountants employed by clients of the author's firm. This contact with accountants gave the author a clear idea of what accountants want and need to know about the law of corporations, partnerships, and agency. Accountants should know about the crucial elements of these areas of the law but not in the detail required of attorneys. The book strives to be a clearly-written, well-organized primer on the subjects it covers but does not pursue oversimplification that talks down to accountants, who are members of a profession known for the degree of detail and sophistication it can handle.

Business is organized and functions in accordance with principles of law. Lack of knowledge of the law is no excuse for mistakes, and a lack of knowledge can cause problems, even disaster, for the accountant's client. In performing professional services for clients, the accountant must have an adequate knowledge of the law of business associations. As an attorney, it is difficult for the author to admit that many older accountants have as much knowledge in this area of the law as sophisticated attorneys who practice it. Good, experienced accountants know that they must be able to see a legal question or situation and understand that preventative, remedial, or other measures need to be taken. Accountants are not a substitute for attorneys, but they often provide the best early warning to alert clients that an attorney needs to be called in.

Three parts comprise this book. Part I (chapters 1–7), covers corporations, Part II (chapters 8–12) covers partnerships, and Part III (chapters 13–15) covers agency. The law of these subjects cannot be found in one single source readily understandable to the accountant. For any one of these topics of law, the source comes from many places—federal laws, state laws, uniform laws, common law, and judicial decisions, commonly referred to as case law. The purpose of this book is to provide a current, accurate, comprehensive, in-depth, lucid, and informationally sound reference of the law of business associations specifically for the accountant. The author earnestly hopes this book fulfills its purpose and is of substantial assistance to the accountant.

PART I

Corporations

1

Nature, Promotion, Formation, and Powers

NATURE OF THE CORPORATION

Definition

A corporation is a legal entity created in accordance with a state incorporation statute to accomplish some purpose that is authorized by its charter or the governing statute. The word corporation is derived from the Latin word "corpus," which means body. A key feature of the corporation is its existence as a legal entity, the fact that it is recognized as a legal "person." This legally recognized artificial person has most of the rights, capabilities, and obligations possessed by a real person. In conducting a business, for example, these rights include the right to own, control, and convey property; carry on a commercial enterprise; sue or be sued; be subject to criminal prosecution; and pay taxes. A corporation, when properly formed, exists in the eyes of the law as an entity or separate being from its owners, who are usually called *shareholders* or *stockholders*.

Sources of Corporation Law

A corporation is an artificial person authorized to exist by state law, usually called an *incorporation statute* or a *general corporation* law. Each state has such a statute that establishes incorporation requirements, rules for financing a corporation, the rights and duties of directors and shareholders, and the procedure for dissolving the corporation. These statutes differ from state to state in various regards—some major, others minor. Most states have been influenced by the *Model Business Corporation Act*, which was first drafted by the American Bar Association in 1946 and subsequently revised. The Model Act has been partially or substantially adopted by a majority of states, with the notable exceptions of California and Delaware. In the remaining states, the basic principles of corporation law are sufficiently similar enough to each other and the Model Act that it is possible to generalize about their key features. However, unless otherwise indicated, the material presented in this chapter is based on the provisions of the widely adopted and extremely influential Model Act.

Most but not all of the law concerning corporations is in a state's incorporation statute. Some common law principles have made their way into corporation law. State court decisions and state constitutional provisions also provide some of the content comprising the total body of the corporation law. Apart from general incorporation statutes concerned with the formation of the corporation, the states have adopted laws for the purpose of regulating, and often restricting, the business activities of existing corporations after they are formed. These laws are state regulatory statutes and include securities laws (called "blue-sky" laws) regulating the issuance and sale of stock and other corporate securities; corporate tax legislation; antimonopoly laws, portions of the Uniform Commercial Code (UCC) that deal with the transfer of corporate securities and the use of stock as borrowing security; laws regulating out-of-state (foreign) corporation business activity within the state; and laws specially regulating certain kinds of corporations like banks, public utilities, and insurance companies.

Federal law also is significantly relevant to corporate activities. The U.S. constitution extends to the corporation, of course. For example, federal courts have determined that a corporation is a "person" entitled to due process of law within the Fifth and Fourteenth amendments of the U.S. constituton. The most significant impact of federal law is found in the form of antitrust, labor, and securities laws for regulating the activities of corporations in these areas. Two federal securities laws in particular have a significant relationship to corporations, and these are the Securities Act of 1933 and the Securities Exchange Act (SEA) of 1934. These acts regulate public corporations in the issuing and selling of their shares of stock. Taxation is a primary concern of any business, and the Internal Revenue Code governs corporate taxation. The Foreign Corrupt Practices Act regulates international corporate ethics and disclosures.

Characteristics of the Corporation

Corporations have some significant attributes that define them and make them attractive as a business form. The principal attributes of a corporation are that it (1) is a legal entity, (2) has limited liability for its owners (shareholders), (3) is a creation of state law, (4) has freely transferable ownership (shares of stock), (5) has continuous existence, and (6) has centralized management.

Legal Entity

As noted before, the corporation is recognized as a legal entity that has a legal existence of its own. It is a person in the eyes of the law, and, although it is really an artificial person, it has virtually all the rights and liabilities of a natural person. It is a legal entity that is separate and distinct from its owners, with rights and liabilities entirely distinct from theirs. A partnership or sole proprietorship, in contrast, does not have a separate legal existence. The only legal existence of these two forms of business organization is in the rights and liabilities of their owners. A corporation can own property, make contracts, sue and be sued, pay taxes, be subjected to criminal prosecution, and generally perform all the normal functions that an individual can perform. By comparison, partnerships do not pay taxes and are not subject to criminal prosecution. Corporate property belongs to the corporation, not to the stockholders, even though they are the owners of the corporation. Corporate liabilities are the liabilities of the corporation not its stockholders, the result being that the stockholders have limited liability. The separate legal entity that characterizes the corporation is respected whether one individual stockholder owns all the shares or thousands of people do.

A corporation has constitutional rights, although not nearly to the same extent as does a natural person. Because the corporation is considered a person, it is protected under the constitutional provisions that prohibit unreasonable searches and seizures, guarantee due process and equal protection under the law, and extend the right not to be tried twice for the same offense (double jeopardy). On the other hand, because the corporation does not have all the constitutional rights of a natural person, it does not enjoy the privilege against self-incrimination under the Fifth Amendment.

Limited Liability

One of the most important effects of treating the corporation as a specific and separate legal entity is that generally the owners (stockholders) and managers (officers and directors) are not personally liable for corporate debts. Moreover, stockholders are not normally liable for the acts of the corporation's directors, officers, or employees. The investor usually sees an advantage in choosing corporations over other forms of business organizations because the stockholder's potential loss is limited to his investment in the corporation's shares. In a partnership or sole proprietorship the owner is personally liable for the business's debts, something called *unlimited liability*. In sum, a stockholder may, at most, lose his investment in the corporation, but the creditors of the business that is incorporated cannot reach the stockholder's personal assets.

Creature of State Law

A corporation's existence and status as a legal entity—as an artificial person—is conferred by the state. The corporation is a creature of state law, deriving its existence and all of its powers from the state where it is incorporated. The first and essential step in the formation of the corporation is the filing of articles of incorporation with the state. If the articles are properly filed and have the proper contents, the business will be granted a *certificate of incorporation* by the state authorizing it to exist as a corporation. A corporation's charter, the *articles of incorporation*, and the provisions under which the corporation is formed constitute a contract between it and the state. A corporation can do no more than it is authorized to do by state incorporation and regulatory laws and the charter that has been approved by the state.

Free Transferability of Corporate Shares

The ownership of a corporation is divided into shares, each of which represents a proportionate ownership interest in the corporation and which can be freely transferred. The transfer of a sole proprietorship or partnership interest is a complicated transaction requiring paperwork, permission, notice, and other legal steps. An ownership share is generally evidenced by a *stock certificate*. To transfer the shares, the owner needs only to endorse and deliver the stock certificate to the transferee.

Continuous Existence

A corporation continues regardless of the death, incapacity, or withdrawal of any of its directors, officers, or shareholders and regardless of the transfer of ownership when stock is transferred by a shareholder. This is completely different from a partnership or sole proprietorship, which ends when the owner dies, becomes incapacitated, or transfers an ownership interest. Unless its duration is specifically limited in the articles of incorporation, the corporation can go on forever or until it is properly dissolved. A few states limit the duration of a corporation or certain kinds of businesses that incorporate, but permit renewal of the term.

Centralized Management

Management of a corporation is in the hands of a management group consisting of directors and officers, who need not be shareholders. This centralized form of management authorized by incorporation statutes is unlike the management of a partnership or sole proprietorship, both of which are managed by their owners. While the shareholder owners of a corporation select and remove directors, they have virtually no control over the day-to-day operations of the corporation.

Classification of Corporations

Corporations may be classified as private, public, public service, special services, profit, nonprofit, domestic, foreign, professional, closely held, holding, or Subchapter S.

Private Corporations

Private corporations are organized by private parties for other than governmental purposes that may include charitable or benevolent (nonprofit) purposes or commercial (profit) purposes. Most corporations are private corporations. The private corporation may be a *stock corporation* or a *nonstock corporation*. In a stock corporation, shares of stock are issued, and the company may distribute dividends to the shareholders. A nonstock corporation is every other kind of private corporation that has a membership rather than shareholders. Private corporations are often called ''public,'' which in business parlance is a shorthand term for ''publicly held corporations'' whose stock is sold to the public or traded on a stock exchange.

Public Corporations

A public corporation is organized for governmental purposes and usually consists of substate political units or subdivisions of government or entities concerned with some special public purpose or with provision of some public benefit. Public corporations are so called because they are established or authorized by a state, federal, or other government for governmental puposes. Cities, towns, counties, villages, school districts, sanitary districts, or other territorial divisions of the state are often incorporated pursuant to state laws. Examples of public corporations created for some special public purpose include the Federal Deposit Insurance Corporation, the Federal Land Bank, and the Corporation for Public Broadcasting. Management of these entities does not answer to shareholders but instead to government-appointed boards. A public corporation can also be established to operate a business providing a public benefit, such as the Tennessee Valley Authority or a state toll road. As noted above, the term "public corporation" (shorthand for publicly held corporation) is often applied to private corporations whose stock is sold to the public or traded on stock exchanges.

Public Service Corporation

A public service or quasi-public corporation is a term that is largely meant to cover public utilities and financial service businesses. These corporations are private for-profit corporations that provide basic services upon which the public is particularly dependent or which so significantly affect the public interest that they need to be subject to extensive regulation. Examples of public utilities in this category of corporations include those supplying gas, electricity, water, and telephone services. As a result of the general importance of the utilities to the public, they are usually given monopolistic privileges and special powers such as eminent domain. Public service or quasi-public corporations are also heavily regulated because of the public's heavy dependence on their important services. In most states the quasi-public corporations are formed under general business corporation statutes, but a regulatory body usually must approve the articles of incorporation before they can be filed with the state official responsible for accepting filings.

Special Service Corporations

Some corporations provide specialized functions that are of significant public interest and require extensive regulation. Corporations formed for transportation, savings and loans, banking, and insurance are examples. These corporations are subject to separate regulatory and incorporation statutes. Their activities are normally regulated extensively by an administrative agency.

For-Profit Corporations

A for-profit corporation is founded for the purpose of operating a business for a profit. The profits, to the extent they are not reinvested, are distributed to the shareholders in the form of *dividends*. A profit corporation is expected to make profits, but it is not required to distribute them to shareholders, that is, to declare dividends. Whether or not shareholders receive dividends is up to the discretion of the directors. A for-profit corporation is established in accordance with the general business incorporation statute in the state, such as the Model Act. For-profit corporations can either be publicly traded or privately traded. The shares of publicly traded corporations are bought and sold by members of the public. Publicly traded corporations usually are the largest and best-known corporations. Nonpublicly traded corporations constitute the vast number of corporations and usually are small businesses. The most common type of nonpublicly traded corporations is the *close* and *closely held* corporation, consisting of a small number of shareholders who are usually friends, relatives, or close business associates. The closely held corporation is described below.

Nonprofit Corporations

Nonprofit corporations are formed for charitable, religious, educational, social, fraternal, or civic purposes. Schools, churches, colleges, service organizations, libraries, athletic clubs, and fraternities are examples of nonprofit corporations. A nonprofit corporation may make a profit, but the profit cannot be distributed to its members and instead must be used exclusively for the purpose for which the group was organized. In fact some nonprofit corporations run profit-making businesses. *Mutual companies* are special forms of nonprofit corporations; the kinds of businesses that can be formed as mutual companies include banks, thrift institutions, and insurance companies. Mutual companies are considered nonprofits because they are made of members rather than stockholders and their earnings must be reinvested in the business rather than distributed to the members. Nonprofit organizations are usually run by boards of trustees, rather than directors, and they have members, not shareholders. Special tax considerations are given to nonprofits. Special procedures normally apply to incorporation of nonprofit corporations, with detailed scrutiny given to the spending and raising of money for the enterprise. Nonprofit corporations are allowed to obtain capital by issuing bonds or other debt securities. Usually the approval of an appropriate state regulatory agency is required to issue such securities. This chapter will not address nonprofit corporations.

Domestic Corporations

A corporation is called a domestic corporation in the state where it is incorporated.

Foreign and Alien Corporations

A corporation is referred to as a foreign corporation in all states except the state in which it was incorporated. For instance, a corporation that is incorporated in Iowa is a domestic corporation in Iowa and a foreign corporation in the other forty-nine states. A corporation incorporated under the laws of another nation is called an alien corporation. A state may exclude a foreign corporation from doing intrastate business in the state but not from conducting business in that state as part of the interstate business. A state can also impose reasonable conditions on a foreign corporation doing intrastate business in the state. Before *doing business* within a state, a foreign corporation must obtain a license or certificate of authority to do so from that state. Doing business means actively engaging in multiple transactions for the purpose of financial gain. A single transaction or activity does not constitute doing business within the state. As part of the license or certificate requirements, a foreign corporation must designate a local registered agent, file annual reports with the state, and adhere to the restrictions upon the use of certain corporate names and types of businesses permitted in that state. A foreign corporation that transacts business without filing a certificate of authority in the state is subject to significant penalties. For instance the foreign corporation cannot enforce its contracts in that state without filing a certificate, although it can defend a suit. A foreign corporation is subject to fines if it fails to qualify to do business in that state.

Professional Corporations

Most states allow certain professionals to form what are called professional corporations. This business form was primarily created to permit professionals to take advantage of federal tax advantages relating to establishing pension and retirement plans available to corporate employees. Another feature of professional corporations is some degree of limited liability granted professionals that is lacking in the partnerships in which they traditionally joined together to practice their profession. The kinds of professionals normally allowed to group together as shareholders in professional corporations include doctors, lawyers, veternarians, dentists, architects, and accountants. Professional corporations are formed under statutes that differ from general business incorporation laws. These statutes often limit ownership of shares of stock to licensed professionals. The corporate status of the professionals is indicated by using letters P.A. (Professional Association), P.C. (Professional Corporation), or S.C. (Service Corporation) after the corporate name.

Close or Closely Held Corporations

A closely held corporation is a private corporation whose stock is held by either a single stockholder or a small, closely knit group of shareholders, usually close family relations or friends. The small number of shareholders is usually active in managing the business and function much like partners or, if there is just one shareholder, function like a sole proprietorship. The stock of a close corporation is not available for sale to the public. The shareholders usually enter into a *buy-sell agreement* with each other at the time of incorporation to keep the stock from being obtained by outsiders. Since the shares of a close corporation are not offered for sale to the public, raising capital is not usually the reason for incorporation. Instead, the close corporation is formed to obtain the advantages of limited liability or a tax benefit while at the same time retaining the type of control that marks a partnership or sole proprietorship. If substantially all the stock in the close corporation is held by members of the same family, that corporation sometimes is referred to as a *family corporation*. Professional corporations are another form of close corporation. General incorporation statutes originally did not recognize or accommodate the close corporation as a different kind of corporation requiring special treatment and thus it is difficult to organize a close corporation under a statute primarily designed to apply to publicly held corporations. Many states have altered their general incorporation statutes to allow the flexibility to create and operate close corporations. These measures include allowing incorporation by a smaller number of persons, allowing one director, and eliminating the requirement of formal meetings.

Subchapter S Corporations

A subchapter S corporation is a kind of closely held corporation, which is taxed in many respects like a partnership in that its owners, the shareholders, rather than the corporation, are taxed directly. The subchapter S corporation is not established under state laws, but instead is a creation of the Internal Revenue Code. The Internal Revenue Code allows the shareholders of the closed corporation to unanimously agree to free the corporation from corporate income tax on its profits. Instead the shareholders will, as individuals, pay a pro rata share of the profits or losses of a subchapter S corporation. In order for a closed corporation to acquire subchapter S status, it must have only one class of stock, consist of no more than twenty-five shareholders who are American citizens or resident aliens, and derive most of its income from an active goods or service business rather than a passive source, such as investments.

PROMOTION OF THE CORPORATION

Promotion consists of individuals starting the corporation and obtaining the capital necessary to finance it through getting subscribers to purchase stock in the new venture.

The person who brings about the birth of the corporation is called a *promoter*. It is the promoter(s) who takes the beginning steps to organize and finance the corporation. The promoter secures a charter, arranges for financing, and makes necessary arrangements to obtain equipment, services, land, buildings, personnel, licenses, leases, and inventory that the corporation will need to begin operations. The promoter also prepares and files the certificate of incorporation, which is necessary to the legal formation of the corporation. Once the corporation has received its certificate of incorporation and is in actuality incorporated, the promoter's organization task is done. A promoter can be any legal person, including a corporation or partnership.

Promoter Financing Through Stock Subscriptions

In order to get a business started, capital is usually required. The most important function of the promoter in launching a corporation is raising capital. In addition to securing loans, a common way to raise capital is to sell ownership in the future business to get it going. This is done by assembling investors who wish to purchase stock prior to incorporation of the business. The promoter seeks out persons, groups, or entities who will submit offers to purchase shares of stock in the corporation. One who offers to puchase stock is called a *subscriber*, and the offer itself is called a *subscription*. An existing corporation may also seek stock subscriptions. When a corporation has not yet been formed, the promoter is seeking *pre-incorporation subscriptions*. A prospectus prepared by the promoter normally precedes his solicitation of subscriptions. A subscriber becomes a shareholder when the corporation comes into existence. The sub-scribers may include the promoter alone or other parties.

Because the corporation has not yet been formed in the case of a pre-incorporation subscription, the important question arises as to if and when the subscriber can back out of his offer to purchase stock. States hold one of three different viewpoints as to whether a pre-incorporation is revocable by a subscriber and when. The traditional view, which had been adopted by a majority of courts in the past, is that a pre-incorporation subscription is a continuing offer to purchase stock from a nonexisting entity and hence can be revoked any time before incorporation because the corporation is not yet in existence. Incorporation is said to occur when the state issues a certificate of incorporation to the business. A smaller number of jurisdictions regard a pre-incorporation subscription as a contract among the subscribers is obtained. The Model Act adopts a compromise; namely, subscribers may not revoke their subscription agreements for up to six months unless the agreements provide otherwise or all the other subscribers consent.

Promoter's Pre-Formation Contracts

Promoters will negotiate contracts in anticipation of the creation of the cor-poration and necessary to its eventual operation. These agreements can include leases, purchase orders, employment contracts, or sales contracts. The corpo-ration is not normally liable on a promoter's pre-incorporation contract, while the promoter is normally personally liable for such pre-incorporation contracts because the promoter is not an agent of the corporation. An agent requires a principal, and one cannot be an agent for a nonexistent principal, for example, a corporation that has not yet come into existence. Promoters cannot bind the corporation even if they will be its controlling stockholders. Thus, the promoter is personally liable on pre-incorporation contracts if the corporation is never formed or fails to act on the contract. The promoter is personally liable on pre-incorporation contracts even if he enters into the contract in the corporation's name and clearly indicates the contract is for the corporation.

There are exceptions under which a promoter can completely escape liability for pre-incorporation contracts. One exception exists in *contingency contracts*. In a contingency contract the promoter is not liable if the contract's performance is clearly made conditional on the corporation coming into being and adopting the contract. Another exception is through a *novation agreement*. In a novation the promoter, the other contracting third party, and the corporation, once it is formed, enter into an agreement whereby the corporation agrees to substitute for the promoter in the performance of the contract.

The corporation, after it is formed, can become bound to the promoter's contracts with third parties if it either adopts or ratifies the contract. There are two kinds of adoption—express or implied. An express adoption is formal adop-tion of the contract by the board of directors. An implied adoption occurs when the corporation accepts the benefits of the promoter's pre-incorporation contract, such as allowing a contract to continue to be performed by the other contracting third party for the corporation after it is incorporated. Even when the new corporation expressly or implicitly adopts the promoter's contracts, the promoter remains personally liable until the pre-incorporation contracts are fully performed or a novation (described above) is entered into by the parties. If the promoter is held liable, the corporation must indemnify him to the extent of the benefits it has received from the performance of the contract by the third party.

The corporation is also not automatically liable to reimburse promoters for the expenses of its own incorporation, such as filing fees or franchise taxes, nor is it liable for the attorney fees incurred in formation or for compensation promoters for selling stock. However, the board of directors can afterwards agree to voluntarily pay the promoters for the corporation's formation expenses. Furthermore, the corporate charter or a statute might impose the cost of the pre-incorporation expenses of the promoter upon the corporation once it is formed.

Promoter's Fiduciary Duty

The promoter has a fiduciary responsibility for other promoters, subscribers, and the corporation that is to be formed. This fiduciary relationship means the promoter owes them a duty of full disclosure, good faith, and fair dealing. A promoter breaches his fiduciary duty if he sells property to the corporation for more than its value or fails to disclose his interest in the transaction—in other words—if the promoter makes a secret profit at the expense of the corporation. In this case, most courts allow the corporation to recover only the overvaluation (the unfair profit). A minority of courts allows the corporation to recover the entire profit. All courts allow the corporation to rescind the transaction. A common example of secret profits is the purchase of property by the promoter in anticipation of selling at a profit to the prospective corporation once it is formed. A promoter can avoid liability to the corporation if he fully discloses his interest in the transaction and the shareholders unanimously *ratify* the deal after the full disclosure. The promoters are also not liable if they took all the stock in the corporation for themselves, under the theory that they cannot be liable for concealing something from themselves.

Promoters are considered partners for the purpose of forming the corporation. They thus owe each other the fiduciary duty partners owe each other, including the duty not to secretly profit at the expense of each other.

Fraud Against Future Shareholders

Promoters owe a fiduciary duty to future shareholders. A common example of a breach of this duty is stock promotion fraud by the promoter. This occurs when a promoter starts a corporation with few, if any, assets, overvalues the assets, and then transfers the overvalued property to the corporation in exchange for its shares. In such cases the transaction is approved by a dummy board of directors appointed by the promoters and all the shareholders, who again, are the promoters. Because the property is overvalued, the promoter gets more shares than he should or the shares have a worth that is far in excess of their true value. The promoter is then able to sell the shares for more and can pull out of the corporation, leaving the corporation with overvalued assets for which it paid too much and leaving the new shareholders with stock for which they paid too much.

There are two kinds of lawsuits that can be brought against promoters for stock fraud. First, individual shareholders who are defrauded can bring a suit to recover the unfair profit of the promoter-seller. Individual fraud actions are usually ineffective when there is a large number of individual shareholders proceeding singly against the promoter-seller. Second, the corporation can bring a usually more effective lawsuit on behalf of newly subscribing shareholders. There are two views on the promoter's liability when such a corporate action is pursued. One is called the *Massachusetts Rule*, followed by a majority of courts, which allows the corporation to recover the promoter's wrongful profit gained from misrepresenting the value of property given in exchange of stock, provided that it was clear at the time of the transaction that the promoter-seller contemplated selling to the public the shares obtained. The other view provides no relief and is called the *Federal Rule*, which is followed by a minority of courts. Under the Federal Rule the shareholders are deemed to have no rights because they were not shareholders at the time of the transaction and at the time of the transaction there was full disclosure to all the shareholders.

FORMATION OF THE CORPORATION

Formalities and Procedural Requirements of Incorporation

The word *incorporation* refers to the procedural requirements and process that must be followed to create the corporation.

Selection of State for Incorporation

As pointed out previously, the corporation is an artificial entity that the state allows to be created and recognizes. The first step of the incorporation process is selecting the state of incorporation. For small corporations the business is usually incorporated in the state where it is operated, and since the vast majority of corporations are small closely held corporations, incorporation is where the shareholders live and intend to do business. However, for larger and more sophisticated businesses that are national and regional in operations, there are important legal and practical factors to consider in selecting the state of incorporation. Often a closely held business will incorporate where it does most of its business. However, a corporation can be formed in one state, have its headquarters in another state, and conduct its operations in these or other states. Such sophisticated businesses often choose to incorporate where the corporation laws are liberal or most advantageous. One such state is Delaware, a state where many of the nation's largest businesses are incorporated, although they usually maintain their corporate headquarters elsewhere and conduct only a fraction of their business in this small state. Delaware is desirable because, in addition to its liberal incorporation law, its courts have thoroughly interpreted its corporation statutes and eliminated the uncertainty as to the statutes' meaning. Other states whose courts have similar expertise concerning corporate issues are chosen for incorporation. Many other factors come into play when a business selects a state in which to incorporate. States vary greatly in the liberality of their incorporation laws, organization fees, franchise taxes, income taxes, securities laws, stock issuance and transfer taxes, sales taxes, inventory taxes, labor laws, and business climate.

Incorporators

Incorporators are the persons who apply to the state for the incorporation of a business. The function of the incorporators is to prepare the articles of incorporation and file them with the state as the application for a certificate of incorporation. Usually the promoters will act as incorporators, but they are not required to do so. Subscribers can also act as incorporators, and a few states require each incorporator to be a subscriber. The qualification and number of incorporators vary from state to state. Most states require one or more natural persons at least eighteen or twenty-one years of age. In addition to any natural or actual person, a domestic or foreign corporation can also act as an incorporator. The required number of incorporators varies from state to state. In some states the incorporator must be a citizen of that state, and in others someone from out-of-state can be an incorporator. Many states allow a single incorporator. It is possible in many states for one person to incorporate a business and be the sole shareholder. The services of the incorporator are perfunctory and short-lived, ending with the first organization meeting of the initial board of directors following the issuance of the certificate of incorporation.

Application for Incorporation (Articles of Incorporation)

All states require the drafting and filing with the state a corporate charter, commonly referred to as *articles of incorporation.* The articles describe the organization, powers, and authority of the prospective corporation. In sum, the articles serve as a constitution for the corporation—its basic governing document. A signed set of articles and required filing fees are sent to the Secretary of State or other official designated by the incorporation statute. Some states also require that a certified copy of the articles be filed in the county where the corporation's office is located. And a few states require the articles to be published in a local newspaper. A properly prepared and filed articles of incorporation is needed in order for the state to issue a certificate of incorporation to the incorporators, which begins the legal existence of the corporation. The articles must be executed by the requisite number of incorporators. A few states require the signature of only one incorporator, but most states follow the traditional requirement of three.

Contents of the Articles of Incorporation

In most states the articles filed with the state must include the following:

Name. Subject to certain limitations, the incorporators may select any name. The name must include at its end one of the following terms (or its abbreviation): corporation (Corp.), company (Co.), incorporated (Inc.), or limited (Ltd.). The name cannot be the same or deceptively similar to that of an existing corporation doing business within the state. For example, "General Motors Automobile, Inc." is too close to "General Motors." Before approving a name, the state will run a check of all the corporations on file to determine whether it is the same or similar to the names of other corporations. The Model Act allows parties to reserve a corporate name while assembling the corporation and paperwork for incorporation. The name reservation is filed with the secretary of state, and a fee is paid. The reserved name cannot be used by any other incorporators for a period of up to six months.

Purpose. Most states also have special statutes for incorporation for charitable, religious, educational, or civic purposes. The purpose of the corporation must be stated, but it usually can be stated in broad terms, such as "for general business" or "for business operations" or "to transact any and all lawful business for which a corporation may be incorporated." In most instances, it is best to state the purpose of the corporation in broad terms to avoid the problem of *ultra vires*. The doctrine of *ultra vires* prohibits a corporation from engaging in a business outside the scope of its stated purpose. For nonprofit or charitable corporations, some states require a statement of the means to be used to attain the objectives of the corporation. Although most states allow a corporation to be established for any lawful purpose, some prohibit corporations from practicing medicine, law, or other professions. Many states and the Model Act do not allow banks, savings and loan, public utilities, and insurance companies to be formed under the general incorporation statutes. Most states have special statutes for the incorporation of these types of corporations.

Duration. The life of the incorporation may be perpetual or for a limited time or purpose. Most states allow a corporation to have a perpetual existence. Some states have imposed limitations on the number of years a corporation may exist, the maximum ranging from 20 to 100 years, and allow for renewal or extension. The Model Act specifies the duration of a corporation is perpetual unless the articles specify otherwise. A corporation can be formed for a limited purpose, such as completion of a particular project.

Financial Structure. The quantities, value, and types of the shares of stock the corporation is authorized to issue must be stated in the articles.

The total number of shares of stock to be authorized must be specified. The articles may authorize more shares than the corporation issues. Authorized shares are the maximum number stated in the articles that the corporation can issue; issued shares are the number that are actually put up for sale by the corporation. The board of directors can at any time approve the issuance of authorized shares that have not been issued. Issued shares are called outstanding shares, and outstanding shares that are purchased by the corporation are called treasury shares.

If the shares of stock are to be divided into classes, the class designations, the number of shares in each class, and the limitations and relative rights of the shares in each class must be specified. There are generally two types of stock a company can issue: *preferred* and *common*. Common shares are generally voting shares. Preferred shares give their holders preference in the distribution of dividends or the liquidation of assets. Even these kinds of shares can be of various types, such as *cumulative preferred* shares, which entitle their shareholders to yearly dividends. If cumulative preferred shareholders are not paid one year or for a number of years, their dividends accumulate and they must be paid their cumulative amount before common shareholders get their dividends. If there is a preferred stock to be issued by the corporation, the preference must be stated.

Many states require the *par value* of their shares be stated unless *no par* stock is issued. The true value of the shares will be determined by the market place and par value does not govern the price of the shares, except to represent a minimum price the corporation will take in its sale of the shares. No par stock has no stated par value, that is, no stated dollar floor on the value of the stock.

Place of Business. This designates the name and address of the corporation's primary place of business.

Statutory or Registered Agent. The articles must state the name and address of the person within the state authorized to receive legal notices for the corporation, such as service of process for lawsuits.

Directors. The number and identity of the directors constituting the initial board of directors must be identified for the first year. This first board of directors provides the corporation with a body to govern the company during the short interval between the moment the corporation receives its certificate to begin legal existence and the first annual meeting of the shareholders to elect a new board. In some states the naming of the first board of directors is not required, and they allow the incorporators to have the power of management during this period.

Incorporators. The names and addresses of the incorporators must be stated, along with the number of shares subscribed by each.

Internal Regulation of the Corporation. Many states require provisions concerning the conduct and scheduling of meetings of shareholders and directors, and other measures governing the conduct of the business. Examples of these provisions are location of shareholders' meetings, quorum and voting requirements at the meetings of shareholders and of directors, removal of directors, filling director vacancies, and the like.

Certificate of Incorporation

If the filed articles of incorporation meet the requirements of the law, the state will issue a certificate of incorporation or charter. The certificate represents permission from the state to conduct business as a corporation and begins the legal existence of the corporation. After the certificate is issued, the certificate and an attached copy of the articles of incorporation are returned to the incorporators.

The certificate of incorporation is regarded as a contract formed between the state and the corporation. Article I, Section 10 of the federal constitution provides that no state can pass any law "impairing the obligation of contracts," and this protection applies to contracts between a state and a corporation. In early American law this meant that subsequent state laws regulating business activity could not apply to the corporation since each corporate charter was a product of a state statute passed by the legislature to create the particular corporation. Today, the states have adopted general incorporation laws that expressly reserve the power to amend or repeal the rules governing the corporation in subsequent legislation or regulation. Moreover, the courts have universally adhered to the view that independently of that reservation the corporation is subject to the police power of the state to advance the public health, safety, morals, and general welfare. This means the state can by its regulations modify existing contracts, including corporate charters.

Initial Organization Meeting

Most states require the board of directors named in the articles to hold an organization meeting to adopt bylaws, elect officers, and "transact other business as may come before the meeting." Such other business typically includes issuing shares of stock, approval of preincorporation contracts made by promoters, selection of the corporation's bank, and approval of the form of stock certificate. During this initial organization meeting the board may also consider approval of a corporate seal, which, while not usually required by law, is for practical reasons a good idea since many other statutes require a corporate seal on certain documents for those documents to be valid. In the states where the board of directors is not named in the articles, the incorporators must, as the first act of the organization meeting, elect the directors, who will carry on the rest of the business of an initial organization meeting.

Bylaws

The most important purpose of the initial organization meeting of the directors is the adoption of bylaws, which are the rules that govern the actions of officers and the company operations. Bylaws are not required as part of the incorporation filing nor do they need to be filed with the secretary of state, but as rules for internal management they are necessary for the corporation to operate in a proper and orderly fashion. The bylaws cannot conflict in any way with the articles of incorporation, since the latter are the basic constitution of the business. The bylaws also cannot conflict with the statutes of the state of incorporation. Unless reserved by the shareholders, the power to alter, amend, or repeal the bylaws or adopt new ones is vested in the board of directors.

Mistakes in Formation—Effect

There are many requirements, as described in previous sections, which must be followed to properly form a corporation. Mistakes are sometimes made. The effect of defects in the formation of the corporation range from no effect at all to the business not being recognized as a corporation. When a business is not recognized as a corporation it loses the attributes of "corporateness," the very attributes the founders and subscribers of the business are seeking when trying to incorporate the business. These important attributes that are sought in forming the corporation can be lost because of a defect in its formation and include limited liability for shareholders, perpetual existence, centralized management, and the application of the corporate law of the state of incorporation—all of which are counted on by those individuals forming the corporation and investing in its stock.

Various parties who would find an advantage in a corporation's not having been formed might attack it if it has been formed defectively. Creditors may maintain that the shareholders of the defectively formed corporation are partners with unlimited personal liability for the debts of the business. Debtors who are sued by the business may dispute its capacity to sue as a result of not being properly formed as a corporation. Shareholders who are displeased with the actions of the board of directors or officers could take on management powers if the corporation has not been formed. Subscribers wishing to avoid liability for subscription contracts might claim the proposed corporation never came into being. The business itself might want to deny it became a corporation in order to avoid paying creditors. And a state might contend that the failure to comply with statutory formalities dictates the business forfeit its charter or cease its operations. The consequences of an error in forming the corporation depend on the seriousness of the mistake and, sometimes, on the intent of the people who represent the corporation.

In addressing the issue of defective formation the courts have come to recognize the existence of and to distinguish between three types of corporation: (1) De Jure Corporation; (2) De Facto Corporation; and (3) Corporation by Estoppel. All types have "corporateness." Unless a business fits into one of the three categories it is not a corporation.

De Jure Corporation

A corporation "de jure" means that a corporation exists by virtue of law. The actual corporateness, that is, legal existence, of a de jure corporation cannot be attacked by anyone, including the state in which it was incorporated. This kind of corporation is not defectively organized but instead was formed in strict compliance with all the mandatory provisions of the incorporation statute and fulfilled all the prerequisites for its organization. The Model Act, which most states have adopted, provides that the state's issuance of a certificate of incorporation raises the irrefutable presumption that a de jure corporation has been formed. Note that some mistakes can be made in compliance with the incorporation statute, so long as they are with the *directory* conditions imposed by the statute rather than the *mandatory* conditions. Mandatory provisions use terms like "must" or "shall," while directory provisions use terms like "may."

De Facto Corporation

De facto means "in fact." A corporation de facto is one recognized in fact, as opposed to one recognized in law, as is the case for a corporation de jure. A de facto corporation is formed when a defect in complying with the incorporation statute is substantial enough to deny de jure status to the corporation, but compliance is sufficient enough for the law to recognize that the corporation in fact exists in most cases. The corporate existence of a de facto corporation cannot be challenged by anyone except the state in a *quo warranto* proceeding. Thus, it is a corporation for most purposes. A de facto corporation exists when the incorporators fail to comply in some material respect with the mandatory provisions of an incorporation statute. There are two requirements for a de facto corporation: (1) there must be a good faith attempt to comply with the state's incorporation statute, and (2) the business must have been a "corporate user," that is, must have operated as a corporation. Examples of defects that would cause a de facto corporation to come into existence include an incorrect business address in the articles, a failure of an incorporator to sign the articles, or oversight to file the articles and certificate in the appropriate county recorder's office.

The Model Act provides that the issuance of a certificate of incorporation by the state is conclusive evidence of the legal existence of the corporation against all persons except the state. The state can take an action against a de facto corporation in a quo warranto proceeding, which literally questions "by what right" the corporation has the authority to exist. The state may sue to cancel or revoke the certificate of incorporation on the grounds that the corporation had not complied with the mandatory provisions of the incorporation law. No one else could challenge the existence of the de facto corporation.

Corporation by Estoppel

A corporation by estoppel is treated as formed only against a party for whom it would be unjust to deny the existence of the corporation because that person dealt with the business as if it were a corporation and benefited in some measure. That person is *estopped* from denying the existence of the corporation, although the business does not legally exist as a corporation for the rest of the world. Corporation by estoppel is often used against a third party who dealt with the corporation as if it were valid and then seeks to escape the obligation. An example follows: A person contracts with a defectively formed corporation to buy goods and services from the business and then refuses to pay for them because the provider of the goods and services did not substantially comply with the incorporation statute. The law believes a recipient of goods and services should have to pay for them. Commonly corporation by estoppel is claimed by shareholders to avoid unlimited liability when a creditor dealt only with the corporation.

Disregarding the Corporate Entity—Piercing the Corporate Veil

The major appeal of the corporation as a form of business is liability—its "corporateness" normally shields its officers, directors, and shareholders (especially, the shareholders) from personal liability for contracts, torts, or crimes. The corporation is a separate and distinct legal entity from the people who manage, work for, or own it; and, thus, these people are not liable for the acts of the corporation. However, in some circumstances, a court will refuse to recognize the existence of a de jure corporation in order to hold its shareholders, directors, and officers liable for contracts, torts, or crimes. When this happens, the court is said to be "piercing the corporate veil" associated with the separate corporate existence that shields these parties from liability. In such situations, it does not matter that the corporation has been formed in strict compliance with the incorporation statute and is recognized as a de jure corporation. Piercing the corporate veil, or disregarding the corporate existence, most often happens in the case of a closed corporation (where the separation between the corporation and its owners is paper-thin at best), although it can and does happen in publicly held corporations, too.

Only third parties, not the corporation or its shareholders, can attempt to disregard the corporate identity. Thus a corporation cannot defend a suit by asserting that its entity should be disregarded so that the shareholders, not the corporation, should be the defendant. Some cases hold that all shareholders are jointly and severally liable to creditors when the corporate entity is disregarded. Others require the shareholders to be active; that is, they must have taken part in management or perpetuated the injustice to be personally liable.

A court will not disregard the corporate identity merely because the corporation is formed to obtain the advantages of a corporation, chiefly tax savings for the business or limited liability for shareholders.

The circumstances under which the corporate veil and its protection are disregarded occur when the corporate entity is used to perpetrate a fraud or circumvent the law, to escape contractual obligations; when stockholders mislead outsiders; or when the shareholders and officers themselves disregard the corporate existence and allow use of it as a shield to avoid personal liability.

Fraud, Illegality, or Circumvention of the Law

Courts will disregard the corporate entity when a corporation is formed or used for the purpose of undertaking a fraud or hiding illegal actions. An example would be a sole or principal shareholder of the corporation setting fire to corporate property and the corporation then suing to recover on its insurance policy. Another example would be an alien forming a corporation to buy specific kinds of property that the law prohibits aliens, as individuals, from purchasing. It is not fraud to form a corporation to take advantage of the virtues of this form of business organization, chiefly tax savings or limited liability for shareholders. However, the situations discussed above indicate that there are some instances when the law will not recognize the corporation if it was formed for a motive harmful to society.

Evasion of Contractual Obligations

The corporate entity cannot be used to evade contractual obligations and civil sanctions associated with these obligations nor can it be used to violate public policy, commit frauds, or achieve criminal objectives. An example of using the corporation to evade civil sanctions would be an individual, bound by covenant not to compete, trying to avoid this by forming a corporation and having it compete.

Misleading Outsiders

The corporate identity will be disregarded if by not doing so a court will cause an injustice to creditors or other persons to whom an obligation is owed. These cases occur when a stockholder misleads the creditor into thinking that the stockholder would accept liability for claims or obligations against the corporation.

Disregard of Corporate Existence by Owners and Resulting Injustice

The corporate identity can be pierced by a court under the following two conditions: (1) there is a functional disregard of the separate corporate identity by those owning or running the business, and (2) an injustice would result if the court fails to disregard the entity. The first condition occurs when an *identity of interest and ownership* between the corporation and the shareholders indicates the latter have disregarded the separateness of the corporate entity. In other words the corporation becomes the *alter ego* of its owners; that is, the corporation is merely an extension of the shareholder and his activities. The identity of interest and ownership occurs when the shareholders have intermingled and confused their identities with the corporation's identity. The identity of interest and ownership similarly appears when shareholders fail to conduct the business on a formal corporate basis.

An example of the confusion and intermingling of identities would be shareholders mixing corporate and personal funds or failing to maintain corporate records separate from personal records. Another example is when corporate property, assets, or cash are used for personal as well as corporate purposes. Stockholders who own several corporations may mix up the affairs of these businesses. The failure to conduct the business as a corporation would include instances when the owners fail to issue any stock or observe such formalities as electing directors, holding directors' meetings, or maintaining minutes for meetings of directors or shareholders.

Disregard of the corporate identity by the owners themselves is only one side of the equation a court will consider in deciding whether to pierce the corporate veil. The other side of the equation requires that an injustice would result if the court did not hold the owners of the corporate entity accountable for its obligations or wrongful acts. Most cases require intentional *undercapitalization* to show injustice. A corporation is undercapitalized if it was formed with insufficient capital to meet reasonably expected business obligations. For example, a corporation is formed to offer boating excursions on a scenic lake. The corporation has no assets, but the shareholders want to enjoy the benefit of limited liability protection. Because of the boat captain's negligence, the boat sinks and drowns several passengers. The shareholders will be liable for damages because the corporation was undercapitalized. Adequate insurance is seen by the courts as a major means to cure undercapitalization. Another example of undercapitalization would be when a newly formed corporation buys inventory on credit, the cost of which is far in excess of the capital it has in the bank or available to it from lenders. If the business fails when it cannot sell enough goods to meet its bills, the unpaid corporate creditors who are harmed by the inadequacy of corporate assets may reach the personal assets of the shareholders to satisfy their claim. It should be emphasized that the sufficiency of capitalization is measured at the time the business begins. Thus, a corporation will not be ignored merely because the corporation does not have sufficient assets to pay its creditors.

Although the case law says that both the *identity of interest and ownership* and the *injustice* conditions must exist, the undercapitalization circumstance has been given great importance by the courts and in some courts will pierce the corporate veil upon a showing of undercapitalization alone. It is also possible for the injustice requirement to be satisfied upon a showing of loss to creditors even without undercapitalization. Consequently, a creditor could prevail merely by showing an identity of interest and ownership.

Close Corporations and Parent-Subsidiary Relations

The two most frequently occurring situations in which the courts disregard the corporate veil are *close corporations* and *parent-subsidiary* relationships. It is easy to understand why the corporation entity is disregarded for close corporations, which are predominantly formed by a single individual or by several members of the family who own stock. The joint or active management of such shareholders frequently results in a tendency to ignore corporate formalities. Some corporations form other subsidiary corporations to eliminate the parent corporation's liability. The parent corporation will be liable for the debts or wrongs of its subsidiary under the similar circumstances of a shareholder of a close corporation being liable for the corporation's wrongs or debts. This means a parent corporation is liable for its subsidiary if that subsidiary is being used to perpetrate a fraud or circumvent the law, to escape contractual obligations; when the parent mislead outsiders that it will be liable for the subsidiary; or when the parent corporation itself is disregarding its separate existence from the subsidiary and an injustice would result if the court did not hold the parent liable for its subsidiary's wrongs or obligations. Similarly, the subsidiary may be held responsible for the parent company's wrongs or obligations when the parent is being used to shield the subsidiary. A parent corporation and its subsidiary may be considered one entity rather than two separate corporations when there is intermingling of funds and accounting records, interlocking directorates, failure to observe separate corporate formalities, inadequate capitalization of the subsidiary, domination by the parent to the degree that the subsidiary is merely an agent or instrumentality of the parent, or failure of the two companies to hold themselves out to the public as separate entities. If a subsidiary is in fact operating independently of the parent, its separate identity will be honored. The two corporations will be considered distinct from each other when each is operated by its own management that makes decisions independently of the other.

CORPORATE POWERS

Nature and Limitation of Corporate Powers

A corporation is a creature of law, deriving its existence and all of its powers from the state of incorporation. The constitution and statutes of the state of incorporation are the sources of authority for corporate authority and establish the limits within which a corporation must operate. The corporation can do no more than it is authorized to do by these sources of law.

The powers a corporation confers upon itself are found in its articles of incorporation and bylaws. These self-conferred powers in the charter may be less than those allowed by state statutory and constitutional laws but cannot be greater. Therefore, the power of a corporation is both founded and limited by the laws of a state and its own corporate rules.

All corporations do not have the same scope or kind of powers. For instance, corporations that operate banks, insurance companies, savings and loan associations, and railroads generally have different and special powers—some greater than ordinary corporations, and some lesser.

Express and Implied Powers

A corporation has two kinds of power—express and implied powers. The express powers expressly come from state law (statutes and constitutions) and corporate rules (articles of incorporation and bylaws). The implied powers are those that custom and reasonableness allow to be exercised, such as those powers that are necessary and appropriate to help carry out the corporation's express powers.

Express Statutory Powers

The chief source of express powers is those specified in the general incorporation statute under which a corporation is created. In the Model Act, Section 4, all corporations are automatically granted the following general powers:

1. To exist perpetually unless a limited period is stated in the articles.
2. To sue or be sued in the corporate name.
3. To have a corporate seal.
4. To buy, own, possess, lease, and sell real and personal property.
5. To sell, convey, mortgage, pledge, lease, exchange, transfer, or otherwise dispose of all or any part of its property and assets.
6. To lend money to its employees.
7. To buy, own, vote, pledge, sell, or otherwise deal in securities (stocks and bonds) of other businesses.
8. To make contracts; borrow money, incur liabilities; or issue notes, bonds, or other obligations.
9. To lend money for corporate purposes and hold property as security for loans.
10. To issue stock and certificates representing such stock.
11. To invest its surplus funds and acquire its own shares.
12. To conduct its business and carry on its operations within and outside the state of incorporation.
13. To elect and appoint officers and agents, define their duties, and fix their compensation.
14. To make and alter bylaws, not inconsistent with the articles of incorporation and statute of incorporation, for the administration and regulation of corporate affairs.
15. To make charitable donations.
16. To establish pension plans, profit sharing, stock bonuses, and other incentive plans for directors, officers, and employees.
17. To be a promoter, partner, member, associate, or manager of a partnership, joint venture, trust, or other enterprise.
18. To amend its articles of incorporation.
19. To merge or consolidate with other corporations.
20. To indemnify against personal liability, officers, directors, employees, and agents who act on behalf of the corporation in good faith and without negligence.
21. To conduct any lawful business.
22. To have and exercise all powers necessary and convenient to accomplish the purposes stated in the articles of incorporation.

Express Charter Powers

The corporation can have express powers conferred by the articles of incorporation. The articles cannot permit the corporation to do anything that exceeds or conflicts with the powers allowed by the incorporation statute. The Model Act does not require the articles to restate the powers listed in the incorporation statute or state in detail every particular type of act the corporation can perform. The corporate charter or articles often contain a broad and general provision that simply grants the corporation all the powers that the law permits it to exercise, rather than specifying in detail the corporate powers or restating the powers conferred by the incorporation statute. The articles may require the corporation to do less than the incorporation statute allows, for example, when the company's shareholders vote to amend the articles to prohibit charitable contributions, which is allowed by most incorporation statutes.

Implied Powers

Corporations have the implied power to do things that are reasonably necessary to carry out the express powers and purposes of the corporation. Merely because an action or endeavor is not specified by the articles of incorporation does not mean the corporation does not have the power to engage in that act or endeavor. Implied powers are used to fill in the details because the statutes and articles usually provide only the general powers. Another term for implied powers is *incidental powers*. Implied powers are determined by custom. The doctrine of implied powers is resorted to when defending against claims that an act or purpose of a corporation is not stated or exceeds those stated in the incorporation statute or articles of incorporation. If the articles or state statute does not authorize a corporation action, the courts examine the facts and custom to determine that the corporate interest is being pursued. Courts generally construe implied powers quite liberally.

Ultra Vires Acts

Acts that are within the express or implied powers of a corporation are called *intra vires*. Acts that do not conform with the corporation's express or implied powers are called *ultra vires*. Ultra vires means "beyond" or "outside" the powers of the corporation.

Ultra vires is typically used in two instances, first, as a defense asserted by the corporation or a third party in lawsuits concerning the enforcement of contracts between them and second, as the grounds for a direct lawsuit by the state or shareholders to stop or nullify an action in which a corporation is engaged.

Ultra Vires Defense in Contract Suits

The law in the past treated ultra vires contracts as absolutely void, with no rights and duties created between the corporation or the third party entering into the contract, which called for an act that was outside of the powers of the corporation. Hence, ultra vires was used as a defense by the corporation or third party in suits for breach of contract. The defending party would claim that there could be no liability since the contract was ultra vires, that is, outside the corporation's powers.

The ultra vires defense in contract actions has been greatly diminished by the law and in most jurisdictions has for all practical purposes been eliminated as a defense in contract actions between a corporation and third parties. The few courts that do recognize ultra vires as a defense limit its applicability to contracts that are wholly unperformed on either side: that is when neither the corporation nor the third party has performed, neither can enforce the ultra vires contract against the other. If both parties have performed in these jurisdictions, the contract will stand and cannot be rescinded. If only one party has performed, the courts disagree on the result, but most permit the party who has performed to enforce the contract if the equities of the situation favor it.

Most states have abolished entirely the defense of ultra vires in an action for breach of contract by or against a corporation, with the Model Act leading the way in this regard.

Ultra Vires in Direct Suits

The Model Act abolishes ultra vires as a defense for contract actions but does not relieve the corporation or its directors from ultra vires as the grounds for a lawsuit brought by shareholders or the state against the corporation. The Model Act allows ultra vires to be used to redress wrongs done by a corporation in three instances: (1) the state is allowed to sue to dissolve the corporation or enjoin it for unauthorized acts, (2) shareholders can sue for an injunction or damages for the performance of an ultra vires act by the corporation, and (3) the corporation can sue directly or through shareholders in a representative suit (derivative suit) against the officers or directors of the corporations.

Liability for Contracts, Torts, and Crimes

The liability of a corporation for contracts, torts, and crimes must be distinguished from the liability of the owners of the corporation, namely the shareholders. A corporation is liable as a legal entity for its contracts, torts, and crimes done by its directors, officers, or employees while acting as corporate agents. The corporate liability is not the personal liability of the shareholders. The shareholders have only limited liability, that is, they are liable only to the extent of their investment in the business.

Contracts

A corporation enters into contracts with third parties through its agents, which are those directors, officers, or employees possessing authority to bind the corporation to a contract with another. The person acting for the corporation binds it as an agent if he possesses express, implied in fact, apparent, or implied in law authority from the corporation; or if an unauthorized contract by him is subsequently ratified by the corporation. Ordinary agency law applies in determining whether a person purportedly acting for the corporation is an agent that can bind it. See Chapter 14. A corporation is not liable for contracts made on its behalf by the corporate promoters prior to incorporation, unless the contracts are expressly or implicitly adopted. A corporation is bound, usually, by its ultra vires contracts.

Torts

Under the agency doctrine of respondeat superior (vicarious liability), a corporation is liable for the torts committed by its officers, directors, and employees while acting within the scope of their employment or authority. The corporation is liable for the unintentional tort of negligence as well as intentional torts such as fraud, assault, fraud, or conversion committed by one of its agents within the scope of his employment. It is no defense that the acts were not authorized by the corporation, so long as they were committed within the scope of employment.

Crimes

The courts have traditionally embraced the position that a corporation could not commit a crime because, as an artificial entity, it lacked the mind capable of criminal intent and the body capable of imprisonment. In part, out of the understanding that while the corporation cannot be imprisoned but can be fined or dissolved, the approach today is to hold the corporation criminally liable under certain situations. Courts and statutes have held corporations criminally liable for crimes that high ranking managerial officials have committed during the performance of authorized duties. Many regulatory statutes specifically will hold the corporation criminally responsible for violations of certain statutes, such as labor, pollution control, securities, and antitrust laws. Many of these statutes impose strict liability for their violation, therefore not requiring proof that a corporate official committing the wrongful act did so with criminal intent, which is normally necessary for finding an individual liable for a criminal act.

2

Management of Corporations

DIRECTORS

Directors are elected at the first shareholders' meetings and each annual meeting thereafter. The directors operate collectively as a board of directors. The function of the directors is to manage the normal business operations of the corporation. The board of directors has the policy-making responsibility for the corporation. The board does the goal setting and long-range planning for the corporation. The board occupies the top of the management structure of the corporation. The shareholders own the corporation and elect and can remove directors, but they do not have the right to participate in corporate management. It is the board of directors who has exclusive control of the ordinary business decisions of the company. The directors are not usually expected to run the day-to-day business affairs of the corporation and normally delegate this responsibility to officers. The officers do not have dominion and control over the corporation's affairs as do the board of directors. Moreover, the officers are hired and fired by the board. In sum, ultimate management responsibility is vested in the board of directors, not shareholders or officers.

Powers of the Directors

The Model Act directs that *all* corporate powers are to be exercised by or under the authority of the board of directors, which emphasizes the complete and exclusive control directors possess over the affairs of the corporation. The Act clearly places management control in the hands of the board of directors. The power of the directors to manage the corporation is vested in the board collectively and not in the directors individually. Thus directors individually or in subgroups do not have the authority to exercise the powers of the directors. Only the directors acting formally as a board after a vote have such authority. The management powers of the board of directors are, in most instances, primarily exercised in the following five areas: (1) selecting, supervising, and removing corporate officers and other managerial employees; (2) establishing compensation of management employees, pension plans, and similar matters; (3) declaring dividends; (4) initiating fundamental changes; (5) determining the financial and capital structure for the corporation; (6) establishing corporate policy and ensuring compliance. A brief explanation of these functions follows.

No one but the board of directors has the responsibility to select corporate officers. The board also has exclusive authority to remove officers and may do so at any time, with or without cause. The responsibilities of the officers are determined and supervised by the board. The board determines the salaries, bonuses, commissions, and expense reimbursement for the corporate officers. Moveover, in some jurisdictions the directors rather than shareholders have the authority to fix compensation of the board members.

Only the directors, not the shareholders or officers, have the authority to declare and set the amount of dividends. The authority of the directors to determine dividends is subject to any restrictions in the incorporation statute, the articles, and agreements concerning corporate loans and preferred stock arrangements. The directors can only pay dividends from earned surplus (retained earnings).

The capital structure and financial policy of the corporation are in the hands of the directors. Among the financial decisions made by the directors are (1) establishing the selling price of newly issued shares of stock; (2) setting the value of property or prior services received in exchange of newly issued shares of stock; (3) purchasing the corporation's stock and canceling and retaining these shares as treasury stock; and (4) selling, leasing, or mortgaging assets of the corporation in the regular course of business.

The board of directors sets basic corporation policy in such areas as product lines, services, prices, wages, and labor-management relations. The directors normally approve or ratify reports and authorize the officers to take important actions, such as borrowing money and entering into contracts.

One of the most important fundamental changes that the board can undertake is to make, alter, amend, or repeal bylaws, unless such power is reserved for shareholders by the articles of incorporation. The board also has the power to initiate actions that nevertheless require additional and final approval by the shareholders; for example, the board must initiate the proceedings for amending the articles of incorporation, changing the corporate financial structure, dissolving the corporation, selling or leasing all or substantially all of the corporate assets of the corporation other than in the usual and regular course of business, and changing the corporate name or the corporate duration.

Qualifications of the Directors

The qualifications of a director are determined by the incorporation statute, articles of incorporation, and bylaws. Only a few states require directors to be of a minimum age, shareholders of the corporation, or residents of the state of incorporation.

Election, Number, Term, and Replacement of Directors

The initial board of directors is generally named in the articles of incorporation and serves until the first shareholders' meeting, when new directors are elected by a majority of shareholders. Thereafter, directors are elected at the annual shareholders' meeting.

There are two methods for board elections that a corporation can use—*straight voting* or *cumulative voting*. If the articles do not provide for a method, the corporation must employ the straight method. In the straight method each shareholder typically has one vote per share for each seat to be filled, and a simple majority of votes elects a director. The straight method has the effect of holding a separate election for each seat on the board. As a means to provide for minority representation, which is not favored by the straight method, a corporation can adopt cumulative voting. Cumulative voting gives every shareholder more votes. In cumulative voting a shareholder is entitled to one vote per share for each director to be elected. There is one ballot for all the directors to be elected, and a shareholder may cast all his votes for one candidate or split them among several directors.

Directors may be *inside* or *outside* directors. Directors who are officers or major shareholders are inside directors. All other directors are outside directors.

Directors typically serve a one-year term, with all the director seats being subject to election at every annual shareholders' meeting. It is permissible for the articles to provide for longer terms. Many states and the Model Act allow a *classified* board in which the directors serve longer than one year. The classified board is divided into classes, most commonly three classes, with only one class elected each year. As a result, the directors serve staggered terms, with one-third of the directors being elected every year for a three-year term. The Model Act requires the board to have at least nine members when a classified board is used. A classified board is meant to provide greater management continuity by preventing complete or substantial replacement of the board at any one time.

The Model Act permits a corporation to have just one director, although some states follow the traditional rule of requiring a minimum of three. The number of directors generally cannot exceed the number of shareholders. Thus, if there is only one shareholder, there need be only one director.

Any vacancy on the board caused by the death or resignation of a director may be filled for the unexpired term by a majority vote of the remaining directors, even if less than a quorum. If the board votes to increase the size of the board, the new seats may be filled with a vote for a term to continue until the next shareholders' meeting for the election of directors.

Rights of Directors

Every director has the inherent and unconditional right to be recognized as a director and to participate as one in corporate affairs. A director who has been excluded from such recognition or participation by other directors can obtain a court order to enforce these rights. Directors have strong inspection rights into corporate records. Complete and unqualified access to corporate records must be given directors so they can competently and fully perform their duties. The director cannot abuse his right to inspection by using it for an improper purpose, and if he does, it is grounds for removal from the board.

Compensation of Directors

There is no right to compensation for a director, but many corporations provide compensation. Under the common law a director has no right to indemnification by the corporation for expenses or losses associated with a lawsuit against him even for acts committed on behalf of the corporation. Most states permit indemnification of corporate directors under certain circumstances.

The common law did not allow directors to receive salaries, but it was usual for them to be paid an honorarium for their attendance at meetings. The Model

Act allows directors to fix their own salaries unless the articles prohibit it. Outside directors usually receive a nominal amount for their service. Inside directors who are officers usually receive only their salaries as officers. In nonprofit corporations, the directors serve for free.

Removal of Directors

The Model Act permits removal of one or more directors or the entire board by the shareholders at any time, with or without cause, at a meeting specifically called for that purpose. In other words, under the Model Act adopted in most states, directors serve at the pleasure of the shareholders. Some states allow removal only for cause. A cause would be breach of fiduciary duty, embezzlement, failure to attend meetings, or failure to perform any other important function of the position. Removal by shareholder vote is a relatively simple procedure if the election of directors is done by straight voting; only a simple majority of shareholders is needed to remove a director. The removal procedure is more complicated if the election of directors is by cumulative voting. In this case, unless all board members are being removed, a director will not be removed if he has enough votes to be elected in a cumulative election. When a director is removed, the remaining board members fill the vacancy until the next annual shareholders' meeting. A director may resign his seat on the board anytime.

Some states also permit the board to remove a director who has been absent from his duties, adjudicated bankrupt, unable to perform his duties due to illness or disability for six months or more, adjudicated insane, or convicted of a felony.

Exercise of Board of Directors' Functions

The directors must function as a board, not as individuals. Directors do not have the authority to make decisions for the corporation or bind it by acting alone. The power of the directors is vested in the board, and they may only take action as a board. The board traditionally takes action at board meetings—in fact, at common law they can only take action at a formal board meeting. Today most states allow the board to take action without holding an actual meeting. The Model Act allows decisions to be made by conference call. The Model Act also allows directors to take an informal action without a formal meeting, but only by unanimous agreement in writing and signed by all of the directors on the board. The action taken by the board at a formal meeting is expressed by its adoption of resolutions, which are positions established after a formal vote.

Meetings

Boards have meetings of two types—*regular* and *special*. Regular meetings have their time and place normally prescribed by the corporate bylaws, and they may also be established by a standing resolution of the board or by custom.

Regularly scheduled meetings do not normally require notice (although notice is often given) unless expressly required. Special meetings do require prior notice, to be given to the directors in a manner prescribed by statute or the bylaws. Where notice is required for a meeting, the action of the board is not valid unless the absent directors have received notice. A director may waive notice of any meeting by attending the meeting, since the law presumes that a director at the meeting had notice of it. Notice can also be waived if the director signs a written waiver of notice before or after the meeting.

Before an action can be validly taken at a board meeting, a *quorum* must be present. A simple majority (more than 50 percent) of directors present at the beginning of the meeting constitutes a quorum in most states. The bylaws may require a greater number to constitute a quorum than that specified by statute. Some state statutes place a maximum and a minimum on the quorum requirement.

For the board to act there must be a majority vote of the quorum number. The majority must be disinterested. The board's actions are reflected in formal board resolutions. Directors cannot vote by proxy. Each director has only one vote on each matter presented to the board.

The resolutions of the board are recorded in the corporate minute book.

If permitted by the articles or bylaws and if all directors agree in writing, the board may take an action without a meeting.

Delegation of Board Powers

An individual director cannot delegate his responsibility to act as a director to another person, even another director.

The board itself as an entity can delegate some of its powers as a board to committees of board members. A board may create an executive committee and any other committees authorized by the articles or bylaws. An executive committee is usually made of two or three members of the board and is given the same authority as the board. Publicly held corporations often have audit committees, which is a prerequisite for a company to list its shares on the New York Stock Exchange. The audit committees supervise corporate finances. Many publicly held corporations have nominating committees, which establish the qualifications for directors and nominate candidates for board seats. The board may establish a compensation committee, which reviews the salaries of top management and makes other recommendations on corporate compensation, profit sharing plans, and benefits. Another common type of committee is a public policy committee, which deals with the corporation's involvement in community affairs.

The board's ability to delegate its functions is not unlimited. There are certain fundamental functions that the Model Act prohibits the entire board from delegating to committees, such as declaring dividends, amending bylaws, approving a merger, authorizing the sale of stock, or (in some states) designating candidates for director seats.

The board normally can delegate only managerial duties to committees, and these committees must be composed of directors only. However, ministerial (i.e., routine and nondecision-making) duties can be delegated by the board to persons other than the directors. In other words, the delegated matters must relate to only ordinary corporate affairs and can only give the officer or employee managerial responsibilities that are limited in scope and under adequate guidelines.

DUTIES AND LIABILITIES OF DIRECTORS

Directors are held to a high standard of conduct in carrying out their responsibilities to the corporation. The directors owe three principal duties to the corporation: (1) fiduciary duty, (2) duty of due care, and (3) duty of obedience.

Ordinarily the liability of directors for their civil wrongs is to the corporation itself, and the directors are not liable to third persons for the effect upon them due to breaches of duty to the corporation by the director. Moreover, the liability of the director to the corporation may only be enforced by the corporation or by shareholders bringing a derivative action on behalf of the corporation. While a director may not be liable to a third person for breach of his duties to the corporation, the corporation in turn is liable to the third person to whom the corporation had owed a duty that was breached as a result of the director's action. The directors are not liable for the economic consequences of their advice and actions to third persons, even though they caused the corporation to refuse to deal or not contract with these third persons, so long as the directors acted in good faith and in the interests of the corporation.

There are exceptions to the rule that directors who breach a duty to the corporation are not liable to third persons. One exception is when they commit a wrong or direct the commission of a wrong on a third person, such as when they take an active part in causing the corporation to conspire or engage in an illegal act or to enter into a monopoly agreement to the detriment of the third person. Furthermore, a director acting in a personal capacity, such as entering into a contract and agreeing to assume personal responsibility, is not protected from liability by the fact that the motive was to act on behalf of the corporation. Finally, when a director is liable to a third person, it is no defense that the corporation may also be liable to the third person.

Fiduciary Duty

Directors owe a fiduciary duty to the corporation. The fiduciary duty obligates the director to act with the utmost loyalty, good faith, and fair dealing in his relationship with other directors and the corporation. The director first and foremost has only one master, and that is the corporation. As a result, the director must be influenced by no consideration other than the welfare of the corporation. Three major categories of breach of the fiduciary duty are commonly seen: (1) seizure of a corporate opportunity, (2) unfair transactions with the corporation, and (3) self-dealing and secret profits by a director. All three kinds of breach of loyalty are a variety of conflict of interest—namely when the director places his interest over that of the corporation.

Corporate Opportunity

The director may breach his fiduciary duty if he takes advantage of any business opportunity of possible use to the corporation. This action is called the *corporate opportunity doctrine*. An opportunity is a corporate opportunity if it was reasonably foreseeable that the corporation would have been interested. The factors that help determine whether a business opportunity is a corporate opportunity include if it was discovered while in the course of duties for the corporation, whether the corporation had interest or expectancy in the property, how closely related the opportunity was to corporate business, and if it was competitive with the corporation. The remedies available to the shareholders or corporation in a lawsuit for breach of corporate opportunity include the return of the director's profit, reconveyance of the property at the director's cost, and payment of damages by the director. A director is not liable for breach of a corporate opportunity under three circumstances: (1) the corporation is financially unable to take advantage of it; (2) the opportunity is ultra vires for the corporation; or (3) the director discloses the opportunity to the corporation and by a majority vote (not including the vote of the interested director) the board rejects the opportunity.

Unfair Business Dealings with Corporation

A director may breach his duty of loyalty if he deals unfairly with the corporation in a business transaction. In early corporation law the director could not do business with the corporation. Current laws allow a director to do business with the corporation, such as buying property or services from, or selling property or services to, the corporation. However, the business transaction is only valid under either of two conditions: (1) the transaction was fair and reasonable, or (2) after full disclosure of the director's financial interest the board by a majority vote (not including a vote by the interested director) approved or ratified the transaction. In other words, the transaction is voidable by the corporation when the director failed to make full disclosure to an approving board or when the deal is unfair. Some states require that the transaction also be approved by the shareholders.

Self-Dealing and Secret Profits

A director cannot engage in self-dealing in any activity that is in conflict with the interests of the corporation. Examples of self-dealing include using corporate funds or employees in an outside venture; selling property to the corporation through an intermediary; selling trade secrets or customer lists to other companies; using influence to prevent the corporation from competing with an outside business; using corporate funds, assets, or employees for personal affairs or other outside activities; being employed by a competitor; embezzling corporate funds;

owning a competing business; and accepting secret profits or commissions on corporate transactions.

In a lawsuit against the corporation for self-dealing, the corporation or shareholders acting on its behalf have available to them the remedies of recovery of secret profits and damages.

Directors are not *per se* precluded from competing with the corporation, but it is a breach of the fiduciary duty if their positions are used to compete unfairly. Unfair competition is usually shown by divulging corporate information, luring away corporate employees, diverting corporate customers, or working at the competing business while being paid by the corporation. Another possible conflict of interest issue occurs when the director purchases a debt owed by the corporation. There is no conflict when the director acquires, even at a discount, a liquidated, unmatured, and undisputed debt against the corporation and enforces at maturity at face value. There is a conflict, however, when the director acquires a matured claim or unliquidated or disputed claims against the corporation. In such cases, any gain must be returned to the corporation.

Disqualification of Interested Directors

Board members must disqualify themselves when the board votes on any matter in which they have an interest. A director who does have such an interest is considered lacking the ability to exercise independent judgment and is called an *interested director*. Only *disinterested directors* can constitute a quorum and provide an affirmative vote.

Duty of Due Care and Good Faith

A director has the duty not to act negligently in exercising his functions as a director. Under the principles of ordinary negligence, the director owes the corporation a duty of care in managing the corporation that an ordinarily prudent man would exercise in respect to his own affairs in the same or similar circumstances. Thus most states will hold a director liable to the corporation if he is negligent in carrying out his functions and such negligence leads to damage to the corporation. A few states will only hold the director liable if he is grossly negligent, and not merely exhibiting ordinary negligence.

A director can make mistakes and still not be liable for negligence if the errors are honest errors in exercising business judgment. This protection for director's mistakes is called the *business judgment rule* or *defense*. In order to take advantage of the business judgment rule there must be no bad faith, fraud, conflict of interest, gross negligence, or abuse of discretion. Courts generally defer to a director's or board's business judgment because of this defense, and thus it is difficult to obtain a negligence judgment against a director or board. The courts are reluctant to second-guess the directors when they exercise their honest business judgment. The business judgment rule is buttressed by the presumption that a director acts in good faith when carrying out his functions.

In addition to the business judgment rule, a good faith reliance on expert advice is a good defense to a negligence suit. This defense is most effective for outside directors who often must rely on data provided by inside directors and officers regarding the company's performance and activities. The directors can also rely on information, reports, statements, and the like prepared by corporate employees, legal counsel, public accountants, and so on. However, the defense of good faith reliance on such advice is not available when the directors have reason to believe reliance is not warranted.

Situations in which directors must exercise due care and, obversely, in which they are most likely to be subject to negligence suits, include hiring honest and competent employees, supervising officers and employees, detecting and preventing wrongs by fellow directors and company personnel, examining corporate books and records, attending board meetings, taking an active part in management, obtaining sufficient information in order to vote in an informed manner on matters presented to the board, and keeping advised of the financial condition (especially solvency) of the corporation.

"Dummy" directors are especially prone to negligence problems. A dummy director is no more than a puppet or added warm body on the board controlled by a major shareholder. A dummy director is often uninvolved in the corporate affairs and as a result is usually liable for omissions in conduct, such as failing to attend meetings, to stay abreast of corporate affairs, or to review financial statements or legal opinions presented by the corporation's accountants or attorneys.

Duty of Obedience (Ultra Vires Acts)

Directors owe a duty of obedience to the corporation, that is, to act intra vires or within their authority. As described earlier, ultra vires activities are those that are beyond the powers of the corporation.

As a general rule, the corporation is liable on ultra vires contracts, and the directors who participated in committing the corporation to an ultra vires contract are liable to the corporation for losses or damages that result. Ultra vires acts include issuance of shares at a discount, paying a dividend when the corporation is insolvent or when paying would make it so, agreeing to a loan of corporate funds or assets to any other director or officer which is not authorized by the shareholders, unauthorized purchasing or selling of corporate property, or acquiring of the company's stock that would make it insolvent.

A defense available to a director for an ultra vires act of the board is to *dissent* to the act at the time it is made by the board. A director who is present at a meeting of the board at which the ultra vires action is taken is presumed to have assented to the action unless, in addition to dissenting, the director makes the dissent evident by having it entered in the minutes of the meeting, by filing a written dissent at the meeting, or by sending a written dissent to the secretary of the board immediately after the meeting.

The legal remedies for ultra vires acts include an injunction, damages against the directors responsible, or revocation of the certificate of incorporation by a suit brought by the attorney general of the state of incorporation. Unless they have properly dissented to such acts, directors are personally liable for the ultra vires acts of the corporation, including declaring dividends that impair the capital of the corporation.

Criminal Liability of Directors

A director is personally liable for any crimes he commits, even when the acts considered criminal were done on behalf of the corporation. Directors may be liable for violation of criminal laws on the local, state, and federal level. Good faith on the part of the director is no defense for a criminal violation. The Model Act imposes criminal liability on a director who knowingly signs false articles of incorporation, reports, or other documents filed with the secretary of state. Examples of laws for which directors may be criminally liable include violations of antitrust statutes, employee health and safety laws, environmental legislation, taxation laws, securities laws, and food and drug legislation.

Indemnification of Directors

A corporation may indemnify (reimburse) directors for the expenses of defending civil or criminal lawsuits or of administrative proceedings or investigations against them in their official capacities. To be entitled to indemnification, the director must have acted in good faith, without negligence, and in a manner he reasonably believed to be in or not opposed to the best interests of the corporation. In addition to the foregoing requirements for indemnification, in a criminal prosecution the director must also show he had no reason to believe his conduct was illegal. Ordinarily indemnification is up to the discretion of the corporation and is addressed in the articles. If the articles do not address the issue, the court may order it. If the director wins the lawsuit or is acquitted, the corporation may indemnify.

In some states the corporation must indemnify the director if he wins the suit. A corporation may indemnify the director even if he loses a tort suit brought by an outsider, or if he is found guilty of a criminal act. In derivative suits brought by shareholders, however, indemnification is generally not allowed if the defendant director loses.

Insurance may be obtained to protect the director against the cost of lawsuits for torts. Insurance companies do not, however, insure against conduct involving bad faith, malice, dishonesty, fraud, or criminal acts.

OFFICERS

Unlike a director, each officer is an *agent* of the corporation. Consequently each officer may bind the corporation, as its agent, by his individual acts within the actual or apparent scope of his authority. In contrast, an individual director, by virtue of the fact that alone he is not an agent of the corporation, cannot legally bind the corporation. Keep in mind, however, that officers and directors may be the same persons, unless the articles prohibit occupation of both roles. Like directors, the officers have a fiduciary responsibility and other duties and liabilities to the corporation. Officers are usually appointed by the board of directors, although sometimes they are elected by shareholders. While directors make policy and fundamental decisions for the corporation, the main function of the officers is to run the day-to-day operations of the business.

The Model Act requires that there be a president, vice president, secretary, and treasurer. Larger corporations generally have more than one vice president and often have a recording secretary and a corresponding secretary. Most state statutes, like the Model Act, allow a person to hold more than one office at the same time, except for the offices of secretary and president. The articles or bylaws of a corporation may prohibit a person from occupying more than one corporate office. The board is free to add other officers by its bylaws. Some corporations have other kinds of officers such as chief executive officer, chairman of the board, general manager, comptroller or controller, and general counsel.

Roles of Officers

The state corporation statute provides the general requirements for officers. The authority, powers, and functions of the officers are found in these statutes, the articles of incorporation, corporate bylaws, and board resolutions. The usual place for a description of each officer's job duties is found in the bylaws.

The *president* is the principal executive officer and, subject to the control of the board of directors, normally supervises and controls the business and operation of the corporation. He presides at meetings of shareholders and directors. The president usually must be a director, as well. The president has the authority to sign for the corporation deeds, bonds, notes, stock certificates, mortgages, and other instruments that the board has authorized to be executed. His general authority to bind the corporation includes broad substantial implied authority in transactions that are part of the usual and regular course of business.

The *vice president* normally does not possess individual power to act for the corporation. His authority arises while acting in the president's absence, death, illness, inability, or refusal to act. Vice presidents can sign stock certificates and other corporate documents.

The *secretary* performs the clerical work for the officers. The secretary maintains minutes of shareholder and board meetings, sees to it that notice is duly given for shareholder and board meetings, maintains the corporate records and the seal of the corporation, keeps shareholder transfer records, and signs the corporation's stock certificates along with the president.

The *treasurer* takes care of corporate funds. His charge and custody of these funds include responsibilities such as giving receipts, making deposits, issuing checks, and maintaining financial records.

Authority of Officers as Agents

The officers are agents of the corporation. As a result the rules of the law of agency govern the powers of the officers. Therefore the corporation is bound by the actions of its officers if they are acting within the scope of their authority—whether express, implied, or apparent—like any other agent. The corporation may also ratify an officer's unauthorized act committed on its behalf.

The express authority of any officer arises from the incorporation statute, the articles of incorporation, the bylaws, and the board resolutions. Most of the express authority arises from the bylaws and resolutions of the board. The implied authority is that which is reasonable and necessary to function as a particular kind of officer.

The states do not agree on the amount of implied authority possessed by the president. Traditionally, the courts tended to hold the president had no implied authority by virtue of his office, his actual authority being restricted to that expressly conferred by the corporation. In states following the traditional line, the president is regarded as a mere "figurehead" unless specific powers have been given to him. In other states the president is presumed to be like a "general manager" with the broad automatic authority a general manager would have to make contracts within the scope of the corporation's regular and usual course of business. Moreover, the president, in either role, does not have authority by virtue of that office to make a contract that due to its unusual or extraordinary character would require action by the board of directors. As a result, the president cannot, without a specific resolution from the board, make a contract for long-term or unusual employment to bind the corporation as a surety, to release a claim against the corporation, or to promise the corporation will later repurchase shares when issued to a subscriber. Any act requiring board approval is outside the implied authority of the president or any other officer.

The implied authority of the corporate secretary and treasurer is relatively easy to determine, since the former has custody and control of corporate books and all powers implied in that role, and the treasurer is the fiscal officer, likewise with the powers implied from these functions. The vice president carries little implied or apparent authority.

Apparent authority in the law of agency arises from the acts of the principal, in this case the corporation, which leads third parties to believe reasonably and in good faith that the officer has authority. An example would be when a third party relies on the fact the officer exercised the same authority in the past with the approval of the board of directors.

Finally, even when an officer exceeds his authority, the corporation can choose to ratify his actions.

Selection and Removal of Officers

Officers are selected by the directors, unless the articles provide otherwise. Officers hold their positions at the pleasure of the board and can be removed with or without cause and regardless of any employment contract. Nevertheless, while the directors can remove an officer who has employment contract without cause, the corporation may still be liable for breach of contract. If the board has authority to dismiss officers, the shareholders cannot vote to fire the officers.

Compensation of Officers

Compensation is determined by the board of directors. If a director is also an officer, he cannot vote on his own salary. Where officers make up a majority of the board of directors, shareholders determine their salaries. The courts generally give great deference to salary decisions made by the boards, but where the salaries are excessive and exceed good business judgment, a legal remedy may be obtained in court.

Liabilities of Officers to the Corporation

An officer's liability to the corporation is the same as the liability of an agent to the agent's principal. See Chapter 14. The duties of loyalty (fiduciary duty), due care, and obedience associated with directors likewise apply to officers.

Criminal Liability of Officers

Officers can be held liable for the criminal acts performed by the corporation if they were responsible or participated in any way. The officer cannot use the corporation as a shield for criminal liability, under the theory that the corporation has no mind nor can it form intent; its officials, however, can. One example would be when a machine shop owned by a corporation is violating a worker safety code. If the violations are brought to the officer's attention and he fails to follow through in having them remedied, he would be liable even if subordinates were responsible for correcting the problem. Officers can also be held liable for securities acts violations and violations of antitrust laws and many other laws where they instigate or participate in an act deemed criminal by a statute.

3

Shareholders' Rights and Responsibilities

POWERS OF SHAREHOLDERS

Shareholders own the corporation. Regardless of the number of shares they own, whether one or one million, all shareholders have certain rights and responsibilities. The very definition of a corporation requires shareholders, since there cannot be a corporation without shareholders. Shareholders are not generally regarded as part of "management," as are the functionaries who oversee the details of corporate operations, such as directors, officers, and managerial employees. Although shareholders are not involved in the day-to-day running of the corporation, as owners they have ultimate control over its policies. The most important control functions of shareholders are: (1) election and removal of directors, (2) amendment of bylaws or articles, and (3) approval of extraordinary corporation transactions or fundamental changes in the corporation. While all shareholders are entitled to vote on these control functions, they are decided by the way a "majority" of shareholders vote. Rightfully it can be said that these control functions are exercised by the majority of shareholders. The control of shareholders over corporate affairs can be viewed as either direct or indirect. The majority of shareholders exercise indirect control over the running of the corporation by electing and removing directors. Their direct control is over the amendment of articles and bylaws and approval of extraordinary corporate transactions.

Election and Removal of Directors

Elections for directors are held each year at the annual meeting of shareholders. Directors hold office until the next annual shareholder meeting or until their successors are qualified. When a board consists of nine or more directors, the bylaws often divide the board into two or three classes as nearly equal in number as possible and stagger directors' terms. If the board is divided into two (three) classes, the directors in each class can be elected once a year in alternate years for a two-year (three-year) term. Under these arrangements one-half the board is elected every two years (or one-third every three years). This arrangement allows for continuity of membership.

During his term of office a director cannot be removed *without cause* unless the articles or bylaws expressly reserve this power for the shareholders. Shareholders have the power to remove directors *for cause* such as misconduct, dishonesty, neglect of duties, gross abuse of discretion, and so on. Some state laws require a specified percentage of outstanding shares to vote for removal of a director. New York and California laws allow only ten percent of the shares of a corporation incorporated in these states to remove a director for cause if a majority of shareholders are unwilling to act. California and the Model Act allow majority shareholders to remove directors with or without cause at a meeting called for the purpose of removing them.

Amendment of Bylaws and Articles

Usually the bylaws are initially adopted by the incorporators, directors, or shareholders. By a majority vote, shareholders have the power to amend or repeal the bylaws and can do so for any reason whatsoever.

The original articles of the corporation are formulated by the incorporators. A majority of shareholders can amend the articles. Usually the amendment is first proposed and approved by the board and then offered to the shareholders to approve at the annual meeting. All shareholders eligible to vote must receive proper notice of the proposed amendment and of the meeting where it is to be voted upon. If approved by the shareholders, the amended articles are filed with the secretary of state, and he issues a certificate of amendment.

Approval of Extraordinary Transactions

Certain matters are of such unusual or fundamental nature that they are beyond the authority of the managers of the corporation to determine, namely directors and officers, and require decision making by the owners of the corporation, namely the shareholders. A matter is considered an extraordinary transaction when it is outside the ordinary course of business and substantially affects the ownership interest of the stockholders. Such extraordinary corporate matters requiring shareholder approval include (1) merger, consolidation, or voluntary dissolution of the corporation; (2) sale, lease, exchange, or other disposition of substantially all corporate assets other than in the regular course of business; (3) reductions in stated capital; (4) loans to directors; and (5) stock option plans benefiting officers and directors. Approval of these transactions by the shareholders is ordinarily expressed in the form of a "resolution" voted on at a shareholders' meeting.

RIGHTS OF SHAREHOLDERS

Right to Stock Certificate

Each shareholder has the right to receive a properly executed certificate as evidence of ownership of shares. The certificate(s) indicates the class and number of shares in the corporation. When the shares are uncertificated the shareholder has the right to an *initial transaction statement*, which specifies ownership of stock.

Right to Transfer Stock

Subject to certain valid restrictions, a shareholder has the right to freely transfer his shares, whether through sale or as a gift. A stock certificate is a negotiable instrument allowing it to be transferred, although it can be made nonnegotiable by properly authorized restrictions on transfer. The restrictions on the transfer of stock may be imposed by the articles, bylaws, or by an agreement between the stockholders and the corporation. The restrictions must be reasonable. If the restriction places an unreasonable burden on the transfer of stock or makes the stock totally untransferrable, it is against public policy and invalid.

Stock restrictions are commonly used to maintain control against outsiders. Limitations are often imposed as a means for insiders to maintain control of close corporations. The most common restriction on stock transferability, and one of the most common means of maintaining insider control of a close corporation, takes the form of options to purchase. An option to purchase prohibits the stockholder from selling his stock to another without first giving the corporation or the other shareholders the option of buying it. This kind of restriction is valid if a reasonable time limit is set for exercise of the option. A restriction requiring the shares to be offered back to the corporation at book value or at a value set by the directors is unreasonable and invalid.

In order for a restriction to be valid against third parties to whom the stock is transferred, the restriction must be conspicuously noted on the certificate.

The method for validly transferring stock can be delivery of the certificates duly endorsed or delivery of the certificate accompanied by a separate assignment.

Right to Vote

The voting rights of a given share are determined by state statutes, the articles and bylaws, board resolutions, and the limitations printed on the stock certificate.

Corporations are permitted to issue both voting and nonvoting stock. The right to vote does not have to be specified in the articles of incorporation, since it is regarded as an inherent right associated with ownership of shares. The articles usually make some provision governing voting rights, however, and can expressly exclude or limit the right to vote. Every corporation must have at least one class of common stock that gives owners of such stock the right to vote. Typically, common stock gives its owners the right to vote, while preferred stock does not. In most corporations common stock is voting stock. If the articles are silent on the rights of different classes of stock, owners of both preferred and common stock have the same voting rights. Un-issued shares and treasury stock (shares that have been issued and later repurchased by the corporation) carry no voting rights. Owners of preferred stock may be given the right to vote in the case of a merger or consolidation or if dividends remain unpaid for a specified period.

The right to vote entitles each shareholder to one vote for each voting share. The right to vote means the right to vote at shareholders' meetings for the election or removal of directors, amendment of bylaws or articles, extraordinary transactions, and policy decisions.

Shareholders vote at the annual meeting of the corporation and at any special meetings called by the board of directors. A corporation must hold an annual meeting of its shareholders at which they elect directors and vote on matters of corporate policy. If an annual meeting is not held in thirteen months, a shareholder can obtain a court injunction to order a meeting. The bylaws often establish the time and place of the annual meeting. Provision for shareholder meetings can be in the bylaws as well. Typically, bylaws will give the president, the board, or ten percent of the shareholders the right to call a special meeting.

Shareholders are entitled to receive notice of the meeting's time, place, and agenda. Under the Model Act, notice must be given at least ten days before the meeting but not more than fifty days before. Shareholders waive inadequate or improper notice if they attend the meeting and stay after protesting the notice. Shareholders can also waive notice by signing a waiver.

Who is given notice and who can vote is determined by the record date set by the corporation. Shareholders who own voting stock at the date of record may vote. The date of record is the time when corporate stock transfer books are closed to determine the shareholders entitled to vote, and this is usually for a period of not more than seventy days before the meeting at which the shareholders can vote. The corporation will send notice of the meeting to anyone listed as a shareholder as of the record date. If stock is bought after the record date, the shareholder cannot vote, unless he obtains a proxy from the seller. When a shareholder pledges shares as security, generally the shareholder may continue to vote the shares.

As noted in an earlier chapter, the two methods for shareholder voting for the election of directors are the cumulative and straight methods. Cumulative voting facilitates minority representation on the board of directors by giving the minority the chance to place one or more of its members on the board. Cumulative voting can be only used for the election of directors and for no other purpose. In cumulative voting all director vacancies that are to be filled in a given year are voted for at the same time, and each share has as many votes as the directors to be elected. By concentrating their votes for only one or a few candidates the minority shareholders can obtain at least some representation on the board. Allowing for minority representation is regarded as so important that some states require cumulative voting, although under the Model Act it is optional. In many states, if cumulative voting is not provided by the articles or bylaws, it automatically is used. Some states prohibit election of directors by classes because it impairs the right of cumulative voting. In other jurisdictions election of directors by class is allowed so long as there is cumulative voting for directors within each class at each election.

A shareholder may vote either in person or by written *proxy*. Proxy is a power of attorney in which the shareholder grants the authority to another to vote in his shares at a particular meeting or for a particular question at a meeting. A few states allow oral proxies, but most statutes require the proxy to be in writing. Statutes generally limit a proxy to no more than eleven months, unless the proxy declares otherwise. A proxy is a form of agency, and like most agencies it is revocable unless coupled with an interest, such as when the shares serve as security for a loan. Proxies can be revoked in writing, by the shareholder appearing at the meeting and voting, by the shareholder giving his shares to another person, or by the death of the shareholder. Securities Exchange Commission (SEC) rules allow the solicitation of proxies from shareholders of publicly held corporations.

Shareholders may aggregate their stocks' voting rights and vote their shares as a block as a means to gain or maintain control of the corporation. This can be done either through a *voting trust* in which the stock from a group of shareholders is transferred to a trustee who votes it or through a *pooling agreement* in which shareholders bind themselves to vote as a block.

The voting trust is the most durable means for accumulating votes necessary to maintain control of the corporation. Title to the shares is transferred to a voting trustee in return for voting trust certificates. The trustee is the registered owner of the shares on the corporate records and votes them. Shareholders retain all their rights as shareholders except the right to vote during the duration of the agreement. The stock's ownership can be transferred, but the voting rights remain subject to the voting trust. As a result the stock usually brings a lower price than it would if its new owner was able to vote the shares. In order to be valid, a voting trust must be in writing and cannot last for more than ten years. A voting trust is irrevocable for its specified duration. A copy of the agreement must be filed with the main office of the corporation. Voting trusts are used for several reasons. First and foremost they are used to gain or maintain control of a corporation by a group of shareholders or by the corporation itself. A corporation's creditors may insist on formation of a voting trust as a condition to the extension of further credit. In this way the creditors can assure continuity of management. A voting trust is used in bankruptcy to keep a company stable during reorganization. A court will void a voting trust if it is against public policy, for example, if it promotes monopoly, suppresses minority representation, or perpetrates a fraud.

Pooling agreements, sometimes called *voting control agreements*, allow shareholders to agree in advance to vote in a specified manner. These agreements are often used in close corporations, usually together with restrictions on the transfer of shares. Most states do not impose specific requirements on these agreements. Pooling agreements are governed by the rules of contract law because they are contracts. Pooling agreements are not binding on the corporation or on unknowing transferees of the stock. The courts will invalidate pooling agreements for improper purposes such as being used to suppress the rights of minority shareholders.

Minority shareholders are bound to the decision of a majority but may sue to restrain the majority when the proposed action is detrimental to the corporation; ultra vires; illegal or fraudulent; or in violation of the articles, bylaws, or statute.

Preemptive Right

The common law gave the shareholder the right to preserve his percentage share of total stock ownership and dividend interest by providing him with the first opportunity to purchase any newly issued shares in proportion to what the shareholder already owned before the newly issued stock was offered to any others. This was called the *preemptive right*. The preemptive right applied to any new offering of stock only of the *same class* at its *offering* price and not to any other class of stock, nor at the original stock's offering price, if lower.

A number of state incorporation statutes have abolished the preemptive right. The common law preemptive right applied unless it was expressly denied in the articles of incorporation or by the incorporation statute. The preemptive right usually was not applied to the purchase of treasury shares, shares issued for noncash consideration, or shares issued as a result of a merger or consolidation. Preferred shareholders were often regarded as lacking the right of preemption. Preemptive rights had to be exercised within a reasonable period or they were lost. A thirty-day period is frequently used and seen as reasonable.

Preemptive rights are an essential tool for the owners of the close corporation to protect their substantial interest and influence when new shares are to be sold. Preemptive rights have little or no use in a publicly held corporation where the number of shares and share owners are quite large. Furthermore, preemptive rights also may be detrimental to a publicly held corporation. Preemptive rights make it difficult for a business to authorize new stock for executive bonuses, acquisition of assets, mergers with other firms, transactions in which the corporation transfers stock as consideration, and other business needs.

There are some exceptions to preemptive rights. When the corporation does not issue all its authorized shares in the first issuance, preemptive rights do not apply to any shares that are originally authorized but issued later. The result is that preemptive rights apply only to increases in authorized stock. Preemptive rights do not apply to shares issued for considerations other than cash (such as property, services, or settlement of a debt). Treasury shares, having once been issued and reacquired, are exempt from the preemptive right when resold.

Because of the difficulties posed by preemptive rights, modern legislation limits or eliminates preemptive rights unless they are specifically granted by the articles or an agreement among the stockholders. Today virtually all states recognize preemptive rights, but most permit the articles to limit or deny them. While as a general rule articles of incorporation can be amended to eliminate preemptive rights, it cannot be done when doing so violates the fiduciary duty of controlling shareholders toward the minority. Under the Model Act, in order for preemptive rights to exist, the articles of incorporation must expressly provide for them since they are not automatic rights under the Act. Corporations now have wide latitude as to the preemptive rights they can allow. Some corporations limit preemptive rights to just newly authorized shares or to authorized but unissued shares, or may even confer them for treasury shares. Moreover, some statutes and many courts prohibit preemptive rights for shares issued for noncash consideration, shares issued as a result of merger or consolidation, or shares issued for an employee stock option plan.

There are various enforcement measures available to the shareholder to protect his preemptive rights. He can enjoin the offering or obtain a court order to compel the issuer to offer him his prorata share of the issuance first. He can obtain a court order to have the new shares cancelled, provided the purchaser knew of the violations. If the shareholder must purchase shares on the market to preserve his proportionate voting and dividend interest, he can recover damages from the corporation for the difference between market price and the issue price of the shares he was denied an opportunity to preempt.

Right to Dividends

A person who purchases stock in a coporation is making an investment for which a profit is expected. The shareholder may make profit either from an increase in the market value of the shares, from dividends, from both, or make no profit from either. A *dividend* is a payment made by the corporation to its shareholders that represents income or profit on their investment. The dividend paid on the stock entitled to receive dividends is a portion of the company's earnings distributed pro rata among the shares.

Stockholders do not have the absolute right to receive dividends. Whether dividends are to be paid ("declared"), how large they will be, and when they will be paid are left virtually entirely up to the discretion of the board of directors. Furthermore, any dividends declared by the board must be valid and lawful, that is, they are subject to the relative rights of other shareholders as to preferences, accumulation of dividends, and participation; they are subject to a proper source of available funds from which to pay dividends; and they cannot be given if the corporation is insolvent or would become so because of the dividends. A corporation is insolvent if it cannot pay its debts and obligations as they become due.

Dividends ordinarily can be paid only from a particular source, and that source is in the earned surplus account. The earned surplus account is the retained earnings account that represents a cumulative figure (earnings of the corporation that over the years have exceeded its losses). By requiring the dividends to come from an existing surplus in corporate funds, the corporation is prevented from paying dividends out of the original capital investment in the company. The earnings or surplus from which dividends are drawn must be in the form of available cash, not in accounts receivables or inventories.

Some states have adopted an exception to the requirement that the earned surplus account be in the black—the *nimble dividends rule*. Nimble dividends are paid out of the year's current net earnings (net profits for the current year or the year just ended) even though the net figure in the earned surplus account is still negative (that is, the prior year's deficit has not been made up). The purpose for the nimble dividends exception is to allow a previously unprofitable company the opportunity to give shareholders a return on their investment without waiting for full recovery in the earned surplus account and thus encourage more investment in the company.

Some states are much more restrictive than others regarding the source of dividends. For instance, a number of states only allow dividends to be paid from current net earnings, that is, the source of funds must be the net profits of the corporation for the current fiscal year or the fiscal year just ended. The Model Act allows companies to make distributions from their capital surplus account. These distributions have the same requirements as dividends, such as approval by the board of directors, but such distributions are not dividends and the shareholders must be told they are receiving a capital surplus distribution and not a dividend.

The idea behind requiring dividends to come from some corporate earnings "surplus" is to prevent dividends from impairing the capital or leaving the corporation unable to pay its debts. There is an exception to this principle that allows corporations with *wasting assets* to impair capital while declaring a dividend. The wasting assets corporation is in businesses that are designed to exhaust or use the assets of the corporation (such as mines, oil fields, and other natural resource extraction activities). A wasting corporation may also be established for the purpose of buying and liquidating the assets of a bankrupt business.

Dividends can be paid in cash, property, or in the stock of the corporation. Normally dividends are paid in cash, but occasionally the corporation makes noncash dividends of property or stock. Property dividends consist of corporate assets, including stock of another company the corporation has been holding as an asset. When the corporation declares its own stock as a dividend, it is said to have issued a *stock dividend*. This kind of distribution is technically not a dividend because it does not involve a transfer of property from the corporation to its shareholders. The stock dividend is an accounting transfer in which the company moves retained earnings into the shareholder equity, or capital account. Each shareholder becomes an owner of a larger number of shares but gets no real immediate benefit as a result because the value of the preexisting shares are diluted. The benefit is long-run, however, because there is a tendency for the shares to increase in value.

A *stock split* is not a real dividend, the corporation simply exchanges an existing share for two or more new shares. A stock split should not be confused with a stock dividend although in both the proportionate interest of the shareholder remains the same. The stock split is a kind of restructuring of shares with no commitment to transfer capital. This is because the stock split does not increase the capital account but instead reduces the shares' stated value.

Once a dividend is declared and is valid, the dividend becomes a debt the corporation owes the shareholders. The shareholders can, as creditors, sue the corporation to recover the amount of the lawfully declared dividends the corporation owes them. The dividend is irrevocable and cannot be recalled unless the declaration is illegal, ultra vires, in fraud of creditors, revoked at the same meeting it was declared, made payable in the future but not made public or communicated to the stockholders, or unless the stock has not been issued.

Whether a dividend is to be paid and how large it will be are normally decisions within the exclusive discretion of the board. The shareholders cannot compel a declaration of a dividend except when a surplus of cash exists and the directors are withholding a dividend dishonestly, out of spite, for their own private purposes, or for some other reason that is a clear abuse of discretion. A court will give great deference and refuse to substitute its judgment for the judgment of the directors on whether or not to declare a dividend but will, however, allow a challenge to the board's decision if (1) the funds were not legally available for a declared dividend, (2) the division among shareholders was not fair and uniform, or (3) the special rights of any particular class of stock were not observed.

When the dividend is declared, the corporation will set a payment date, which is the final one allowed for payment of the obligation, after which a shareholder can sue if the dividend is not paid. A record date, the cutoff date for closing the corporate books in determining which shareholders will be paid dividends, is also set. Persons buying shares before the record date will receive the dividend from the corporation, and those who purchased stock from the corporation after the record date must make arrangements with the seller to have the dividend turned over to them. The buyer of the stock can sue the seller for return of the dividend.

Right to Inspect Books and Records

The shareholder has the right to inspect the books and records of the corporation. Shareholders have the right to inspect significant corporate records, provided the inspection is for a "proper purpose." The important records that shareholders have the right to inspect for any proper purpose include the general books of accounts, minutes of director or shareholder meetings, stockholder lists other than those available at shareholder meetings, and other records and files containing accurate information of corporate affairs.

Proper purpose is defined as any purpose that is relevant to one's status as a shareholder. Proper purpose would include to determine the financial condition of the corporation, the quality and conduct of its management, propriety of dividends, and any matters relating to the rights and interests in corporate business; to obtain information related to a lawsuit against the corporation or its officers or directors; to organize shareholders into an opposition group to remove directors at an election; or to buy shares of other shareholders. Many of the purposes considered improper involve minor shareholders who buy a share or two and try to use their status as shareholders to gain access to the corporation's trade secrets, formulas, or customer lists and then use the information for personal or business gain. Inspection can be denied when the corporation can show the shareholder's motive is for an unwarranted purpose (e.g., to obtain a shareholder list for junk mailing or to sell to another business) or for a purpose hostile to the corporation (e.g., to aid a competitor). Inspection can be denied when it is sought merely out of idle curiosity or for speculative purposes. Inspection can be refused when the purpose of the shareholder is to further political or social beliefs without regard to the welfare of the corporation. Many courts denied the right to inspection when it would have been harmful to the corporation or was sought solely for the purpose of annoyance, harassment, or causing vexation.

The Model Act provides safeguards, in addition to the proper purpose re quirement, to protect against abuses of the shareholder inspection right. Under the Model Act the shareholder must either own 5 percent of any class of out standing shares or must have been a shareholder for at least six months. The Model Act also requires that the request for inspection be in writing and state its purpose.

If a shareholder is denied inspection rights, he may seek a court order to compel access to corporate records. The burden of proof is on the corporation to show the stockholder sought the information for an improper purpose. A shareholder comes before the court with a presumption of good faith when he requests to be permitted to make inspection of corporate records.

Some statutes provide for penalties for an improper refusal of a shareholder's inspection rights. The Model Act makes the corporation liable for 10 percent of the value of the stock owned by the shareholder, in addition to any other remedy available to the shareholder. The corporation is also liable for the shareholder's legal fees in getting a court order for inspection, unless the corporation had a good faith doubt about the right of inspection under the circumstances.

An inspection need not be made personally. The shareholder can employ accountants, attorneys, stenographers, or other assistants who may be reasonably required to get the necessary information. The right to inspect includes the right to copy corporate records.

The right to inspect corporate records is derived from the common law. All the states have adopted statutes that give shareholders additional rights and access to information from the corporation. Corporations must mail an annual financial statement to shareholders. The Model Act requires a corporation to send a financial statement to any shareholder who makes a written request for one. The major corporate records must be made available at the corporation's registered office. Shareholders have an absolute right to shareholder lists at the shareholder meeting.

Right to Sue

Shareholders have the right to sue the corporation to enforce their rights and also have the right to sue the corporation to enforce rights it has itself neglected to enforce. There are two types of shareholder suits: a *direct suit* or a *derivative suit*. Direct suits can be categorized as either being brought by an individual shareholder or by one or several shareholders on behalf of a larger group, a *class action*.

A direct suit is brought by a shareholder to enforce his rights or to redress an injury to his interests as a shareholder. In a direct lawsuit any recovery goes to the shareholder plaintiff. Situations in which direct suits can be brought include to enforce the shareholder's preemptive rights, inspection rights, or voting rights;

to compel payment of dividends properly declared or on preferred stock ahead of common; to enforce rights under a share contract; or to compel dissolution. A direct suit can also be brought against the corporation when it performs an ultra vires act or when a corporate insider fails to disclose material information when trading corporate stock.

The suit is an individual suit if brought by one shareholder on his own behalf. In some instances one or several shareholders can institute a suit against the corporation, which is brought on behalf of a larger group of shareholders in the same position. This is called a *class action*. There are two key requirements for a class action: (1) a common question (e.g., to force the directors to pay validly declared dividends) and (2) a class too large to make it practical for the courts to hear multiple individual suits (e.g., a million shareholders of IBM suing for a $5 dividend each). In a class action the recovery, if any, goes to the shareholders represented by those bringing the suit, not just to those instituting the action.

A derivative lawsuit is brought by one or more shareholders on behalf of the corporation to enforce a right that belongs to the corporation. The term "derivative" refers to the fact that the shareholders' right to bring the suit is derived from the corporation. The suit is brought on behalf of the corporation because it refuses to bring a suit. This concept also allows shareholders to defend suits against the corporation in its name when the directors unjustifiably fail to do so. The recovery a shareholder obtains from an offending director, officer, employee, or shareholder in a derivative action belongs to the corporation. The suit is not brought in the name of the shareholder(s) but in the name of the corporation. Examples of a derivative suit include actions to recover damages for an ultra vires act, to recover damages for a breach of duty by management, and to recover improper dividends.

Before a shareholder can sue derivatively, he must meet several requirements. He must first make a *demand* on the directors or officers to take action on behalf of the corporation, and unless such a demand is futile or useless he must show the directors refused to sue. And he must show the refusal was in bad faith.

Right to Dissent

Some shareholders may disagree with an extraordinary corporate transaction approved by a majority of shareholders, such as a merger, consolidation, or liquidation. These minority dissenting shareholders are given what is called the *right of appraisal*, that is, the right to have the corporation purchase their shares for fair value. The value of their shares is determined as of the time immediately prior to the extraordinary transaction. A dissenting shareholder who is not satisfied with the proposed payment can bring a suit to have the fair value determined. Shareholders who wish to exercise their appraisal rights must file a written objection either before or at the shareholder meeting and must vote against it.

Right to Shareholders' Meeting

Most states require the bylaws to fix a time for an annual shareholders' meeting. The primary purpose of an annual meeting is to elect directors and review corporate operations. Any shareholder—big or small—can obtain a court order compelling an annual meeting if none is held for thirteen months. Special meetings may be called by the board or shareholders as authorized in the articles or the bylaws. Typically the bylaws or articles allow a special shareholders' meeting to be called by holders of 10 percent or more of the shares entitled to vote. Special meetings are not to be held instead of, but in addition to, the annual meeting. Special meetings are for handling matters requiring special attention.

Every shareholder has the right to participate at the shareholders' meeting by offering resolutions and by arguing and voting for or against the resolutions that are presented by shareholders or the board.

In some states the bylaws dispense with notice of the annual shareholders' meeting if the date and hour are specified in the articles or bylaws. Most states require written notice to be given for annual and special meetings to any shareholder eligible to vote. The notice ordinarily must include all matters the board plans to bring up at the meeting. Actions taken at a meeting for which proper notice has not been given are not legally valid unless shareholders waive notice requirements by attending the meeting or unless all of them sign a written notice of waiver.

A shareholder may vote in person or by written proxy. A shareholder is entitled to one vote for each share on each matter submitted to a vote at the meeting unless cumulative voting is being used for the election of directors.

A quorum is required to conduct a meeting. If a quorum is not available at the meeting, the shareholders cannot vote on any action, and the meeting must be adjourned. States vary on quorum requirements. Some states require a quorum of at least one-third of the corporation's outstanding voting shares eligible to vote. As a device to protect minority shareholders, the articles or bylaws of close corporations often provide for higher than normal quorum and voting requirement at a meeting.

If a quorum is present, an affirmative vote of the majority of shares at the meeting is normally required for a valid action by the shareholders. The bylaws or articles may provide that certain actions require approval of more than a simple majority of shareholders.

As a general rule, the shareholders can only act at a formal meeting. Most states provide an exception whereby shareholders may act, without a meeting, by a unanimous agreement in writing and signed by all the shareholders.

LIABILITIES OF SHAREHOLDERS

Probably the most important reason people form corporations instead of partnerships or other forms of business organizations is that the owner's (shareholder's) personal liability is limited. If the corporation is legally formed and operates within the laws, the shareholders, even if one or a very few, are generally immune from liability over and above the investment they made in the corporation—the amount they paid into the corporate treasury for their shares. The capital contributed by the shareholders, in the form of what was paid for shares purchased from the corporation, may be lost to the claims of creditors, but there is no personal liability for any unpaid balance. In other words, a person dealing with the corporation can look only to the corporation's assets to satisfy its obligations. In sum, the most the shareholder can lose is his investment in the shares he purchased.

There are some exceptions to unlimited liability in situations involving abuse of corporate privilege when courts "pierce the corporate veil" and impose personal liability on shareholders. Furthermore, as was also discussed previously, if the corporation has been defectively formed, shareholders who actively participated may be personally liable for the business's obligations. Other liabilities that frequently arise are explained in the following paragraphs.

Wage Claims

State statutes impose liability on major shareholders for wages of employees whose shares are not publicly traded. New York, for instance, imposes joint and several liability for the corporation's wages on the ten largest shareholders of such a corporation.

Unpaid Stock Subscriptions

A stock subscription is an offer by a prospective investor to buy shares of stock in a corporation. Most states provide that a subscription is irrevocable for a certain time period, unless the subscription expressly provides it can be revoked. The Model Act, for example, makes subscription agreements irrevocable for six months. In addition, the promoters of a corporation, before it is formed, may agree among themselves that their subscriptions are irrevocable for an agreed time period.

When the shares issued by a corporation are not fully paid for, the original subscriber or any transferee who does not give value or who knows the shares were not fully paid may be liable for the unpaid balance if the corporation is insolvent and the money is needed to pay creditors.

Watered Stock

Shareholders who are issued *watered stock*—stock sold for less than its par or stated value—are liable to the corporation or its creditors for the deficiency (the "water"), provided the facts show the undervalued price involved fraud on the part of the shareholder or bad faith on the part of the directors. Stock watering often occurs when the stock is issued as fully paid in return for property or services that were so overvalued that the stock is not actually paid in full. The watered stock rule is primarily meant to protect the corporation's creditors, who are harmed when investors in the corporation underpay for their shares rather than pay for their true value. As in the case of unpaid subscriptions, when shareholders underpay for stock, they are liable to creditors to whom the corporation owes money. The watered stock liability applies only to the initial purchase of shares from the corporation upon their issuance, not to shares purchased on the market nor to purchases of treasury shares.

Improper or Illegal Dividends

Shareholders are usually liable for the return of any dividend that was improperly paid. If a dividend is paid while the corporation is insolvent, shareholders are always liable for its return, whether or not they know of the illegal dividend. This rule is for the protection of creditors. The shareholders' liability is either to the corporation or its creditors. When the corporation is not insolvent, shareholders are liable to the corporation or creditors for an improper dividend only if the shareholders knew the distribution was illegal.

Liability of Controlling Shareholders

Normally shareholders owe no fiduciary duty to the corporation or other shareholders. An exception to the lack of a fiduciary duty applies to controlling shareholders. Controlling shareholders are shareholders who own a sufficient number of shares to have effective control over the corporation. In many jurisdictions, but not all, controlling shareholders owe a fiduciary duty to minority shareholders, much like that which partners owe each other in partnerships.

One major area in which the fiduciary duty arises is the selling of controlling shares in a block by a majority shareholder for more than other shareholders can—at a "premium," at more than the market value of the shares held by smaller shareholders. Controlling shareholders are able to do this because a controlling interest is usually worth more than a minority interest. Many courts compel the majority shareholders to redistribute the premium to the other shareholders.

Many courts require sales of controlling interests to be made with due care. The controlling shareholder must make a reasonable investigation so as not to transfer control to corporate looters who plan to wrongfully convert the assets of the corporation or act in a manner that is detrimentally to the best interest of the business.

Controlling shareholders, much like directors, cannot seize a corporate opportunity. Controlling shareholders cannot, in bad faith, use their power to suppress dividends for wrongful purposes. Such improper purposes include forcing minority shareholders to sell their stock, depressing the price of the stock, or advancing the personal interests of the directors. Remedies can include a court order directing the declaration of a dividend or awarding damages to the minority shareholders. Controlling shareholders cannot make changes in the corporation's structure that harm the minority, changes which might happen when the controlling shareholder attempts to liquidate the corporation.

4

Financial Structure of the Corporation

A corporation, like any other form of business, needs capital to function. Capital can be raised in three ways: (1) from selling ownership, (2) from borrowing, and—after business begins—(3) from earnings.

All for-profit corporations must issue and sell shares of stock, also called *equity securities*. This method of financing is known as *equity financing*. A share of stock represents an ownership interest in the corporation; thus, when a corporation sells shares to raise capital, it is selling ownership.

The two principal methods a corporation borrows are by procuring a loan from others, such as a bank, or by selling bonds. Bonds are essentially promissory notes that obligate the corporation to pay the bondholder the principal (amount of loan) on a stated maturity date and at a fixed rate of interest on the principal, which is payable at regular intervals until maturity. Bonds are sold to institutions and individuals and this method of financing is called *debt financing*. Bonds are also called *debt securities*. Share of stock represents an ownership interest in the corporation. Bonds, or debt securities, do not represent an ownership interest. They create a debtor-creditor relationship between the corporation and the bond-holder. Viewed another way, a corporation is owned by its shareholders and indebted to its bondholders.

After a corporation has been in operation for some time, a variety of financing alternatives are available to it, including obtaining capital through retained earnings, short-term borrowing, and accounts receivable financing. However, the options for the newly formed corporation are considerably more limited. The principle methods for initially financing a corporation attempting to get started are the sale of debt or equity securities.

The corporation *issues* equity and debt securities, and the corporation is known as the *issuer*. A change of ownership after the issuance of a security is called a *transfer*. Securities that have been issued by the corporation are said to be *outstanding*. In order to issue debt or equity securities, the corporation must be authorized as described in the articles of incorporation, bylaws, or the corporation statutes. A security is either *certificated* or *uncertificated*. Certificated securities are represented by a written instrument issued in bearer or registered form. Uncertificated securities are not represented by a written instrument, and their transfer is registered in corporation books maintained for that purpose. Certificated securities are negotiable instruments, which means they are readily transferable by simply endorsing and delivering the stock certificate. The transfer of a certificated security occurs with the transfer of the certificate itself. The transfer of ownership of an uncertificated security can be accomplished with or without a written instruction directing the corporate issuer to register the security in the name of the transferee. Although a written instrument is not needed for a valid transfer of an uncertificated security, an expression of intent to make the transfer is required.

DEBT SECURITIES

A bond creates a debtor-creditor relationship between the corporation issuing the bond and the bondholder. Virtually all state statutes allow the board of directors to incur debt for the corporation without shareholder approval. However, corporate borrowing may be restricted by the corporation itself through articles and bylaws and by the state in its laws.

A bond is a *negotiable security* (readily transferrable) when issued in a bearer or registered form and used as a medium of investment. An *indenture* is a bond agreement that specifies the contractual rights and duties of the corporation and its bondholders. Debt securities are normally issued under an indenture that specifies in great detail the terms of the loan.

Bonds or debt securities can be classified according to different types, depending upon their characteristics. A particular bond may be a combination of several of these types. Bonds are classified as follows:

1. *Registered Bonds*. These bonds are issued to owners whose names and addresses are registered by the owners themselves on the books of a corporation. Payments of principal and interest are made only to the bondholder of record. The payments are mailed to the registered owner of the bond.

2. *Bearer Bonds*. These are sometimes called coupon bonds. Such bonds are not registered in the name of any person. Bearer bonds have interest coupons attached to them, and this is why they are sometimes referred to as *coupon bonds*. Principal and interest are payable to the person in possession of the bond and its coupons.

3. *Redeemable Bonds*. These bonds are payable before maturity at the option of the corporation. They are sometimes termed *callable* bonds. A redemption provision in the bond agreement allows the corporation to redeem or call (pay off) all or part of the issue before maturity at a specified redemption price.

4. *Convertible Bonds*. These bonds may be exchanged, usually at the option of the holder, for shares of the corporation at a specified ratio of stock to bonds.

5. *Secured Bonds*. These are secured by specified assets of the corporation. The bondholder is a secured creditor of the corporation. The secured bondholder has not only a lien on specified property but also a claim, as does any creditor, against the general assets of the corporation.

6. *Debenture Bonds (Unsecured)*. These are unsecured bonds, and their holders have the status of general creditors. Debentures ordinarily are not issued for longer than fifteen-year terms. As a protection for unsecured bondholders, the debenture agreements often impose restrictions upon the corporation's subsequent borrowing, payment of dividends, and redemption and reacquisition of its shares.

7. *Income Bonds*. Debt securities usually bear a fixed interest, which is payable without regard to the financial condition of the corporation. Income bonds, in contrast, condition payment of interest to some degree upon corporate earnings. It is not unusual for an income bond to make interest payable only if, and to the extent, it is earned. Some income bonds provide a stated percentage of return regardless of earnings and confer additional payments dependent upon earnings.

STOCKS

Stock Subscriptions

When a corporation wants to sell new shares of its stock, it seeks offers from parties to buy the shares. These offers for the new corporate stock are called *subscriptions*. Stock subscriptions are used both before incorporation to raise capital to get the corporation started and after incorporation to raise capital when money is needed during the operation of the corporation. Thus subscriptions are either pre-incorporation or post-incorporation.

Subscriptions are used to sign up for shares before the shares are actually available. A subscription is a contract to take and pay for a certain number of shares from the corporation by a subscriber. When the board of directors decides to accept the subscription, a formal contract for the purchase and sale of the shares is created.

Pre-incorporation subscriptions sought by promoters of the corporation present a problem in that the offers are made to the corporations and therefore cannot be accepted until after incorporation. As a general rule a stock subscription, like any offer, is revocable prior to acceptance. However, most states have adopted the rule, as in the Model Act, that a pre-incorporation subscription is irrevocable for a period of six months, absent an agreement to the contrary. Making the subscription irrevocable for a definite, reasonable period of time solves the pre-incorporation problem for promoters who, without such a rule, could not count on having any set amount of capital necessary to get the corporation organized until the corporation is actually formed and able to accept offers.

There are other conditions in which pre-incorporation subscriptions become irrevocable, even in states that do not provide for a period of irrevocability or where that period has expired. A pre-incorporation subscription is irrevocable if each subscriber in a group has subscribed in consideration of the promise of the others to subscribe. In this case, all of them must agree before any one of them can revoke. A subscription is irrevocable if a subscriber gave the corporation an irrevocable option to sell him shares in return for consideration furnished by the promoter.

A post-incorporation subscription may be revoked by a subscriber any time prior to its acceptance.

Certain conditions must exist before a subscription is enforceable by the corporation. Some states require a subscription to be in writing and signed. A corporation must be fully organized as a *de jure* corporation. The corporation must be as described or proposed to the subscriber, that is, it cannot be materially different in purpose or function from that which is represented. The shares subscribed for must be legally issuable by the corporation—the shares of the corporation must not be oversubscribed. And finally, the shares subscribed for must be promptly called, that is, be accepted without unreasonable delay by the corporation. Solvency of the corporation is not a condition to the enforceability of a subscription by the subscriber.

If the subscription by a promoter or the corporation is fraudulent, the offer can be revoked, even if consideration was given for it or there is a statutorily imposed period of irrevocability. Some jurisdictions will not impute the promoter's fraud to the corporation unless the directors knew of the fraud prior to acceptance.

A corporation cannot release a subscriber unless *all* the shareholders and other subscribers consent *and* the release would cause no harm to the creditors.

When the subscription is accepted by the corporation, the subscriber becomes a shareholder even though he may not have paid for the stock or received the certificates. With such acceptance by the corporation, this person as a shareholder can receive dividends and vote.

A post-incorporation agreement to sell stock may be a contract to purchase shares rather than a subscription, and the difference is important. A subscriber is liable for the full price of the shares when the subscription is accepted by the corporation. A purchaser under the contract to buy the shares does not become a shareholder and is thus not liable for the price of the shares until a stock certificate is tendered and a price is paid. However, he is liable on the contract for its breach if he fails to perform. If the contract of sale calls for installment payments, the buyer does not become a shareholder with all the attendant rights and liabilities until all payments are made. If purchase of stock is an installment sale rather than a subscription, the corporation's insolvency is a defense to the obligation to pay. An insolvent corporation, of course, can enforce a subscription liability. Subscription liability can also be enforced by a trustee of the corporation in bankruptcy or by a receiver. A creditor also can enforce a subscription if the corporation is insolvent.

Authorization and Issuance of Shares

Shares must be *authorized* by the articles of incorporation before they can be validly *issued* by the corporation, that is, before they can be offered and sold. The total amount of stock authorized in the articles is referred to as *authorized capital stock*. As the authorized shares are sold by the corporation, they become *issued* and *outstanding*. Unauthorized shares of stock that the corporation attempts to issue are void.

The articles should specify the classes of shares and the maximum number of shares per class that are authorized. The classes and amounts of shares set forth in the articles are the *authorized stock*. Once the classes and amount of shares the corporation is authorized to issue have been established in the charter, they cannot be increased or decreased unless an amendment to that effect has been made to the charter and approved by the shareholders. A corporation may issue fewer shares than it is authorized to issue, but not more. If the shares of stock issued by the corporation are unauthorized, the subscriber can rescind his subscription agreement and recover any consideration given to the corporation in exchange for the shares.

Shares of stock, like bonds, may be issued in certificated or uncertificated form and are transferable accordingly.

Un-issued stock is authorized stock that has not yet been issued. *Issued* stock is stock that has been sold and delivered to shareholders. Issuance requires a resolution by the board of directors. Issuance creates shareholder status in the purchaser. The issuance of shares can precede distribution of the certificates, which are merely evidence of shareholder status. Stock issued by the corporation that is in the hands of shareholders is *outstanding* stock.

Treasury stock is stock that has been issued to shareholders and is later repurchased by the corporation. Treasury stock thus is authorized and issued but not outstanding. Treasury stock must be paid for with the corporation's unreserved and unrestricted surplus funds (earned surplus, capital surplus, or paid-in surplus), but the corporation cannot use original capital funds to repurchase stock. Treasury shares may not be voted, dividends cannot be paid on them, and they do not have preemptive rights. The corporation may resell, hold, or cancel its treasury shares. A corporation may transfer ownership of treasury stock without receiving par value or stated value in exchange. Cancelling the shares reduces the number of shares issued, and the corporation can then issue new stock so long as it does not exceed the authorized number of shares. Sale or purchase by a corporation of its own shares usually does not result in a taxable gain or deductible loss.

Types of Stock

The stock of a corporation may be divided into two or more classes. *Common* and *preferred* shares are the two principal classes of stock issued by corporations, but there are many kinds of common and preferred shares.

Common Stock and Preferred Shares

Common stock is the basic class of stock issued by the corporation. All corporations must have at least one class of stock, common stock. If the corporation has only one class of stock, it is usually deemed to be common stock, even if the articles do not use the term. Common stock is the voting stock of the corporation, unless the common stock is designated as nonvoting. Each share typically entitles the holder to one vote. The common stockholder has no right to dividends unless the directors, in their discretion, declare them. The common shareholder has the right to share in the general distribution of assets upon dissolution of the corporation. The corporation may have several classes of common stock. Stock is regarded as "common" in the sense that it has the lowest priority in relation to other classes of shares when the corporation pays interest or dividends, or distributes capital upon dissolution. Common stock is ordinary stock that has no special rights or preferences for such payments and distributions.

Preferred shares have a contractual preference over other classes of stock, normally with respect to dividends and the distribution of assets upon dissolution. Other types of special rights or privileges are not generally regarded as removing a stock from the classification of common stock. The contractual rights of preferred shares are superior to those of common stock, which is last in line for dividends and payments when the corporation is liquidated. Thus, for instance, if the corporation decides to pay a dividend, it must pay the preferred shareholders first if the priority is dividends. Preferred stock that is often issued provides a fixed dividend, payable even if there is no dividend on common stock. If the preference is distribution of assets upon dissolution, the preferred shareholders are first in line to receive payments for the sale of assets before any money is returned to the common stockholders. The common shareholder is given no guarantees or special preferences, as distinguished from the preferred share-holder, who is. Preferred shares are ordinarily nonvoting, although they may be given voting rights if there has been no preferred dividend for a set time period. Preferred shares are often held by corporate rather than individual investors because corporations pay no tax on most dividend income. Preferred stock is frequently used in corporate mergers and reorganizations as a means of payment or raising capital without giving up voting control of the corporation.

Cumulative and Noncumulative Preferred Stock

Preferred shares in which dividends are required to be paid may be classified as *cumulative* or *noncumulative*. In the case of cumulative preferred stock, if dividends have not been paid to the preferred shareholder in one or more prior years, he is entitled to receive the dividends in arrears when the corporation is capable of paying them and before they can be paid to owners of common stock. Noncumulative preferred stock implies that regular dividends do not build up upon the failure of the board to declare them, and all the rights to a dividend for the period omitted are completely gone. Cumulative preferred dividends do not require the corporation in lean years to pay dividends it cannot afford, only that the obligation to pay such dividends continues and accumulates and must be eventually paid when the corporation is able to pay them.

In order to have the right to cumulative dividends, it is not necessary for the articles to expressly state that the right to dividends by preferred shareholders is "cumulative" or that dividends are guaranteed. A provision in the articles that does guarantee dividends is usually interpreted to mean that dividends are cumulative. Any manifestation of intent that preferred stock is cumulative is sufficient, such as the articles stating that no dividends can be paid upon common stock until unpaid dividends for all preceding years have been paid to the preferred shareholders. The courts have typically held that, unless expressly issued as noncumulative stock, preferred stock is to be regarded as cumulative, particularly with respect to each year in which there was a surplus available for dividend declaration.

Participating and Nonparticipating Preferred Stock

Preferred shares may be classified as either *participating* or *nonparticipating*. Participating stock receives not only the basic stipulated preferred dividend but also shares on a prescribed basis in earnings with common stock earnings that are over and above those delared for the common stock. For instance, the preferred shareholder typically is entitled to receive only a specific percentage dividend, such as five percent. Should the corporation have a highly profitable year, the amount left to divide among common shareholders might exceed the percentage to which the preferred shareholder is entitled. If the corporation has preferred shareholders, the common shareholders are entitled to receive no more than the prescribed percentage dividend due preferred shareholders—in this case five percent, and the money left over is to be divided on a proportional basis between the preferred and common shareholders. Preferred shares can also be participating as to any excess profits from the liquidation of the corporation. In sum, participating preferred shares get a "second helping" of dividends.

Redeemable and Convertible Stock

Stock ordinarily exists for the life of the corporation. However, *redeemable* and *convertible* shares may be made terminable at an earlier date. Redeemable shares are subject to redemption (recall by the corporation) at a fixed price, usually above the issuing price paid to the corporation by the stockholder. Redemption is the involuntary sale of the shares to the corporation. The redeemed shares cease to exist after redemption, as distinguished from treasury shares, which are owned by the corporation after repurchase. The call price is generally fixed in the articles of incorporation, but it also may be subject to an agreement among the shareholders themselves. Redemption by the corporation is not allowed when the corporation is insolvent, when the purchase of shares would make the corporation insolvent, or when the purchase would reduce the net assets in a way that would adversely affect the corporation.

Convertible shares may be recalled by the corporation in exchange for a different type of share or for bonds of the corporation. For instance, convertible common stock might be exchanged for preferred stock. Common stock and preferred stock may be convertible or redeemable.

Voting and Nonvoting Stock

Stock may be made *voting* or *nonvoting* by the articles of incorporation. If the articles are silent as to voting rights, each outstanding share of stock is deemed to be voting. However, the right to vote in board elections is usually restricted to common stock and denied to preferred shares. The New York Stock Exchange will not list companies with publicly held, nonvoting common shares in order to preclude a situation in which a small number of voting shares is purchased by promoters to control the company while leaving the public only as investors in a large class of nonvoting shares.

Par and No-Par Stock

The corporation issues either *par value* or *no-par value* stock, terms that refer to whether or not the corporation sets a value on stock when it is initially issued and sold.

Par value shares are shares issued with an arbitrary value printed on the face of the certificate, such as one dollar per share. The par value of stock must be stated in the articles of incorporation. The person subscribing to the stock and acquiring it from the corporation must pay no less than that amount. The corporation may sell the stock for more than the par value, but not less (discount). Corporations typically set par value, when they use it, at a very low amount, such as one dollar—far below what the shares will actually sell for. The consideration received for the shares constitutes *stated capital* and is allocated to the *capital account* to the extent of the amount represented by the par value of the shares. Any excess of the purchase price over par value is allocated to *capital surplus*. When the stock is issued in excess of par value, the excess is known as *paid-in capital* or *premium*. The total amount received on the sale of par value stock is known as *contributed capital*.

Shares that are issued with no value fixed on the certificate are called no-par shares. In this case the board fixes the amount the subscriber will pay the corporation. The amount the board sets for no-par stock is called its *stated value*. The consideration received for no-par stock is allocated to stated capital unless within sixty days after issuance the directors allocate any or all of the consideration to capital surplus. Par value shares allow the directors great latitude in establishing capital surplus. Some states bar the issuance of no-par stock, and others bar the issuance of par stock. The revised Model Act deletes the terms "par" and "no-par" stock but does not prohibit the use of either type of stock if the articles so provide.

Par or no-par value should not be confused with the *book value* and *market value* of the stock. Book value of shares is found by dividing the value of the corporate assets by the number of outstanding shares. The market value of a share of stock is the price at which it can be voluntarily bought or sold.

Corporate Capital

Corporate capital represents the monetary value of the combined ownerships of shareholders of a corporation. A portion of the price of stock issued by the corporation must be set aside in the *capital stock* account, which is generally referred to as the *stated capital* of the corporation. Stated capital is the sum of the value of shares issued at their par value and their stated value, in other words, the contributed capital equal to par value or stated value. The stated capital of the corporation appears on the equity side of the corporate balance sheet. Stated capital is the measure of a corporation's capital strength. Statutory safeguards protect shareholders and creditors against a diminution in stated capital that would impair a company's financial condition. These safeguards generally require the stated capital to exceed the sum total of the liquidation preferences payable on outstanding preferred shares plus the sum par value of outstanding shares without liquidation preferences.

If shares are issued for more than their par value or stated value (in the case of no-par stock), the excess is called *paid-in surplus* and allocated to the *capital surplus account*. In other words, paid-in surplus is contributed capital in excess of par value or stated value. *Surplus* simply means the excess of the net assets of a corporation over its stated capital. Capital surplus is also called *capital in excess of par* or *unearned surplus*. *Earned surplus*, also referred to as *retained earnings*, is that portion of the surplus of a corporation consisting of the balance of its net profits; income; gains earned, retained, and accumulated by the corporation from the date of the inception of the corporation or from the last date on which a deficit was eliminated. Capital surplus should be distinguished from earned surplus in that the former consists of the corporation's entire surplus other than the latter. *Reduction surplus* is created by reducing downward the stated value of outstanding shares. This is done by board and shareholder resolution plus a filing with the secretary of state. *Revaluation surplus* is surplus created by an upward valuation of assets.

Proper Consideration for Shares

Proper consideration, in terms of kind and amount, must be paid to the corporation for stock it issues. It is a fundamental principle that the price of stock must be *fully* paid, and this principle applies to both the kind and amount of consideration.

Kind of Consideration

As to the kind of consideration, shares may lawfully be issued *only* for money, past services (not future services), debts cancelled, or property received. If stock is issued for any other kind of consideration, it is not fully paid. For example, an unsecured promissory note is not lawful consideration in most states. A secured promissory is valid consideration. Pre-incorporation services are not usually considered valid consideration, including commissions paid in stock to underwriters who sell the stock to the public prior to the incorporation. Most stock issued by a corporation is paid for in cash. Any property or services, to be valid payment for shares, must be usable by the corporation in operating its business.

Amount of Consideration (Watered or Discount Stock)

The shares newly issued by a corporation must be issued for consideration (i.e., cash, property, or past services) in an amount at least equal to the par value of par value shares and the stated value of no-par shares. If no consideration is paid for stock, it is called *bonus stock*. If the stock is paid for in cash that is less than the par or stated value, the stock is called *discount stock*. If the stock is paid for in property or services that are worth less than par or stated value, it is called *watered stock*. The term "watered stock" has come to be commonly used to refer to bonus stock and discount stock as well, that is, any stock issued for consideration that is less than the value of the stock. The next section synonymously uses the terms watered stock, watering, discounting, and discounted stock to refer generally to the issuance of stock for less than adequate consideration.

Liability for Inadequate Consideration

As a general rule, shareholders who are issued watered stock must reimburse the corporation for the difference between the price they paid and the stock's greater par, or stated, value. Shareholders are liable for the value of stock received in exchange for a promise to perform services in the future or for a promissory note if they do not perform the services or pay the note. The liability of the shareholders on watered stock is enforceable by both the corporation and its creditors. The corporation can also cancel any shares not paid for in a stock subscription. A creditor can also sue, like the corporation, to recover for any unpaid portion. Most states allow a lawsuit to be brought only by creditors who extend credit after the shares are issued, on the theory that only such post-sale creditors are defrauded. In these states post-sale creditors may not recover if they know about the watering when they extend credit. A minority of states allow recovery by all creditors. Creditors recover through an action called a *creditor's bill in equity*. Shareholders who have paid full value for their shares may also sue the discounter shareholder to pay up in full.

In addition to the original subscriber who bought watered stock, liability may also be imposed upon knowing transferrers of the discounted shares, directors who approved the sale, and the promoters.

Since the value of cash is apparent, watering is not often an issue when cash is given for newly issued stock. Watering is more of a problem when the noncash items of property or services are exchanged for the newly issued stock. When stock is newly issued by the corporation, the directors fix the value of any property and services given to the corporation in exchange for the shares. Watering occurs when the directors knowingly accept overvalued property or services for the stock. In the majority of jurisdictions, the value established by the directors cannot be challenged if they acted in good faith. This is the *good faith rule*. However, in some jurisdictions the good faith of the directors is irrelevant, and the stock is considered watered if the property or services received is in fact worth less than par. This is called the *actual* or *value rule*.

Some states provide an exception to the requirement that stock issued by the corporation be paid for with consideration no less than par or stated value. This exception occurs when the board in good faith decides it cannot get par value or stated value for the stock. Directors are personally liable if they acted in bad faith in approving watered stock.

Dividends

A person who purchases stock in a corporation is making an investment from which a profit is expected. The shareholder may make a profit from an increase in the market value of the shares, from dividend, from both, or from neither. A *dividend* is a distribution of cash, property, or corporate stock by the corporation to its shareholders that represents income or profit on their investment. The dividend paid on the stock is a portion of the company's earnings distributed pro rata among the shares.

Stockholders do not have the absolute right to receive dividends. Whether dividends are to be paid (declared), how large they will be, and when they will be paid are left virtually entirely up to the discretion of the board of directors. A few statutes permit the articles to require "mandatory" dividends, but such provisions are rare. Furthermore, any dividend declared by the board must be valid and lawful, that is, it is subject to the relative rights of other shareholders (regarding preferences, accumulation of dividends, and participation), subject to a proper source of available funds from which to pay dividends, and cannot be given if the corporation is insolvent or would become so because of the dividends.

Kinds of Dividends

Dividends can be paid in cash or property and also in the stock of the corporation. Normally dividends are made in cash, but occasionally the corporation makes noncash dividends of property or stock. Property dividends consist of corporate assets, including stock of another company the corporation has been holding as an asset.

When the corporation declares its own stock as a dividend, it is said to issue a *stock dividend*. A stock dividend is a ratable distribution of additional shares of the capital stock of the corporation to the shareholders. This kind of distribution is technically not a dividend as are cash or property dividends because it does not involve a transfer of property from the corporation to its shareholders. Stock dividends can be characterized as merely "psychological" dividends. Shareholders receive certificates evidencing dividend shares, but the company does not actually distribute any of its cash or assets. Following the payment of the stock dividend, the assets of the corporation are no less than they were before (in contrast to the case of cash or property dividends); only the total of outstanding and issued shares is increased. There is also no increase in the shareholder's relative interest in the net worth of the corporation over what he had before, unless the dividend is paid on only one of several classes of stock. The stock dividend does result in a decrease in the proportionate interest of the shareholder in the assets of the corporation. The book value of each share held by the stockholder is diluted by the increased number of shares, but his total investment remains the same by virtue of the increased number of shares he holds. Each shareholder becomes an owner of a larger number of shares but gets no real immediate benefit as a result because the value of the preexisting shares is diluted. However, there is a long-run benefit since there is a tendency for the shares to increase in value. Stock dividends are not taxable as income because no profit is realized unless the shares are later sold at an appreciated market value.

A stock dividend should not be confused with a *stock split*, which is not a real dividend. In a stock split the corporation simply exchanges an existing share for two or more new shares. What makes the stock split different is that it is restructuring of shares with no commitment to transfer capital. The stock split does not increase the capital account, and instead reduces the shares' stated value, while a stock dividend does just the opposite. In a stock split, unlike a stock dividend, the shareholder's proportionate interest in the assets of the corporation remains unchanged. A stock split does not affect the accumulated earnings account or total assets of the firm. It increases the number of shares outstanding and reduces the par or stated value of the stock; e.g., 1,000 shares of ten dollars par value with two-to-one stock split results in 2,000 shares at five dollars par.

A *liquidation dividend* is a distribution of capital assets in the form of a dividend upon termination of the company. A liquidating dividend also includes a distribution of capital to common shareholders from the company, as opposed to accumulated profits or current earnings.

Sources of Dividends

Dividends can never be from the corporation's stated capital account, which is the sum of the price it received for par value and stated value stock at par value and stated value. Dividends traditionally could be paid only from a particular source and that is the *earned surplus account*. Earned surplus is the total net profits (i.e., all profits less all losses) of the corporation in its history less prior dividends. Earned surplus is also referred to as *retained earnings*. The earned surplus account is a cumulative figure representing the earnings of the corporation that exceed its losses over the years. This accumulated income may be used to pay dividends even in profitless years.

Some states have adopted an exception to the requirement that the earned surplus account be in the black; it is called the *nimble dividends rule*. Nimble dividends are paid out of the year's current net earnings (net profits for the current year or the year just ended), even though the net figure in the earned surplus account is still negative (i.e., prior year's deficit has not been made up). In effect, nimble dividends are distributions out of capital. The purpose for the nimble dividends exception is to encourage more investment in the company by allowing a previously unprofitable company the opportunity to give stockholders a dividend in the current profitable year without waiting for full recovery in the earned surplus account. The earnings or surplus must be in the form of available cash, not in accounts receivables or inventories.

A number of states are less restrictive and permit distributions to be paid out of any surplus—earned or capital. The Model Act allows companies to make distribution from their capital surplus accounts (paid in surplus). The capital surplus account is also referred to as *paid in surplus*. In other states paid in surplus can be used to pay dividends on preferred but not on common stock. The capital surplus account is the entire surplus of the corporation other than its earned surplus. It consists of the amounts paid for stock in excess of its par value or its stated value or from a reappraisal upward of certain corporate assets. These distributions have the same requirements as dividends, such as approval by the board of directors. But such distributions are not dividends, and the shareholders must be told they are receiving a capital surplus distribution and not a dividend.

Reduction surplus can be used in some, but not all, states to pay dividends. Reduction surplus is created by reducing downward the stated value of outstanding shares. Dividends from the reduction surplus require approval by director and shareholder resolution plus filing with the secretary of state.

Revaluation surplus is defined as surplus created by upward revaluation of assets. In very few states can it be used to pay dividends. By requiring the dividends to come from an existing surplus in corporate funds, the corporation is prevented from paying dividends out of the original capital investment in the company.

Some states are highly restrictive about the source for dividends. For instance, a number of states allow dividends to be paid only from current net earnings, that is, the source of funds must be the net profits of the corporation for the current fiscal year or the fiscal year just ended. Some states allow paid in surplus to be used to pay dividends only on preferred but not on common stock.

The idea behind requiring dividends to come from some corporate earnings "surplus" is to prevent dividends from impairing the capital or causing the corporation to become unable to pay its debts. There is an exception to this principle that allows corporations with *wasting assets* to impair capital while declaring a dividend. Wasting assets corporations include businesses that are designed to exhaust or use the assets of the corporation (such as mines, oilfields, and other natural resource extraction activities). A wasting corporation may also be established for the purpose of buying and liquidating the assets of a bankrupt business.

Declaration and Distribution of Dividends

Whether a dividend is to be paid and what its size will be are normally decisions made at the exclusive discretion of the board. With one exception, the shareholders cannot compel a declaration of a dividend. That exception occurs when (1) there are corporate cash earnings or surplus available out of which a dividend can be drawn; and (2) the board is withholding a dividend dishonestly, fraudulently, unreasonably, in bad faith, out of spite, for its own private purposes, or for some other reason that is a clear abuse of discretion. A shareholder seeking a court order to compel the directors to declare a dividend must, in addition to all the other requirements, make a *demand* to the board for a dividend before commencing the suit. A large amount of accumulated surplus in the corporation's hands will not alone justify compelling the directors to declare a dividend when the funds, in their good faith judgment, should be retained for bona fide corporate purposes.

A court will give great deference to, and refuse to substitute its judgment for, the good faith business judgment of the directors on a dividend declaration. In other words, the "business judgement" rule applies to the directors' decision whether or not to declare a dividend. The courts, however, will allow a challenge to the board's decision to declare a dividend if the funds were not legally available for the dividend, the division among shareholders was not fair and uniform, or the special rights of any particular class of stock were not observed.

If a distribution is to be made, dividends must be paid to preferred shareholders before any distribution is made to common shareholders. Discrimination is prohibited in the declaration of dividends among shareholders of the same class. A dividend cannot be made if it is paid while the corporation is insolvent or if distribution will make the corporation insolvent. A corporation is insolvent if it cannot pay its debts and obligations as they become due. A dividend cannot be paid if the assets after the payment are less than debts and the liquidation preferences of preferred stock. If the corporation has watered stock outstanding, most states allow dividends if an appropriate surplus is available out of which to pay them. In other words, the surplus does not have to be applied to squeeze out the water in the shares. A minority of states require earnings to be retained up to the amount of water in the shares.

Once a cash or property dividend is declared and it is valid, the dividend becomes a debt the corporation owes shareholders and cannot be revoked. The shareholders can, as creditors, sue the corporation to recover the amount of the lawfully declared dividends the corporation owes them. A cash or property dividend can be revoked and recalled, however, when the declaration is illegal, ultra vires, in the fraud of creditors, revoked at the same meeting it was declared, made payable in the future but has not been made public or communicated to the stockholders; or when the stock has not been issued. Unlike a cash or property dividend, a stock dividend can be revoked before it is paid.

When the dividend is declared, the corporation will set a payment date, the final one allowed for payment of the obligation, after which a shareholder can sue if the dividend is not paid. A record date is also set, which is the cutoff date for closing the corporate books, to determine which shareholders will be paid dividends. Persons buying shares before the record date will receive the dividend from the corporation, and those who purchase stock from it after the record date must make arrangements with the seller to have the dividend turned over to them. The buyer of the stock can sue the seller for return of the dividend.

Dividends normally will be made payable to the stockholders on the date the corporation sets as the record date, which is the cutoff time for determining who is entitled to payment. Everyone who is listed on the corporation's record will get the dividend.

Liability for Dividends

Shareholders and directors are liable for unlawful dividends, that is, dividends that are contrary to the incorporation statute or the articles of incorporation. Directors who declared an unlawful dividend are personally liable to the corporation for the benefit of corporate creditors for the amount of the unlawful dividend. If the corporation is not insolvent, it cannot recover illegal dividends from directors. The directors do not escape liability by delegation of the power to declare dividends to an executive committee. In most states liability for illegal dividends is not strict liability, which was the traditional rule. Directors are not liable when they rely in good faith upon financial statements showing the availability of proper sources and amounts of funds for a dividend presented by the corporation's officers, public accountants, or finance committee. A director who dissents to the declaration of a dividend at the board meeting is not liable. Absence from the board meeting where the illegal dividend was declared is also probably a good defense if the director has a valid excuse for having missed the meeting.

Shareholders who receive unlawful dividends are liable to return or repay them to the corporation for the benefit of creditors when certain factors are present. These factors include (1) if the shareholder had knowledge of the illegality when the dividend was declared, (2) if the illegal dividend was a result of the shareholder's fraudulent behavior, or (3) if the corporation is or was rendered insolvent by the dividend, regardless of the shareholder's knowledge or good faith. An unsuspecting or innocent shareholder who receives an illegal dividend from a solvent corporation is not liable to make a refund. However, most states require the corporation to identify the source against which the dividend is charged, and thus shareholders are put on notice if it is drawn from an unlawful source.

Stock Options, Rights, and Warrants

A corporation may issue options to purchase its shares. An option holder has the right to purchase a specified amount of shares of stock at a stated price within a specified time period. Options are sometimes offered as an alternative to the outright issuance of stock in order to attract additional investment by the present owners, act as an inducement to obtain the services of new executives, or retain or reward the services of valued executives in the company. Options are classified as securities. Options can also be acquired in the hope the price of the stock will go up.

Written certificates evidencing the options are called *warrants*. Short-term options are called *rights*, and, unlike warrants, they are usually not transferable (negotiable) and expire at a relatively early date. Rights are frequently issued to shareholders so that they may protect their existing stock interests in buying pro rata shares of a new issue.

Redemption and Repurchase of Shares

In a redemption, the corporation recalls stock held by shareholders at a fixed price, pursuant to a provision in the articles giving the corporation the right of redemption for designated classes (usually preferred) of stock. A redemption is called by the directors and is an involuntary sale under which the shareholder is forced to sell the shares to the corporation. The redemption price is usually the issued price paid to the corporation by the stockholder, although it may also be subject to an agreement among the shareholders themselves. Once the directors "call" shares for redemption, the call is irrevocable. The holders of the called shares become creditors of the corporation and can sue it to be paid for their shares. As a general rule, common shares cannot be redeemed, only preferred shares.

A corporation may also *repurchase* its own shares, calling on its shareholders to voluntarily sell their shares to it. Common stock as well as preferred stock can be repurchased. A corporation may validly obligate itself at the time of subscription, or later, to repurchase particular shares at the option of the shareholder. This agreement is enforceable by the shareholders.

Redemption or repurchase of shares by the corporation is not allowed when the corporation is insolvent, when the purchase of shares would make it insolvent, or when the purchase would reduce the net assets in a way that would adversely affect the corporation.

Funds for a repurchase or redemption of shares can be taken from earned surplus, from paid-in surplus, or from reduction surplus in most states. Even if there is no surplus at all, stated capital can be used in some states to make redemptions.

The decision of the directors to repurchase shares can only be made for corporate not personal reasons. Repurchases are often used as a means to repel a takeover by a corporate raider. The repurchase in this case would be lawful if done to prevent a disadvantageous change in business policy that might be brought about by the raider, but not if done by the directors only to save their jobs or for some other personal purpose. It will be relevant whether the board made a careful study of the practices and policies of the raider, as distinguished from having plunged ahead in a massive repurchase program without performing such an analysis. Repurchases similarly cannot be used to unfairly favor some shareholders at the expense of others, e.g., when the directors want to bail out a shareholder who needed to sell his stock to obtain cash to avoid bankruptcy. This would be a breach of the director's fiduciary duty to the other shareholders.

Directors are personally liable for negligence or breach of fiduciary duty in an improper repurchase or redemption of shares. Shareholders whose shares are bought are personally liable to return the money if they had knowledge of the illegality or if the corporation is insolvent, whether or not they took the money with knowledge of insolvency.

A corporation may resell or cancel shares it redeemed or repurchased or may hold them as treasury stock.

Stock Transfer Restrictions

Corporations sometimes restrict the transfer of their shares. Restrictions are adopted for a number of reasons. Restrictions are used to keep ownership among family members in family-owned corporations or to otherwise prevent stock in a closely held corporation from reaching outsiders. Restrictions are sometimes used by corporations to qualify for a securities registration exemption. Common restrictions include a grant to other shareholders of the right of first refusal or a stipulation for redemption in the event of death of a party or the departure from the company of a key executive. A buy-out clause in the company's articles or in a shareholder's agreement is another common kind of restriction used by shareholders in a closely held corporation as a means to restrict transferability.

A buy-out provision enables the shareholders to preserve their existing proportional ownership and to control who might come into the corporation.

A corporation can refuse to recognize the transfer of restricted stock if the transfer is not in accordance with the restriction. A party who is ignorant of the restriction, a good faith purchaser, is not bound by the restriction and gains full title to the stock. A person can claim to be a good faith purchaser without knowledge of the restriction if it is not conspicuously noted on the certificate.

Restrictions on the transfer of stock are closely scrutinized by the courts and strictly interpreted. There are certain requirements to be met in order to make a restriction valid. It cannot be so arbitrary or unreasonable as to make the stock effectively nontransferable or transferable only at an unconscionably low price. In other words, a restriction cannot be absolute; the holder must be able to sell his stock to someone. Unreasonable and invalid restrictions include requiring the consent of the board of directors before a sale of one's stock or requiring a shareholder to first offer the shares to a greater number of shareholders. There must be a valid reason for the restriction, and it must be one of those described above.

TRANSFERRED AND MISAPPROPRIATED SECURITIES

Transfer of Investment Securities

Article 8 of the UCC contains many of the rules governing the transfer of stocks, bonds, debentures, or any other interest in property or the enterprise of the issuer that is a medium of investment. Article 8 establishes rules similar to those in Article 3 of the UCC, which applies to the transfer of ordinary negotiable instruments (commercial paper) other than investment securities. Many rules and practices of custom are also involved, such as stockbrokers' rules for dealing with each other and their customers, regulations adopted by the stock exchanges, and SEC administrative rulings. A number of rules and practices applicable to the transfer of securities are regulated by federal securities laws.

The investor has the right to transfer his securities by sale, gift, pledge, or by will, just as he would have the right to transfer other property he owns. Under Article 8 the transfer of an uncertificated security can be accomplished by delivery of the certificate alone if it is in bearer form or by an endorsement in blank (does not contain the name of the transferee but only has the signature of the registered owner).

A registered security (most stocks and bonds) has on its face the owner's name and is registered in the corporate books. Transfer of a registered security can be by delivery of the certificate with an endorsement by the registered owner on the certificate or by a separate document of assignment or transfer (such as a power of attorney) executed by the owner. Delivery alone, then, is not a valid transfer for a registered security. Conversely, where there is no delivery of an endorsed share certificate to anyone, there is no transfer of ownership of the shares. A delivery from the owner himself of the shares directly to the transferee is not required. It can be made to an intermediary. The transferee may register the transfer on the books of the issuing corporation, but not doing so does not ordinarily affect his title to the transferred shares.

The delivery of the certificate without a necessary endorsement is an effective transfer between the parties because endorsement is only necessary to make a transferee a *bona fide purchaser*, thereby protecting him against the claims of third parties. The delivery of an unendorsed certificate with the intention of transferring title gives the intended transferee complete rights in the securities against the transferer, including the right to compel endorsement. However, the transferee becomes a bona fide purchaser of the certificate only at the time the endorsement is provided. The endorsement on the security by the owner warrants to the transferee for value that the transfer is rightful, the security is genuine, the security is not materially altered, and the owner knows of no fact that would impair the validity of the security.

A *bona fide* purchaser of a security takes title free of all claims by others to the security, even the rightful owner, when such adverse claims are not conspicuously noted on the certificate. Consequently, the bona fide purchaser who buys from a thief, finder, or unauthorized person is protected in his ownership. A person becomes a bona fide purchaser when he pays value in good faith with no notice of any adverse claims, provided the purchaser takes delivery of an endorsed certificate.

The owner of a security can prove continued ownership by showing that what appears to be a proper endorsement on the security is actually forged or unauthorized. Title to a security cannot be transferred through a forged or unauthorized endorsement. Thus one generally does not lose title to a registered security when his endorsement is forged or unauthorized. Ordinarily the issuing corporation and its transfer agent are under a duty to register the transfer of certificated securities and issue new certificates to the new owner. A corporation that honors the wrongful endorsement does so at its peril and is liable for the improper registration. The owner of a security that was transferred by another with a forged or unauthorized endorsement may assert its ineffectiveness against the corporation issuing the security and against any purchasers, with two exceptions: (1) when the owner ratified the unauthorized endorsement; or (2) in the case of a bona fide purchaser who received a new, reissued, or re-registered certificated security from the issuing corporation. In the second case, the remedy of the true owner is restricted to the issuing corporation that exchanged the registered security with a new, reissued, or re-registered security, and to the transfer agent of the issuer. The purchaser of a security bearing a forged or unauthorized endorsement who resells it to a bona fide purchaser is liable to this purchaser on the grounds of breach of warranty that the transfer was rightful, the security was genuine, and the security was not materially altered.

The issuing corporation has a duty to transfer registered securities upon request of the new owner. If the corporation fails to perform this duty, the new owner may recover damages for conversion, obtain a decree compelling transfer, or hold the corporation liable for unreasonable delay. Since it is liable for an improper registration based upon a wrongful endorsement, the corporation has the duty, and right, to inquire into any adverse claim of ownership if timely notice is received before transfer is recorded.

Lost, Destroyed, or Stolen Securities

A certificated security that has been lost, destroyed, or stolen must be replaced by the issuing corporation, provided the owner files a sufficient indemnity bond to protect the issuer and requests the new security within a reasonable time before the issuer has notice that the original certificate has been acquired by the bona fide purchaser. The issuer may demand other reasonable requirements.

If lost or stolen securities were in bearer form or had been properly endorsed by the former registered owner, a good faith purchaser from the thief or finder owns the securities. When registered securities are lost or stolen, the bona fide purchaser is entitled to be registered in the corporate books as the new owner. For securities in the registered form that the thief or finder forged the endorsement or assignment of the owner, the bona fide purchaser does not own the certificates and must return them to the true owner. Large corporations usually appoint a financial institution such as a bank or trust company to act as their *transfer agent* whose function is to record transfer of corporate securities and to issue new certificates in the name of the owners of the newly issued stock. When the bona fide purchaser sends in an old certificate to the transfer agent and the old certificate is cancelled and a new one is issued to the bona fide purchaser, the bona fide purchaser owns the new certificate. The former owner in this situation has a claim against the corporation and its transfer agent for not detecting the forgery.

5

Mergers, Consolidations, and Stock and Asset Acquisitions

Mergers and Consolidations
Purchase or Lease of All or Substantially All of the Assets
Purchase of Controlling Stock

Two or more corporations may be combined to form a new structure or enterprise. There are four ways corporations can form such combinations: (1) merger, (2) consolidation, (3) purchase or lease of assets of another business (asset acquisition), and (4) purchase of controlling stock interest in another corporation (stock acquisition).

MERGERS AND CONSOLIDATIONS

A *merger* is the union of two or more corporations in which one of them acquires and absorbs the others, the absorbing corporation continuing to exist and the others going out of legal existence. In a *consolidation*, two or more corporations combine, each losing its separate existence, with a totally new corporation being formed. Mergers and consolidation thus have the same effect, which is two or more business joining together.

Both the surviving corporation in a merger and the new corporation in a consolidation take on the assets and liabilities of the former businesses. Because the liabilities of the absorbed corporations are assumed by the surviving or continuing corporation as a matter of law, the consent of creditors to the merger or consolidation is not required. Mergers and consolidations are specifically governed by state corporation statutes. In a merger, the acquired corporation ceases to legally exist upon the filing of a certificate of merger with a state official. The shareholders of any acquired corporation are issued shares of the acquiring corporation in place of their old shares. The statutes allow issuance of other consideration to the shareholders of the acquired corporation, such as debt securities or cash. A consolidation is the same except the existence of the old corporations ceases and their shareholders are issued shares of the new corporation. The terms of the exchange of shares are fixed by an agreement of merger or consolidation.

The shareholders of all the companies involved in a merger or consolidation must approve an agreement for it. Approval must come from more than a majority of the shareholders of the companies, in most states by a two-thirds vote of the shares of *each class* of shares. In a few states, the shareholders of the acquiring corporation need not approve if the new shares to be issued to the shareholders of the acquired corporation do not exceed 20 percent of the class to be issued. After shareholder and director approval of the merger or consolidation agreement, the corporation must file it (called the "articles of merger" or "articles of consolidation"), and if it is filed in proper form, the corporation will receive a "certificate of merger" or "certificate of consolidation."

Shareholders who object to a merger or consolidation may *dissent* and have the right to receive the appraised value of their shares in cash. This is called the *appraisal right*. The dissenting shareholder must strictly follow required procedures of the appraisal right, or it will be lost. The dissenting shareholder must file his objection prior to the shareholders' meeting at which the matter is voted upon, then vote (or abstain) against the merger or consolidation, and present a written claim to the corporation within a short time after the meeting. When the merger or consolidation takes place, the surviving or new corporation must make a written offer to each dissenting shareholder for his shares. The Model Act requires the offer to be made within ten days after the effective date of the merger or consolidation and to include the most recent balance sheet and income statement of the corporation whose stock is owned by the dissenting shareholder. If the dissenting shareholder believes the offer of the corporation does not represent the *fair value* of the shares and refuses to accept it, he may bring a suit to have the value determined. Fair value is not the same as market or book value. Fair value is determined by taking into consideration the quality of management, current financial position, past earnings, future projected earnings, nature of the corporate business, and goodwill. If the shareholder accepts the offer, he cannot later sue in court if he believes the price he was paid was unfair. In some states the right of appraisal is the shareholder's sole remedy. In most states the shareholder can seek court action to set the merger aside due to unfairness or fraud even if he has an appraisal right.

If a stockholder fails or refuses to convert existing shares into stock of the new or acquiring corporation, the corporation is required to pay the value of the stock to the shareholder, and the stockholder is required to transfer the shares to the corporation.

Most states allow a *short-form* or simplified type of merger for the merger of a subsidiary corporation into its parent. The streamlined procedure is available to a corporation that owns a high percentage of stock in the subsidiary, either

90 percent or 95 percent. Under this simplified merger procedure, the merger is approved only by the directors of the *parent* corporation, the shareholders of neither parent nor subsidiary vote, and the shareholders of the parent have no appraisal rights. Only a resolution by the board of directors is required. Shareholders of the subsidiary can be "frozen out," that is, they can be offered cash or other property rather than the right to exchange their shares in the subsidiary for shares of the parent corporation. The dissenting shareholders of the subsidiary do retain their appraisal right to receive payment if they believe that the consideration offered is less than the fair value of their shares.

PURCHASE OR LEASE OF ALL OR SUBSTANTIALLY ALL OF THE ASSETS

Generally, the directors can resolve to sell or lease corporate assets, and no shareholder approval is necessary. However, if the directors decide to sell or lease all or substantially all the corporation's assets and such an extensive sale is not in the ordinary course of the business, shareholder approval is needed of the shareholders of the corporation whose assets are to be sold. Such a decision for complete or virtually complete asset sell-off must receive the votes of a majority of the shares entitled to vote. In effect, asset acquisition is the merger of one company into another; however, only the company acquired has to obtain shareholder approval, not the buying company. Generally the shareholders of the acquired company must approve the sale by the same vote required for a merger or consolidation. In most states a majority vote of the outstanding voting shares is sufficient. In the majority of states, there is no appraisal right in the event of the sale of all assets. Some states give dissenting shareholders of the acquired corporation an appraisal right just as in a formal merger or consolidation.

Once shareholder authorization has been given, the board may still cancel the sale or lease, if conditions change, without further shareholder approval.

In a merger or consolidation, the acquiring corporation automatically as a matter of law, without any choice, assumes the liabilities of the acquired companies. In asset acquisition the purchasing corporation does not automatically acquire the debts of the acquired corporation, but may agree to do so in the purchase agreement.

Following the sale of assets, the seller company remains in existence. Although it is usually dissolved after the sale, it need not be.

PURCHASE OF CONTROLLING STOCK

The purchase of all or a controlling interest in the stock of one corporation by another corporation is a means for combining corporations. The target corporation becomes a subsidiary of the acquiring corporation. The purchasing corporation need not obtain all the shares of the target corporation to obtain control. If ownership of the target company's shares is widely dispersed, control can be achieved by the purchase of less than 50 percent of those shares, sometimes substantially less. No shareholder approval is required in either corporation in the event of a stock purchase (unless the acquiring corporation needs to amend its articles). It is up to each individual shareholder of the target corporation to decide whether he wishes to accept the offer of the acquiring corporation. There are no appraisal rights in the shareholders of either corporation. The directors of the acquiring corporation must authorize the transaction, but the directors of the target corporation are not involved. Because management of the target corporation can be bypassed, stock purchase is useful in hostile takeovers.

The rights of the creditors of the target corporation are not impaired by the acquisition. The target corporation retains all debts and liabilities existing against it.

If the number of shareholders is large, individual offers to all the shareholders is not feasible. Moreover, individual negotiations with shareholders could cause artificial inflation in the market value of the target company's shares. As a result the acquiring corporation may issue a *tender offer*, which is an advertised offer directed at all the shareholders of the target company. A tender offer is subject to extensive regulation by the SEC and the states. The tender offer usually is made at a cash price somewhat higher than the current market value.

6

Securities Regulation

INTRODUCTION

Securities Act of 1933 and Securities Exchange Act of 1934

In order to provide an honest marketplace for securities and restore public confidence in the securities market after the stock market crash of 1929, President Franklin Delano Roosevelt's New Deal Congress enacted two statutes—the Securities Act of 1933 and the Securities Exchange Act (SEA) of 1934. Together these two pieces of legislation provided stringent federal regulation of the securities industry, which prior to that time had been feebly regulated.

The 1933 act regulates "primary offerings," which are brand new issues of securities being offered for sale to the public for the first time. The 1933 act has disclosure provisions that require sellers of new issues to provide adequate, accurate, and truthful disclosure information to prospective purchasers—the reason the 1933 act is sometimes called "the truth in securities law." To achieve proper disclosure for securities "going public," the 1933 act requires that issuers register with the SEC, which includes a report (prospectus) describing the offering made available to purchasers. The 1933 act also prohibits misrepresentation, deceit, and other fraudulent practices in the sale of securities, regardless of whether they are subject to the act's registration requirements. While the purpose of the 1933 act is to regulate the *issuance* of new securities by corporations, the purpose of the 1934 act is to regulate the trading (sale and purchase) of existing or seasoned securities, called "secondary offerings." In other words, the 1933 act deals with the primary market, which involves the sale of new or just issued securities, and the 1934 act is directed at abuses and manipulations that occur for previously offered securities that are not bought and sold in the secondary market. The purpose of the 1934 act is essentially the same as the 1933 act; namely to protect investors by requiring full and fair disclosure.

In addition to requiring disclosure of material information when existing securities are bought and sold, the 1934 act requires securities to be registered with the SEC by the issuing company if the securities are traded on a national stock exchange or if the company has 500 or more shareholders, has over $1 million in assets, and issues stock that is sold in interstate commerce. Companies required to register their securities are also subject to the act's reporting requirements, short-swing profits provisions, tender offer provisions, proxy solicitation provisions, and the internal control and recordkeeping requirements of the Foreign Corrupt Practice's Act. The 1934 act applies not only to corporate behavior concerning securities; it regulates all securities trading by anyone, such as the broker-dealer who buys and sells covered securities. Moreover, as an issuer of securities, whether required to be registered under the 1934 act or not, a company must comply with the antifraud provisions of the legislation.

Both the 1933 and 1934 acts are administered by the SEC, which was created by the 1934 act and is an independent government agency with rule-making and adjudicatory power to carry out its responsibilities.

Other Federal Laws Regulating Securities

Although this chapter details the requirements of the two main federal securities laws—the Securities Act of 1933 and the SEA of 1934—there is a diverse assortment of other federal statutes that are important parts of the federal mosaic of laws for regulating securities. They include the following:

1. *Public Utilities Holding Company Act of 1935 (PUHCA).* Administered by the SEC, this legislation is directed at preventing abuses in the financing and operations of public gas and electric utility companies.

2. *Trust Indenture Act of 1937 (TIA).* This law regulates the sale of debt securities, such as bonds, to the public. Debt contracts, such as a trust indenture, must contain certain provisions to protect investors. These provisions are required because the earlier Securities Act of 1933 failed to provide them. Several types of debt arrangements must include a trustee to look out for the lender's interests.

3. *Investment Company Act of 1940 (ICA).* Under this law the SEC regulates publicly owned companies that invest and trade in securities. The ICA allows the SEC to regulate the selection of managers, managers' salaries, size of sales charges, investment strategies, and other related matters.

4. *Investment Advisors Act of 1940 (IAA).* The SEC is empowered to regulate investment advisors.

5. *Securities Investor Protection Act of 1970 (SIPA).* This law established a federal corporation called the Securities Investor Protection Corporation (SIPC), which administers the liquidation of brokerage firms with financial problems. The legislation is designed to protect investors against the insolvency of their stockbroker. For instance, the SIPC settles claims of an investor whose stockbroker has become insolvent.

6. *Foreign Corrupt Practices Act of 1977 (FCPA).* The FCPA prohibits bribes to foreign officials and directs certain businesses to establish systems of internal controls that would allow managers to spot and prevent bribery activities.

7. *Insider Trading Sanctions Act of 1984.* While insider trading is regulated by the SEA of 1934, this law specifically increases possible punishment for insider trading.

State Regulation

The federal securities laws specifically permit concurrent regulation by the states. These laws take two forms: (1) *blue sky* (disclosure) statutes and (2) Antitakeover statutes.

The existence of blue sky laws predates the major federal securities acts. These laws primarily impose disclosure requirements that are meant to protect investors from speculative stock promotion. They are termed "blue sky" laws because they are designed to prevent the sale of stock that is worthless or, as one judge put it, "so many feet of blue sky."

A person selling securities must comply with the securities laws of each state in which he intends to offer the securities. Securities exempt from federal securities legislation are not automatically exempt from any applicable state law. State law frequently regulates securities and transactions that are exempted from federal regulation. The blue sky laws are in fact primarily designed today for the sale of securities in *intrastate* commerce, in contrast with the *interstate* application intended for federal laws. While a seller of securities must comply with both state and federal regulations, in cases when the requirements are often different, the issuer must comply with the stricter requirement of the two. Thus, if a state disclosure request is stricter than a federal one, the state standard requiring greater disclosure must be followed.

Blue sky laws differ from state to state, but most contain five basic kinds of provisions that (1) require the corporate issuer to register security offerings with a designated state agency; (2) require full disclosure of all material information to prospective purchasers of the security; (3) require security brokers and dealers to register or obtain a license; (4) prohibit fraud in the sale of securities; and (5) provide for injunctions and criminal penalties for submitting false or misleading registration data and engaging in fraudulent sale activities.

About half the states have adopted the Uniform Securities Act (USA), which incorporates the aforementioned five kinds of provisions. States that have not adopted the USA or like kinds of comprehensive legislation have at least adopted full disclosure statutes. There is nevertheless significant disparity in state securities laws, and this lack of uniformity is one of the principal reasons for federal regulation. Some states, like Delaware, have chosen minimal blue sky regulation. Others, such as New York and California, have strict and extensive regulation.

Many states have adopted statutes designed to protect their home businesses from being taken over by out-of-state companies, that is, "corporate raiders" who attempt to obtain control by lucrative offers to buy the shares of stockholders. These statutes are commonly known as "antitakeover" statutes, although they are more formally termed "tender-offer" laws because they set up various stumbling blocks to tender-offers by these outsiders seeking control.

SECURITIES ACT OF 1933

Overview

The Securities Act of 1933 requires issuers of newly offered nonexempt securities to publish facts that will enable investors to judge the financial soundness of the issuing company and the quality of the securities offered for sale. The act is aimed at "primary offerings," that is, the first-time offering of a securities issue, not the later trading on stock exchanges or over-the-counter. The underlying purpose of the act is to provide "truth in securities" by protecting the investor from fraudulent or misleading statements by the sellers of securities and by providing the investor all the basic information needed to make a rational decision when buying a security. In sum, the Securities Act requires complete and honest disclosure to the public in the marketing of new securities. It should be emphasized that the 1933 act does not involve governmental approval of the securities, that is, guaranteeing their merit or value or declaring whether they are good or bad investments. The main objective of the law is to ensure investors receive the required data needed to make an informed decision on whether or not to invest in the securities.

Under the Securities Act of 1933, every investor seeking to buy a security must receive a prospectus from the issuer. The prospectus contains the data, in narrative or tabular form, which allows the prospective investor to make an informed decision to buy. The prospectus is the first part and a shorter version of the comprehensive registration statement any issuer of a nonexempt security must file with the SEC before the security can be offered for sale to the public. The registration statement consists of the issuer completing a lengthy SEC form with detailed information about the company. While the registration requirements are meant to apply to primary offerings, securities sold in "secondary offerings"—sales by controlling shareholders of their stock to the public—also must be registered.

Regardless of whether securities are exempt from the registration and disclosure requirements of the act, this legislation contains antifraud provisions that apply to any securities offered for sale in interstate commerce or the mails. Civil and criminal penalties also may be imposed for violations of the act.

Definitions

The definitions of key terms in the 1933 act are extremely important because they determine whether a party issuing securities is subject to the disclosure requirements and anitfraud penalties of the act. These key terms are security, person, sale, issuer, underwriter, controlling person, and dealer and can include or exclude thousands of investors from the protective coverage of the act.

Security

The costs of complying with the disclosure requirements of the 1933 act can be extremely high, often exceeding $1 million, when one takes into account necessary payments to lawyers, accountants, printers, and others to issue a security covered by the law. Moreover, the civil liabilities and criminal penalties can be severe for not complying with the full disclosure requirements of the 1933 act for an offering considered a security under it. As a result, the definition of a security is extremely important for it determines whether an offering is subject to the disclosure requirements and penalties of the act.

The term security has a broad meaning for the purposes of the act. The act provides a long list of instruments and interests that are considered securities, and this is to include any note; stock; bond; debenture; evidence of indebtedness; preorganization certificate or subscription; investment contract; voting trust certificate; fractional undivided interest in oil, gas, or other mineral rights; or, in general, any interest commonly regarded as a security. In addition, the term security includes any certificate of interest or participation in, temporary or interim certificate for, receipt for, guarantee of, or warrant or right to substitute to, or purchase any of the interests or instruments listed in the previous sentence. The long list provided to define securities makes it hard to imagine any investment that is not a security.

Despite the seemingly clear and expansive list of the types of investments included as securities under the act, there can be instances in which an instrument or interest that clearly seems to fall within one of the kinds of securities listed in the act is in fact not a security for its purposes. For instance, although securities usually include shares of stock, the U.S. Supreme Court has determined that shares of stock in a cooperative housing corporation were not securities on the reasoning that the motivation for buying was solely to obtain housing and not to invest for a profit. The Supreme Court has adopted the approach of "substance, not form" in determining whether an investment is a security, stressing economic reality over terminology. Thus the fact that a transaction is labeled a stock, or any other term commonly regarded as a security, does not mean that it is a security for the purpose of the act.

Like the 1933 act, the courts have given the term "securities" a broad definition that is in line with the "substance, not form" approach. The courts have generally interpreted the statutory definition in a manner that expands its already broad coverage of traditional investments to include nontraditional forms of investment. There is usually little trouble in including under the term securities traditional forms of equity and debt issues, like stock and bonds, respectively. The landmark case that established the ground rules for the broad judicial interpretation of securities so as to include nontraditional types was *SEC v. W. J. Howey*, 328 U.S. 293 (1946) In this case the U.S. Supreme Court found an investment contract could be a security, provided it met certain conditions. The trouble in determining whether an investment contract is a security is that no piece of paper exists called a "security" or "stock." But the Supreme Court in *Howey* made it clear that it is immaterial whether or not ownership in a business enterprise is evidenced by a formal certificate. In the *Howey* case the court said that an investment is considered a security if it satisfies a test consisting of three criteria: (1) a person invests in an ownership share of (2) a common enterprise in which (3) management is separate from the investor who expects to profit solely from the efforts of others. The *Howey* case held that investment contracts for selling the fruit from separate rows of orange trees in a grove were securities under the 1933 act. Investments that meet the *Howey* test, and thus are subject to the registration and antifraud provisions of the securities acts, include sales of investments in citrus groves, whiskey warehouse receipts, franchises, pyramid schemes, oil drilling investment programs, beaver raising schemes, savings and loan certificates of deposit, promissory notes, and some types of variable life annuities. In short, the *Howey* test means that for the purpose of securities law, a security is an investment in money, property, or other valuable consideration made in expectation of receiving a financial return solely from the efforts of others. In other words, the investment contract principle is that for a transaction to be a security it is only necessary there exist an oral or written arrangement whereby investors provide money to a common enterprise and are led to expect profit from the significant efforts of persons other than themselves. It is worth noting that *Howey* stands for the principle that the term 'securities" can include many types of investments that do not neatly fall into the categories of debt and equity securities. *Howey* means that the 1933 act not only applies to transactions in securities but also offers to sell investments. Finally, the last condition of the *Howey* test, that profit is sought through the "efforts of others," has become the basic test of whether something is a security.

While *Howey* has the effect of expanding coverage of the 1933 act by including within the meaning of security those investments not traditionally regarded as such, it also correspondingly provides a limit on the coverage of the act. The courts have held that an investment that falls within the plain terms of the statutory definition but does not meet the three criteria of the *Howey* test is not a security and thus not covered by the act. A prominent example of exclusion are notes that are simply for the purpose of formalizing an open account debt incurred in the ordinary course of business. These include notes commonly executed for consumer financing (secured by home mortgages, assignment of accounts receivable, and so forth) or charter loans to bank customers. Notes that resemble these examples do not meet the *Howey* test and therefore are not covered by the 1933 act.

The Supreme Court has also moved toward establishing some boundaries on the *Howey* test that have led to a sensible definition of security that is not too broad. For example, in *International Brotherhood of Teamsters v. Daniel*, 99 S.Ct. 790 (1979) the Supreme Court decided a noncontributory pension plan was not a security for the purposes of the Securities Act of 1933 or SEA of 1934. The court found that such a pension plan was not really an investment by the employee, since he was primarily selling his labor to make a living and his participation in the pension plan was a relatively insignificant part of the total and indivisible employee pay package. More simply, the pension plan was part of the employee's compensation package and not an investment by him. Finally, the 1933 act itself exempts from the term security any note that has a maturity at the time of issuance of not more than nine months.

Person—Issuer, Underwriter, Controlling Person, Dealer

The 1933 act regulates persons. The term "person" has been broadly defined to include individuals, corporations, partnerships, trusts, and unincorporated associations. There are four kinds of persons who must be distinguished to determine whether a particular party or entity is regulated under the act: issuers, controlling persons, underwriters, and dealers. Dealers are not regulated, the others are.

Public offerings are distributions of securities to the general public. Distributions of securities must be registered under the 1933 act. Distributions of securities are usually made in two ways: (1) the person that issues or proposes the securities, known as the issuer, may sell directly to others, or (2) the person may obtain the services of an investment banking firm, known as an underwriter, to sell the securities for the issuing corporation.

Issuer. An issuer is usually a corporation but can involve any of the parties or entities included under the term person, as defined above. An issuer proposes to issue or actually issues *new* securities, that is, those that have never before been offered for sale.

Underwriter. An underwriter is a person who purchases the securities from an issuer with a view or intent to distribute them, or who offers to distribute them, or sells for an issuer, or guarantees the sale of the security. A distribution of securities must be registered by the underwriter under the 1933 act.

Controlling Person. The term controlling person is not specifically defined by the 1933 act but has been adopted by the SEC. The term controlling person is quite broad and includes not only natural persons but also corporations or other entities that control them. A controlling person is included in the term issuer for registration purposes. Generally, a controlling person is one who has the authority or power to influence the management or policies of an issuer, either directly or indirectly. A controlling person is a type of issuer. The term controlling person is used in conjunction with the terms issuer and underwriter above. Exempted from the registration requirements of the 1933 act are *private* offerings of unregistered securities. To prevent the resale (secondary offering) to the public of unregistered securities bought previously by certain private persons called controlling persons, the term issuer has been interpreted to include these controlling persons. Thus, securities that are purchases by a controlling person as part of an exempt private offering are subject to registration if the controlling person resells (or reissues) the securities to the public. A controlling person is someone who can generally influence decisions of a corporation. Majority stock ownership naturally constitutes control, but a person need not have majority ownership to be controlling. Actual or practical control is the test. In general a controlling person has the power to influence the management and policies of the issuer, even when the power is not exercised. A 5 percent owner (or even less) may be a controlling person if he is on the board. If an officer or director is on the executive committee, a lower percentage than 5 percent can suffice. A controlling person may involve a group of persons who vote together and actively participate in management.

The controlling person is regarded as holding restricted stock, that is, stock that cannot be disposed without registration. It does not matter whether the stock was bought from an issuer or in the open market, or whether held for many years or previously registered. It also does not matter if the controlling person sells his stock directly to others or on the open market through a broker.

Moreover, a person who buys the controlling person's unregistered securities with the idea of distributing them to the public is included in the term underwriter, and he cannot resell the securities without first registering them. Consider, for example, a director who purchases controlling shares of an unregistered stock issued by a corporation under the private sale exemption. The director intended to resale one-half the shares to his brother, knowing the brother in turn plans to resell the stock in several lots to friends at the local Rotary Club of which the brother is a member. The director is a controlling person who is regarded as reissuing to the public through his brother, who unwittingly becomes an underwriter because he is buying the unregistered shares with the idea of distributing them elsewhere. Likewise, a broker may be considered an underwriter if he sells securities owned by a controlling person who is in turn regarded as an issuer of securities subject to registration requirements, even when such a controlling person is exempt from registration at the time he obtained the securities in a private offering.

Dealer. A dealer may be confused with an underwriter. The difference is important because an underwriter is subject to registration requirements and a dealer is not. A dealer is a person who is engaged, whether full time or part time, directly or indirectly, as an agent, broker, or principal in the business of offering, buying, or selling or otherwise dealing or trading securities issued by another person. A dealer is not an underwriter except when the buy-sell price exceeds the customary commission payable to brokers who sell for the account of others.

Offered for Sale or Sale in Interstate Commerce

The offer and sale of securities by mail or "*by any means* or instruments of communications in *interstate commerce*" are regulated by the 1933 act.

Offered for Sale. The 1933 act defines offer of securities to include any attempt to dispose of securities for value. An offer can be by oral or written solicitation, by advertisement, or any other means.

Sale. The sale of securities includes any contract for sale or disposition of a security for value. Mergers and consolidations are considered sales by SEC regulations. This term has a major exclusion; namely, preliminary negotiations or dealings between an issuer and a potential underwriter. A principal or agent who actively solicits an order, participates in negotiations, or arranges a sale of securities is subject to the 1933 act.

By any means, instrument, or communication in interstate commerce. This phrase includes the telephone, telegraph, and mail. Any method of advertisement or solicitation can be used for interstate trade or commerce, even though the particular solicitation or advertisement itself was intrastate in nature. For example, the telephone solicitation may be made within a state but because of the character of the means, instrument, or communication, the device is interstate in nature, and the solicitation is regulated by the act.

Registration

Section 5A of the 1933 act bars the offer or sale of newly issued securities in interstate commerce unless a registration statement is filed with the SEC. Put another way, the issuer of securities must register them with the SEC before offering the securities for sale to any member of the public. Once the registration statement is filed, it is subject to public inspection and becomes public information. There can be no important secrets kept by those who sell securities to the public.

In addition to registration of newly issued securities as a precondition to sale, the 1933 act requires that a prospectus be furnished to each buyer before or at the time the sale of the security occurs. The prospectus must be submitted to the SEC along with the registration for review. The prospectus is a liability document and consequently contains hedges, caveats, and limitations. While the registration goes only to the SEC, the prospectus is to be given directly to prospective and actual buyers.

The registration statement contains detailed information about the issuer, chiefly about its assets and business, management, and financial status. Both the registration statement and prospectus must be accurate and complete. The prospectus contains most of the kinds of information required of the registration statement but not necessarily all the details or exhibits that constitute the registration statement. The prospectus essentially summarizes the registration statement. While the prospectus must be given to the security buyer before or when the security purchase occurs, most investors do not ask for it or read it prior to placing an order with their broker.

The registration statement is the principal document for making full disclosure of financial and other information upon which investors may evaluate the merits of the securities. This full disclosure to be achieved by the registration statement is the very purpose of the act. Together the registration statement and prospectus are supposed to supply sufficient information to allow any unsophisticated investor to appraise the financial risk of buying the security. The registration of a security does not signify that the SEC believes the security is a good investment.

Contents of Registration Statement

The registration statement submitted to the SEC must contain certified financial statements and detailed data about the issuer's assets, management, business, capital structure, and kinds of securities to be issued. While not an exclusive list, the following indicates the key kinds of information that generally must be contained in the registration statement submitted to the SEC:

1. Historical and current information about the issuer's business and management.
2. A description of the issuer's properties and business.
3. Financial statement of the issuer, certified by an independent accountant for the current year and the last two previous years.
4. Capital structure of the issuer.
5. Names and renumeration of directors and principal officers, names of persons who control the company and who own ten percent or more of the company's securities, and details about material transactions between such persons and the company.
6. Disclosure of any options or rights in favor of promoters or insiders (major shareholders, directors, or officers).
7. Information about current and pending legal proceedings.
8. Description of significant provisions of the security to be issued and its relationships to the registrant's other capital securities.
9. The plan for distributing the securities (such as underwriting arrangements), estimate of amount of proceeds and anticipated use, and a description of the rights and limitations placed on the securities.
10. Signature of the issuing company, one or more of its principal officers, comptroller or principal accounting officer, at least a majority of the board of directors, and any relevant expert (accountant, lawyer, and so forth) named as having prepared or certified the registration statement.

Information similar to that in above points one through ten is to be included in summary form in the prospectus.

Place of Filing

The registration statement is filed in the SEC's Washington, D.C. office, except for small public offerings under Regulation A (described below).

SEC Review and Response

The SEC has twenty days to review the registration statement and prospectus submitted by the issuer. The 20-day period is called the waiting period because at its expiration the registration statement becomes effective. Registration occurs on the date the registration statement becomes effective.

As noted before, the SEC does not evaluate the merits of the prospective offering to determine whether or not it is a good investment. The SEC review is for the purpose of determining the adequacy of the information to provide full disclosure to prospective investors.

Registration statements are reviewed in detail by the SEC's Division of Corporate Finance to determine whether the company has complied with the disclosure requirements in a manner that provides the investing public with enough information to make a reasoned judgment about the new offering. The registration statement must be accurate and complete. The SEC can (and often does) require amendment or modification of the registration statement through the use of a deficiency letter or letter of comment if it finds the registration statement to be incomplete, inaccurate, or misleading. The SEC does not have the power to disapprove a statement merely because it is a bad investment, but by delaying and requiring negative or unflattering disclosures in the statements to obtain full disclosure, the SEC can discourage the issuer. If an amendment or modification is filed, a new twenty-day period for SEC review begins. The SEC can order an indefinite number of twenty-day periods through successive deficiency letters or letters of comment.

Normally a registration statement becomes automatically effective twenty days after being filed or on the twentieth day after filing the last amendment or modification required by the SEC, unless the SEC accelerates the applicable review period at its discretion. The registration statement becomes effective twenty days after filing, unless the SEC advances the effective date or requires additional data, in which case the twentieth day starts again when the amended or modified registration statement is filed. If the issuer refuses to file an amendment or revision as requested by the SEC, the agency may either issue a stop order to allow the deficient registration statement to become automatically effective on the twentieth day of the waiting period and thereafter initiate enforcement and sanction measures. If the issuer refuses to file an amendment or modification as directed by the SEC (even if the SEC does not issue a stop order), he is subject to criminal sanctions and civil remedies for false or misleading statements.

An issuer may not make written offers to sell or, indeed, actually sell a security until the registration becomes effective. The registration statement and prospectus become public immediately upon filing with the SEC. For violating the prohibition against written offers to sale or actual sales of securities before the expiration of the twenty-day period, the SEC can issue a stop order terminating further consideration of the registration.

While prohibited from making written offers or actual sales during the waiting period, the issuer can exchange with interested investors oral offers to buy and sell, and the issuers may make public announcements touting or advertising the sale of the securities for the future. The announcements may consist of oral communications to investors, dealers, or underwriters. Another kind of permitted announcement is written advertising in the form of a Tombstone Ad, often seen in major business periodicals and newspapers like *The Wall Street Journal*. The purpose of a tombstone ad is to locate potential purchasers of the securities and inform them of the availability of a preliminary prospectus. The tombstone ad can contain only a limited amount of information, and this information pertains to the identity of the security to be sold, where a preliminary prospectus can be obtained, the price of the security, the amount of the offering, and the identity of the underwriters.

Another form of announcement allowed is a preliminary prospectus, sometimes known as a red herring prospectus, so called because it bears a red legend stating a registration statement has been filed but has not become effective. The red herring prospectus can contain only limited, sketchy information, essentially being a summary of information in the registration statement.

Shelf Registration

The SEC has adopted shelf registration, which permits an issuer to file a registration statement with the SEC and let it lie on the shelf until market conditions are right. Large, periodic issuers of debt find shelf registration advantageous. Shelf registration permits the registration of an amount of security that may be reasonably expected to be sold on a delayed or continuous basis over a two-year period. During the two-year period the issuer can make as many offerings as it wishes without registering each offering individually. For such matters as changes in interest rates, redemption, maturities, and prices, the issuer can make the prospectus current by merely affixing a sticker.

Prospectus Requirements

A prospectus must be submitted with the registration statement and is part of the registration statement when filed. A copy of the prospectus must be offered to every security buyer before or when the purchase occurs. The prospectus contains essentially the same information as the registration statement, except in summary form and lacking all the exhibits that might be required for a registration statement. Like the registration statement, the prospectus must be accurate and complete. Even true information, which is misleading in the context in which it is stated, violates the act. A prospectus need not be taken by the security buyer. It must merely be tendered by the issuer, that is, offered to be given to the buyer. As a practical matter, most buyers never ask for or take a prospectus before ordering securities from a broker.

Exemptions From Registration

The Securities Act of 1933 exempts certain types of securities and securities transactions from registration. The exemptions extend only to registration and prospectus requirements. The antifraud and other provisions of the act still apply.

Exempt Securities

Exempt from the registration requirements of the 1933 Act are the following securities:

1. securities sold prior to July 17, 1933.
2. securities of federal, state, and local governments and their public instrumentalities.
3. securities issued by organizations whose issuance of securities is regulated by agencies other than the SEC, such as national or state chartered banks and savings institutions, railroads, and farm cooperatives.
4. securities issued by nonprofit organizations, such as charitable, religious, educational, and other such organizations. To curtail abuses of the nonprofit exemption, the SEC and the courts take the position that this exemption will be lost if there is a single substantial noncharitable purpose for the organization.
5. insurance policies and conventional annuity contracts other than variable annuities.
6. securities issued pursuant to a court order in a bankruptcy reorganization case.
7. securities issued with a sale or a commission paid, for example, when the issuer exchanges its securities currently owned by its existing security holders, such as a stock split or other common types of recapitalization.
8. short-term commercial paper, that is, checks, notes, bankers' acceptances, and similar types of commercial paper that arise out of a current transaction and that have a maturity not exceeding nine months.
9. intrastate issues of securities. Under SEC Rule 147 this exemption is allowed if the issue meets two criteria:

   (a) The issuer is organized (i.e., incorporated) and doing business within the same state as the state of residence of *all* the purchasers.

   (b) 80 percent of all the issuer's gross revenues are from operations within the state, and the issuer plans to use at least 80 percent of the proceeds from the issue within the state.

To preserve the intrastate exemption, the securities must also rest in the hands of the resident purchasers for at least nine months before an out-of-state offer or resale can be made.

Exempt Transactions

TRANSACTIONS BY INDIVIDUAL INVESTORS   This broad exemption is for individuals who are not issuers, underwriters, or dealers. The exemption covers sales by and to most investors in respect to securities already issued. The exemption is meant to facilitate routine trading activities on securities exchanges. The exemption is not extended to sales by a controlling person. A controlling person, defined earlier, is regarded as having direct or indirect control of an issuer or having common control with an issuer. Sales by controlling persons of already issued stock they acquire from the corporation are treated as if they are new issues and thus must be registered when resold. The rationale for this rule is that controlling persons have an advantage over others in the marketplace because of their knowledge of the corporation and should thus be under an obligation to disclose what they know.

The controlling person is regarded as holding "restricted stock," that is, stock that cannot be disposed of without registration. It does not matter whether the stock was bought from an issuer or in the open market or whether it was held for many years or previously registered. It also does not matter if the controlling person sells his stock directly to others or on the open market through a broker.

Limited sales of securities by a controlling person through a broker are exempt from registration, as described in the next section.

TRANSACTIONS BY BROKERS AND DEALERS   Ordinary broker transactions and transactions in which a dealer is not acting as an underwriter are exempt from registration. The purpose of the exemption is not to regulate the public trading in the buying and selling of seasoned securities by ordinary investors or their brokers and dealers on the over-the-counter markets or the securities exchanges.

Limited sales by a controlling person through a broker are exempt from registration if the following requirements are met:

1. The broker performs only usual functions of executing an order and receives only the usual or customary broker's commission.
2. The controlling person pays the usual commission and does not, to the broker's knowledge, pay any additional amount.
3. The securities are owned at least two years by the person on whose account they are sold.
4. The amount of stock issued for sale does not exceed one percent of the class outstanding.
5. Adequate information about the issuer must be available to the public and notice of the sale must be filed with the SEC concurrently with the sale.

A dealer can sell securities without providing the purchaser with a prospectus when the securities themselves have been registered or have been available on the market for a *minimum* period. The minimum period for a regular public offering is forty days or more if the issuer had sold a previous issue under an effective registration, or ninety days or more if the securities were part of the issuer's first public offering.

SALES OF PROMISSORY NOTES SECURED BY A LIEN   This registration exemption is for sales totaling $250,000 or more of first trust-deed notes originated by state or federally regulated lending institutions.

REGULATION D—PRIVATE AND LIMITED OFFERINGS   SEC Regulation D provides exemptions from registration under certain specific conditions for certain small private placements of securities. An issuer subject to Regulation D does not have to file a registration statement or a prospectus with the SEC but must notify the SEC of an issuance and must comply with any applicable state regulations. The Regulation D issuer also cannot make a general solicitation of purchasers and may not advertise the sale. The exemptions of Regulation D apply only to transactions in which securities are issued and not the securities themselves. Securities sold under Regulation D are considered restricted securities and may be resold only by registration or in another transaction exempt from registration.

Regulation D contains three exemptions: (1) private placements; (2) limited offers by noninvestment companies not exceeding $5,000,000, and (3) limited offers by noninvestment companies not exceeding $500,000.

Private Placement. The most important registration exemption is the private placement provision of the act, which exempts private offerings of securities. Rule 506 of the SEC Regulation D provides this safe harbor for private offerings. The registration exemption applies regardless of the dollar amount of the offering. There is a limitation on the number of purchasers, which truly assures the exemption is for private offerings. The issuer must believe there are no more than thirty-five nonaccredited purchasers. There can be an unlimited number of accredited investors, which are normally knowledgeable and sophisticated investors like banks, insurance companies, registered investment companies, executive officers, or directors of the issuer, any person who purchases at least $150,000 of securities so long as the price does not exceed 20 percent of the investor's net worth, any person whose net worth exceeds $1,000,000, and any person with an income over $200,000 in each of the last two years who expects over $200,000 in the current year.

In what is called the sophisticated investor standard, the issuer is required to reasonably believe that each nonaccredited investor, either alone or through his representative, has sufficient knowledge and experience in financial matters to capably evaluate the merits and risk of the investment. The standard is subjective on the part of the issuer. Because the accredited investor is presumed to be sophisticated, there are no disclosure requirements if the securities are sold only to accredited investors. If the sale involves any nonaccredited person, even if only one, then all purchasers, including accredited investors, must be given prior to sale detailed information about the issuer, its business, and the securities being offered. This disclosure must include audited information about management, capital structure, salaries of officers and directors, and financial affairs.

Commission can be paid to dealers and brokers in a 506 sale. The issuers must notify the SEC of a 506 sale by filing an initial, interim, and final report. Securities sold under the Rule 506 exemption are restricted securities (restricted on resale) and may be resold only by registration or in a transaction exempt from registration. No general public advertising or solicitation can be used to promote the sale of 506 securities.

Limited Offerings by Noninvestment Companies under $5,000,000. Rule 505 of SEC Regulation D provides a registration exemption for an offering by a noninvestment company whose issue does not exceed $5,000,000 over twelve months. Investment companies do not qualify for the registration since its purpose is to facilitate capital formation by small businesses. Many of the Rule 506 requirements for the private offering exemption are similarly applied for this Rule 505 limited offering exemption. Like the private offering, under Rule 506 exemption there can be an unlimited number of accredited purchasers but not more than thirty-five unaccredited purchasers. The Rule 506 private placement exemption is limited to sophisticated investors, while the Rule 505 limited offering exemption does not require the issuer to determine whether purchasers are such sophisticated investors. The disclosure requirements for both exemptions are the same; disclosure is required only when the sale includes a purchase by an unaccredited investor and when that occurs all purchasers, accredited investors included, must receive material information about the issuer and the securities. General public solicitation and advertising is prohibited for the Rule 505 limited offering exemption. This exemption does not impose the sophistication standard that the issuer determine that the nonaccredited investor has significant financial knowledge or experience to evaluate the merits or risks of the investment. Unlike Rule 506, the Rule 505 limited offering exemption is not available to certain disqualified issuers that have had previous problems of noncompliance with securities laws.

The issuer must notify the SEC of the sale by filing initial, interim, and final reports. Rule 505 securities are restricted and therefore cannot be resold except where registered or under some other exemption from regulation.

Limited Offerings by Noninvestment Companies Under $500,000. The true small issue exemption is found in Rule 504 of Regulation D. Rule 504 exempts from registration offers and sales of an issue of securities not exceeding $500,000 to be sold within a 12-month period. There is no limitation on the number of purchasers. Investors may be accredited or unaccredited. There are no restrictions on commissions and compensation in connection with the offering. No disclosure is required. There can be no general public advertising or solicitations by the issuer, except if the issue occurs exclusively in states where the security is registered pursuant to a blue sky law that requires delivery of the document to a purchaser. The SEC must be notified of the sale through the filing of initial, interim, and final reports.

The exemption dictates that only noninvestment company issuers can use the exemption.

Only issuers not subject to the reporting requirements of the SEA of 1934 can use this exemption, that is, issuers who have not voluntarily registered a class of securities with the SEC or those that do not meet the $1,000,000 total asset and 500 shareholder test for mandatory registration under the 1934 act. The Rule 504 exempted security is a restricted security and therefore cannot be resold unless registered or subject to another registration exemption.

ACCREDITED INVESTOR EXEMPTION (4[6] EXEMPTION)   Section 4(6) was added to the 1933 act by the Small Business Act of 1980 (the Incentive Act). This exemption borrows some of the features from the exemptions of SEC Regulation D and discards others. All issuers qualify for the exemption. The aggregate offering price is limited to $5,000,000. There is no limit on accredited investors, but *only* accredited purchasers can purchase. The sale must be private, that is, there can be no public advertising or solicitation to promote the sale of the securities. There are no disclosure requirements. Notice of the sales must be given through initial, interim, and final reports. Commissions can be paid on the sale of the securities.

The issuer is required to control the purchaser's right to resell the securities, using the following three methods: (1) investment letter; (2) conspicuous written warning; and (3) stop transfer order. An investment letter, signed by the purchaser, states that he or she knows the securities are exempt from registration and that they are bought for the purpose of investment and not resale. A conspicuous warning must be placed on the stock certificate that indicates the securities are unregistered and cannot be resold unless registered. The issuer must place a stop transfer order with its stock transfer agreement and is thus obliged to refuse to transfer and reregister on the books of the corporation any certificate subject to the stop transfer order.

REGULATION A—SMALL PUBLIC OFFERINGS   Regulation A allows the SEC to exempt small public offerings (no more than $1.5 million in a one-year period) if registration is deemed unnecessary for public protection. Regulation A is not a true exemption. It merely provides a simpler and less expensive method of registering small public offerings with the SEC. Regulation A's provisions still protect the investor, and liability is the same as that imposed for violations of actual registration.

Under Regulation A, instead of registering, the issuer provides an offering statement to the SEC. The offering statement consists of *notification* to SEC of intent to issue securities under Regulation A, an *offering circular*, which will be furnished to investors, and exhibits. The notification is somewhat simpler than a registration statement. The offering circular substitutes for and is a shorter version of a prospectus. Unlike a prospectus, the offering circular does not contain certified financial statements and is not meant to be extensive. Regulation A offerings are not restricted securities and thus can be resold freely after issuance.

The offering statement must be filed with the SEC at least ten days (Saturdays, Sundays, and holidays excluded) prior to the date of the offering. The statement must be signed by the issuers and any other person for whose account the securities are offered. The filing is local, meaning the statement is filed with the appropriate SEC regional office in which the issuer's principal business is conducted. There is a ten-day waiting period for a Regulation A offering during which time the SEC has the opportunity to review and respond. The filing automatically becomes effective on the tenth day unless the SEC issues a stop order that suspends consideration of the filing. SEC can demand amendment or revision of the offering statement in a deficiency letter or letter of comment if it believes the offering statement to be incomplete, inaccurate, or misleading. If an amendment or revision is filed, a new ten-day waiting period is established. If the issuer refuses to file an amendment or revision, the SEC can issue a stop order or allow the deficient statement to become effective automatically on the tenth day of the waiting period and thereafter pursue enforcement remedies. During the ten-day waiting period there can be not written offers to sale or sales of securities.

Oral offers to sell securities may be made during the ten-day period but must be accompanied by a preliminary offering circular. The preliminary offering circular must contain substantially the same information as an offering circular. The preliminary offering circular must conspicuously bear the caption, "Preliminary Offering Circular," on the outside front cover page. At the expiration of the ten-day waiting period, a complete and accurate offering circular must be furnished prior to or at the time of any written offer to sell or actual sale of the securities.

Informational advertising in writing or public advertising is allowed after the ten-day waiting period. The advertisement cannot contain offers to sell and is limited to information on the identity of the issuer, character of its business, the use of the security, amount being offered, its price, and the sources from which an offering circular can be obtained.

The Regulation A issuer must provide the SEC with notice of sales by filing interim and final reports—the interim reports being filed once every six months after the date of the offering circular and the final report being filed upon completion or termination of the offering.

The offering circular can go stale. If the offering is not completed within nine months from the date of the offering circular, the issuer must file a revised offering circular with the SEC.

In general, a Regulation A security is a restricted security and therefore cannot be resold unless registered or subject to another registration exemption.

Resales of Restricted Securities—Rule 144 (Two-Year or Dribble Rule)

SEC Rule 144 establishes the requirements for the resale of restricted securities.

The Regulation D exemptions do not necessarily exempt a subsequent transaction (usually resale) in the same securities. A person who buys a Regulation D security must register any resale or find an exemption from registration, subject to the limited exception provided for some issuances under the Rule 504 exemption for limited offerings under $500,000.

Rule 144 provides the requirements for resales of the restricted Regulation D securities, which, if met, allow the buyer of restricted securities to sell them without registering them. Rule 144 makes certain distinctions among controlling persons, noncontrolling persons, and affiliates of the purchasers (such as a parent or a subsidiary), but all of them can sell limited amounts of restricted securities in ordinary trading transactions. Rule 144 requires that there must be adequate current public information about the issuer (such as a recent annual 10-K report filed with the SEC), that the person selling under the rule must have owned the securities for at least 2 years, that the seller cannot solicit buyers, that the securities must be sold through a broker, and that the SEC must be notified when the securities are placed with a broker. To prevent a disruption in the market from the massive resale of restricted securities, Rule 144 strictly limits the number of shares which can be sold in each quarter. Because of these requirements, SEC Rule 144 is popularly known as the "two year or dribble" rule.

Securities sold under Regulation A are totally unrestricted. Securities sold under the intrastate sales exception and then resold are slightly restricted; they are freely transferable to residents and transferable without registration to non-residents after being held nine months.

Legal Sanctions and Remedies Under the 1933 Act

The 1933 Act provides for legal remedies and sanctions for noncompliance with its requirements. These measures include administrative remedies by the SEC, civil suits by injured investors, and criminal penalties.

SEC Sanctions and Remedies

The SEC is empowered to seek injunctive relief in federal court to halt the sale of securities in violation of the registration requirements. The SEC has the power to issue a *stop order* during or after the registration process. The stop order lasts for an indefinite duration of time. The SEC can refer a matter to the U.S. attorney general for criminal prosecution. The SEC, under Rule (2)e of its rules of practice, may bring disciplinary proceedings against professionals, such as accountants and attorneys, who are involved in securities transactions under SEC's jurisdiction. The SEC, after giving the alleged offender an opportunity for a hearing on the charges, may revoke the privilege of practicing before the commission.

Civil Liability

There are two main sources of civil liability under the 1933 Act; the antifraud provisions and the registration provisions.

ANTIFRAUD PROVISIONS   In addition to its disclosure requirements, the 1933 Act contains a broad antifraud provision that applies to all primary offerings of securities, whether registered or exempt. Securities that are exempt from registration are not exempt from the antifraud provisions. The antifraud provisions are found in Section 17a of the 1933 act.

Under Section 17a a seller is liable to a purchaser for damages caused by the seller's fraudulent conduct or activity in respect to the offer or sale of securities to the purchaser. Liability is imposed on a seller when he employs any device, scheme, or artifice to defraud, obtain money or property by means of any untrue statement of a material fact or by omission of a material fact deemed necessary to make the statements not misleading, or engages in any transaction, practice, or course of business that operates as a fraud or deceit upon the purchaser. The seller may avoid paying damages by proving that he did not know, and in the exercise of reasonable care could not have known of, the untrue statement or omission. Seller's lack of knowledge is not a bar if the SEC is seeking injunctive relief. In that case, negligent conduct is sufficient. The seller is liable to the purchaser for the amount he paid when the security was delivered. If the purchaser no longer owns the security, he can recover damages from the seller.

CIVIL LIABILITY FOR UNREGISTERED SECURITIES SALES   Section 12 imposes civil liability for the sale of an unregistered security that is required to be registered, the sale of a registered security without delivery of a prospectus, the sale of a security by use of a noncurrent prospectus, or offer of a sale prior to the filing or effective date of a registration statement. Liability is absolute and does not depend on fault (i.e., negligence or fraud). The purchaser who no longer owns the security may sue to recover monetary damages from the seller. Rescission and restitution are remedies available to the purchaser. Namely, a purchaser who is still the owner of the security may rescind the purchase and obtain a refund of the purchase price plus the statutory rate of interest, less any income received (i.e., dividends, profits, or interest).

FALSE REGISTRATION STATEMENTS   Section 11 of the 1933 act gave purchasers of securities the right to recover damages for false or misleading statements or omissions of material facts made in a registration statement, including a prospectus. A purchaser can recover losses up to the full price paid for the security.

The following individuals can be sued in a Section 11 claim: (1) issuer; (2) any person who signed the registration statement; (3) any director or partner consenting to be named as such in the registration statement; (4) experts who are named as having prepared or certified any part of the registration statement; and (5) underwriters of the securities. These persons are jointly and severally liable on a Section 11 lawsuit. This means that each liable party could be compelled to pay the entire amount of a Section 11 claim, even if he were only partly to blame and other liable parties were more to blame. However, an expert is only liable for false or misleading statements or omissions in the portion of the registration statement prepared or certified by him.

Liability in a Section 11 claim does not require the injured party to show fault on the part of a liable party for the false or misleading statements or omissions, that is, to show that there was negligence or fraud. All that needs to be proved is the existence of the false or misleading statements or omissions of material fact, even if unwittingly or innocently made.

The false statement or misleading omissions must constitute a *material fact* in an effective registration statement. A fact is regarded as material if a reasonable person operating in the securities market would likely attach importance to the statement or omission and thus be influenced. The purchaser needs to prove he relied on the registration statement or that the loss suffered was the proximate cause of the false statement or omission. The purchaser does not have to prove the violator possessed the intent to deceive, manipulate, or defraud, which is in line with strict liability. Original purchasers as well as subsequent purchasers can recover from the violator.

A party sued for a Section 11 violation is in an unfavorable position due to the strict liability nature of the violation. Generally in strict liability actions the burden of proof is shifted to the defendant rather than the plaintiff, as is the norm in a civil suit.

Despite the significant problems for a person sued in a Section 11 action, there are defenses available.

Due Diligence. The most important defense is due diligence. Most defendants can raise it, except an issuer. This defense advocates the defendant made a reasonable investigation into the truth of what the registration statement said and reasonably believed, in good faith, that what was stated was true. The standard of reasonableness is that required of a prudent man in the management of his own property or affairs. If an expert such as a lawyer is involved, he must meet the due diligence exercised in his profession. The defendant has the burden of proof for a due diligence defense.

Prior Knowledge. Prior knowledge of the purchaser is another defense. While a plaintiff-purchaser in a securities case does not have to provide he specifically relied upon, or even heard, the misstatement, he cannot recover if the defendant can prove the plaintiff-purchaser knew of the omissions or false statements when he entered into the transaction.

Immaterial False Statement or Omission. The immateriality of a false or misleading statement or omission is a defense. If the fact misstated or omitted was not material to the decision to purchase, then there are not grounds for the suit.

Statute of Limitations. The statute of limitations in the 1933 act is relatively short. Suit must be started within one year from the discovery of the violation but in no case later than three years after the security was offered for sale.

DAMAGES FOR FALSE REGISTRATION   In a Section 11 suit, the violator is liable to the purchaser for his out-of-pocket losses. This generally means that the measure of damages is the difference between the price paid for the stock and its price either at the time of the lawsuit (if the purchaser still owns the stock) or at the time the buyer sold it.

Criminal Sanctions

The Securities Act of 1933 has criminal penalties. The penalties apply to any person who willfully violates the provisions of the act or SEC's rules and regulations, makes a material misstatement or omission in a registration statement, or fails to register a security.

Conviction for a criminal violation carries punishment of up to five years in prison, a $10,000 fine, or both. The statute of limitations for criminal offenses is the same as for a Section 11 lawsuit as described above.

SECURITIES EXCHANGE ACT OF 1934

Overview

The 1933 act was primarily directed at the first-time issuing of a security, which is commonly known as the primary issue. The 1934 act (SEA) is primarily aimed at covering abuses and manipulations in the trading of securities after they come onto the market—it concentrates on secondary or previously issued and now resold securities and their markets. The objective of the 1934 act is basically the same as the 1933 act, to protect investors by full and fair disclosure. But while the 1933 act largely confines itself to disclosure, the 1934 act does many more things to rid the securities marketplace of abuses. Other significant matters in the 1934 act and its subsequent amendments include the establishment of the SEC, regulation of securities exchanges and over-the-counter trading, of dealers, brokers, publicly held companies, and of corrupt foreign practices of American companies.

The major provisions of the 1934 act cover the following:

1. Registration requirements.
2. Proxy solicitation rules.
3. Regulation of credit in securities markets (margin requirements and borrowing by brokers and dealers).
4. Antifraud provisions.
5. Insider trading limitations.
6. Tender offer limits.

Registration Requirement for Securities Exchanges, Brokers, and Dealers

The SEA imposes registration requirements on major participants in stock trading to achieve its purpose of regulating securities and securities markets. Securities exchanges, security broker-dealers, municipal securities dealers, publicly held companies, and certain securities must be registered with the SEC.

Requiring national securities exchanges (such as the New York Stock Exchange) to register makes the act and SEC regulations under it applicable to the members and brokers of these exchanges. A registered exchange must adopt disciplinary rules that control the conduct of its members. An exchange's disciplinary rules must provide for the expulsion, suspension, or exercise of other disciplinary measures against members who fail to follow the law and rules.

Brokers and dealers engaged in interstate commerce or dealing in securities listed on a national exchange must register. A broker or dealer that deals exclusively in intrastate commerce and does not use the facilities of a national exchange is not required to register.

Brokers and dealers who must register under the 1934 act are subject to its margin requirements and restrictions on borrowing (Sections 7 and 8), specialized reporting requirements (Sections 15 and 17), recordkeeping and accounting requirements (Sections 11 and 17), rules of conduct for broker-members of securities exchanges (Section 6), financial responsibility requirements (Section 15(c), and potential civil and criminal liability under the act.

Mandatory Registration of Certain Issuers and Securities

Issuers of certain securities are subject to mandatory registration. An issuer of any security listed on a national securities exchange, whether a bond or equity security, must be registered with the SEC and the exchange, unless the security is exempt under the act. Issuers of unlisted equity securities (traded on the over-the-counter market) must register with the SEC if the issuer is subject to three criteria: (1) the issuer has 500 or more shareholders; (2) he owns over $1,000,000 in gross assets; and (3) he engages in interstate commerce or trades the securities in interstate commerce. This means that an equity security traded over the counter and not on a national securities exchange must be registered if the issuer has over $1,000,000 in assets and 500 or more shareholders.

The registration of securities under the 1934 act is a onetime action that applies to an entire class of securities the issuer creates and differs from registration under the 1933 act that relates only to securities involved in a specific offer of a first issue. A class of securities includes all an issuer's securities with substantially similar characteristics and in which its owners possess substantially similar rights. For example, "Class A" common stock. It cannot be stressed enough that SEA registration of any class of securities authorized by a business is in addition to registration that may be required under the 1933 act.

Once an issuer is made subject to the registration requirements of the 1934 act, the issuer becomes subject to its other requirements. For the purpose of updating information contained in the original registration, the issuer must comply with periodic reporting requirements.

The issuer of a registered security is subject to the proxy solicitation requirements of the SEC. There is potential civil and criminal liability for failing to comply with the registration and other requirements of the 1934 act.

Voluntary Registration

The 1934 act allows voluntary registration by issuers of securities, listed or unlisted. Any issuer of an unlisted security can register any class of its securities. For example, issuers of unlisted securities (i.e., traded over-the-counter) who do not meet the $1,000,000 and 500 shareholder criteria for mandatory registration can register nevertheless. The issuer can list and register any class of its securities on a national securities exchange that lists such securities.

Registration Exemptions

Some securities are exempt from registration under the 1934 act. Securities exempted from registration include (1) securities of federal chartered savings and loan associations; (2) securities issued by religious, educational, or charitable nonprofit organizations; (3) securities listed and registered with a national securities exchange; (4) securities in the form of mortgage notes guaranteed by the federal government, such as FHA mortgages; (5) securities issued by agricultural cooperatives; and (6) securities issued by a state regulated insurance company.

Reporting Requirements

Companies required to register their securities must file a registration statement with the exchange on which the securities are traded and with the SEC or, if they are not traded on an exchange, with the SEC. The reporting requirements for these companies is generally comparable to but less extensive than the disclosure requirements of the 1933 Securities Act registration.

Once an issuer is made subject to the registration requirements of the 1934 act, the issuer becomes subject to the other requirements of the act. For the purpose of updating information contained in the original registration, the issuer must comply with periodic reporting requirements. The act requires issuers of registered securities to file annual (form 10-K), quarterly (form 10-Q), and current (form 8-K) reports and other reports. These periodic reports must be filed by corporations with 500 or more shareholders and assets exceeding $1,000,000, even if the corporation issues securities not registered under the 1933 act. The annual report form (10-K) calls for facts about the corporation's management, outstanding securities, and business operations, including a certified financial statement for the previous fiscal year. Annual reports to the shareholders must include the same kinds of information. The quarterly report form (10-Q) requires audited operating statements and a statement of financial condition, which can be summarized. The quarterly report is to reveal changes in the issuer's operations, management, and financial condition or structure in the interim between annual reports. Financial statements in the quarterly report must be certified. The current report (8-K) is an early warning report, which must be filed within fifteen days of any materially important event such as changes in corporate control, significant assets changes, or important legal proceedings. In any fiscal year other than that in which an issuer registers a primary offering, the annual, quarterly, and current reporting requirements may be suspended by the SEC if at the beginning of the fiscal year the securities of the class registered for the corporation are held by less than 300 persons of record.

Insider Trading Restrictions

The 1934 act is concerned with fair dealing in the trading of securities. A major area where fair dealing can be abused is trading by "insiders." An insider is typically an officer, director, or shareholder who has information about a publicly traded corporation that is not available to the public. The 1934 act imposes limitations on insider trading in order to curb insiders from profiting from insider knowledge and to assure noninsiders do not suffer losses from insider trading.

The 1934 act (Section 16 [b]) defines the term insider to include an officer, director, or large shareholder (holder or beneficial owner of more than 10 percent of an equity class) of the issuing corporation. But for the purpose of some punitive provisions of the 1934 act, the SEC rules (Rule 10b–5) have interpreted insider to extend beyond officers, directors, and controlling shareholders to include employees, attorneys, accountants, investment bankers, and others who have access to inside information. Insiders also include "tippees," any individuals who receive information from an insider.

The major limitation on insiders, which is called the "short-swing profits rule," is that they must turn over to the corporation any short-swing profits. Short-swing profits result from either the purchase and sale or sale and purchase of the securities of the issuer within a six-month period. The idea behind the short-swing profit penalty is to put all investors on the same footing and to eliminate an insider's special advantages. The short-swing profit penalty only applies to an officer, director, or ten percent shareholder. If the buying and selling transactions extend beyond six months, then profits need not be returned. The "profit" these insiders must return to the company is calculated by matching the highest sale price against the lowest purchase price within six months of each other. Losses cannot be offset against profits.

Liability is automatic for short-swing profits by an inside director, officer, or 10 percent shareholder. This is called absolute or strict liability. There are no defenses—good faith, lack of inside (nonpublic) information, or lack of intent to profit, for example. If an insider profits from a transaction within the six-month period, the profit must be returned to the corporation without exception.

The company, or any shareholder on behalf of the company in a derivative suit, can sue to require the insider to pay short-swing profits to the corporation.

Section 10(b) of the 1934 act makes it unlawful for an insider who has knowingly obtained *material inside information* to purchase or sell the issuer's securities to a person without first disclosing such information to the person. The insiders covered by Section 10(b) extend beyond directors, officers, and 10 percent shareholders to include any others who have actual access to inside information such as employees, attorneys, accountants, investment bankers, and tippees. The purchase or sale is voidable by the person not possessing the material inside information. Damages may be recovered from the nondisclosing party. Information is material if it is reasonably likely to affect the market price of the issuing corporation's shares. Examples of material insider information are: a significant oil and gas discovery by the issuer, trading on the security that is about to be suspended by the SEC, the existence of a substantial embezzlement by an officer or director of the issuer, and finalization of a merger or substantial acquisition by the issuer.

The Insider Trading Sanction Act of 1984 empowers SEC to bring a civil penalty suit against a purchaser or seller of securities while in possession of material nonpublic information. A maximum penalty paid to the federal government (of up to three times the profit gained or the loss avoided) can be levied by a federal court as a result of such an unlawful purchase or sale.

There are reporting requirements for certain types of insiders. Insiders may be required to report because they are insiders of an issuer that has registered either any class of its securities or because they hold or seek to acquire privately or publicly five percent of any class of stock registered by an issuer.

Proxy and Tender Offer Solicitation

Proxy Solicitation

A proxy is a person who acts for another. In a corporation, it is a common practice for shareholders to give the right to vote their shares to incumbent management or a challenging group. When someone solicits proxies of shares registered under the 1934 act, the act and its rules impose certain requirements. Any solicitation by management or a challenging group must disclose all material facts pertaining to the issues on which the proxy is being sought.

A proxy solicitation must provide each solicited shareholder with a copy of a *written proxy statement*, either before or at the time of the solicitation. A proxy statement describes all material facts concerning the matters being submitted for a vote for which the proxy is solicited. If the solicitation is made on behalf of the management and relates to an annual shareholder meeting at which directors are elected, an annual report must be furnished to the shareholders no later than the proxy statement. A proxy statement must disclose the following information:

1. revocability of the proxy;
2. rights of dissenting shareholders;
3. identity of the soliciting parties;
4. voting securities and owners of record entitled to vote;
5. identity of directors and principal executive officers and their remuneration;
6. information about the issuer's past and present public accountants;
7. stock options, warrants, and rights;
8. contemplated mergers or acquisitions;
9. contemplated modification, authorization, or issuance of securities;

10. certified financial statements if voting is to concern merger or acquisitions or the issuance, authorization, or modification of securities;

11. any other information material to the action for which the proxy is to be utilized.

The proxy to a shareholder must be *written*. The proxy must contain certain information. The proxy must state whether it is solicited on behalf of management. It must have a clear and impartial statement of each matter to be voted upon. The proxy is to explain the means by which the person solicited can choose between approval or disapproval of the matter(s) to be acted upon. Finally, the proxy must contain a statement that the shares represented by the proxy will be voted upon according to the choice specified by the person when the proxy was solicited.

The proxy, proxy statement, and all other solicitation materials must be filed with the SEC and with each securities exchange on which any class of issuer's shares are listed.

In an attempt to promote shareholder democracy, SEC rules require that management must include shareholder proposals in the proxy statement and provide shareholder lists or send out supporting material for the sponsors of such proposals. If management opposes the proposal, it must include in its proxy material a statement of not more than 200 words by the shareholder making the proposal. The management may omit a proposal if, among other things, it (1) is under state law not a proper subject for shareholder action, (2) is not significantly related to the business of the issuer or is beyond the issuer's power to effectuate, or (3) relates to the conduct of the ordinary business operations of the issuer.

An issuer who distributes a false or misleading proxy statement or proxy solicitation to its security holders may be liable to any person who suffers a loss caused by purchasing or selling a security as a result of relying upon the proxy statement or solicitation. Filing with or examination of proxy materials by the SEC does not mean that the statements therein have been found to be accurate, complete, truthful, or not misleading.

Tender Offers

To gain approval of a merger or acquisition, outside corporations may solicit proxies from shareholders of the target corporation. As a more common alternative, the corporate acquirers may make a tender offer, which is an offer to purchase stock at a stated price made either to the company or directly to its shareholders. An offer may be for all or a portion of the company's outstanding shares. A tender offer is most commonly used to acquire voting control of the target corporation.

The 1934 act requires any person or corporation seeking to acquire more than 5 percent of a company's securities, whether by direct purchase or by tender offers, to comply with reporting and disclosure requirements in order to make the marketplace, SEC, securities issuers, and their shareholders aware of the acquisition or takeover.

A "tender offer statement" must be filed with the SEC, sent to the target corporation, and sent to each securities exchange where the shares are listed. The tender offer statement must be filed and sent prior to the making, requesting, or inviting of a tender offer. The tender offer statement must disclose the following: (1) offerors' names and stock interest, (2) source of the funds used to acquire the securities, (3) purpose of the acquisition, and (4) details of any planned merger or disposition of the target corporation's assets. An offeror may not keep shares in a "street name"—in the name of the brokerage through which the stock was purchased—to avoid disclosure. Any special arrangement to obtain shareholder support for the tender offer must be disclosed. A tender offer can offer payment to a large group of shareholders at a higher price than is paid to other shareholders.

Before a recommendation to accept or reject a tender offer can be made by the target company or a competing tender offeror, the company must first file a similar disclosure statement with the SEC and send copies to the issuer of the securities and to any securities exchanges where the shares are listed.

There are exemptions to the reporting requirements for tender offers. These exemptions apply to treasury stock (reacquired by the issuer), call and redemption of equity securities, and offers to purchase fractional interests in equity securities.

It is unlawful for any person to make any untrue statement or omission of material fact or to engage in fraudulent, deceptive, or manipulative practices in connection with a tender offer.

Legal Sanctions and Remedies Under the 1934 Act

The 1934 act provides for sanctions against and remedies for noncompliance with its provisions. These include administrative remedies by the SEC, civil suits by the SEC and injured investors, and criminal penalties.

Trading Violations

Section 17(a) and SEC Rule 17(a)–5 impose liability for failure of exchange members or broker-dealers to keep appropriate books and records. Section 6(b) fixes liability for violation of national securities exchange rules by exchanges or their members. Liability is imposed for violation of *margin requirements* set by the Federal Reserve Board. Section 11(d)(2) imposes liability for failure by a member of a national securities exchange or a broker-dealer to inform a customer in writing in connection with a securities order from a customer as to whether it is acting for its own account, for the account of a customer, or as a broker for some other person. Section 16(c) bars insider short trading (short sales) by an insider who purports to sell stock of an issuer that the insider does not own. Participants in wash sales are liable, such sells being prohibited by Section 9(a)(1). Wash sales are the selling and buying of the same securities by the same parties to give the appearance of market activity. "Churning" is prohibited and a cause of liability under Section 15(c)(1) and Rule 15c 1–7. Churning involves a broker acting under discretionary authority who engages in excessive trading in order to generate increased commissions. Section 18 imposes liability for false or misleading statements made in registration statements or other documents filed under the act. Section 9(a)(1) imposes liability for matched transactions, the buying and selling of securities, knowing that others are taking the other side of the transaction with the intent to affect market prices. Section 9(a)(3) imposes liability for false statements made by broker-dealers to affect prices on a securities exchange. Section 9(a)(5) imposes liability for "touting", which involves a person being paid by a broker-dealer, securities buyer, or seller to influence the price of securities listed on a securities exchange.

Antifraud Provisions

The most sweeping, controversial, and revolutionary section of the 1934 act is section 10(b), which prohibits fraud in the purchase or sale of securities. The most widely known of the SEC regulations is SEC Rule 10b–5, which implements Section 10(b) of the law and potentially covers nearly every aspect of the securities market. SEC Rule 10b–5 makes it unlawful for any person to use the mails, facilities of interstate commerce, or facilities of any national security exchange as a means to purchase or sell security to engage in any of the following acts:

1. employ any device, scheme, or artifice to defraud;
2. make any untrue or misleading statement or omission of material fact;
3. engage in any act, practice, or course of business that operates or would operate as a fraud.

Rule 10b–5 is extremely broad in its scope, covering anyone involved in securities transactions, outsiders as well as insiders. Thus 10b–5 extends potential liability to sellers, buyers, issuers, insiders, directors and officers, controlling shareholders, members of national stock exchanges, brokers, dealers, tender offerors, underwriters, controlling persons of issuers, outside experts (accountants, engineers, geologists, and so forth), or any other person who violates the antifraud provisions in connection with the purchase and sale of securities. Some specific fraudulent acts include knowingly spreading false rumors about securities issuers to affect the issuer's securities prices; nondisclosure of material facts in a proxy solicitation; a corporation publishing a misleading press release regarding a mineral find; a broker's churning a customer's account; high pressure (boiler room) selling of securities to strangers by long-distance telephone; a parent company using its subsidiary to manipulate the market price of its stock; engaging in wash sales (excessive trading for the purpose of giving investors the appearance of active trading to drive up the market value of a security); incorporating false and misleading statements and omissions in an annual financial report filed with SEC; a broker falsely representing a stock as registered.

Rule 10b–5 applies to *all* securities, whether registered or unregistered, publicly or privately traded, listed or not listed on stock exchanges where the mails or instrumentalities of interstate commerce are involved. There are no exemptions.

Unlike the short-swing profit prohibition for insiders (Rule 16b), only a sale *or* a purchase (not both) of securities is required to violate Rule 10b–5. Unlike the liability provisions of the 1933 act, Rule 10b–5 applies to the misconduct of purchasers as well as sellers and allows both defrauded sellers and buyers to recover. It applies not only to the actual purchase and sale of securities but to *any* transaction *in connection with* their purchase and sale.

Recovery by a seller or purchaser in a Rule 10b–5 lawsuit requires he prove the following:

1. purchase or sale of a security took place;
2. the false statement or misleading omission is material;
3. purchase or sale made with *scienter* (actual knowledge of the falsity or reckless disregard of the truth) by the defendant;
4. the false statement was relied upon;
5. action in question was related to the purchase or sale of the security; and
6. the consequence of the preceding factors causes the defendant a loss.

The determination of what is material is crucial. A fact is material if it is so relevant or important to the transaction that it would have influenced the decision of a reasonable investor whether to purchase or sell the security. The rule imposes for material facts an affirmative duty to disclose, unlike the common law. Consequently, a defendant may be under a duty to disclose inside information he possesses. Because of the scienter requirement, the misconduct must be intentional. Negligence is not sufficient for a violation, and certainly a violation is not subject to strict liability.

There is a statute of limitations for lawsuits seeking damages under Section 10b and Rule 10b–5. The suit must be filed within one year after discovery of the false or misleading statement but not later than three years after the false or misleading statement was made.

SEC Remedies and Sanctions

The SEC has the power to impose sanctions or remedies, which include

1. *injunctions* to stop future violations.
2. *suspension of trading* of a security over-the-counter or on an exchange.
3. denial, suspension, or revocation of registration.
4. *delisting* of a security.
5. *censure* of a broker or broker-dealer for unlawful conduct.
6. *limitation* of operations of brokers or broker-dealers.

7. investigation of violations.

8. recommendation of criminal proceedings to the U.S. attorney general.

Criminal Penalties

Criminal penalties of a fine and/or imprisonment are provided for any *willful* violation of any provision of the act, SEC rule, or regulation and for any *willful* falsification or omission of material fact in a registration statement, application, report, or other required document. A securities exchange that commits a violation is subject to a fine of up to $500,000. Other violators are subject to jailing of up to five years and/or a fine of up to $10,000.

FOREIGN CORRUPT PRACTICES ACT

Overview

The Foreign Corrupt Practices Act was enacted in 1977 as an amendment to section 13(b) of the 1934 act. The Foreign Corrupt Practices Act came into being after a series of international scandals involving bribes by American corporations to foreign officials to obtain business. The purpose of the 1977 act is to prevent an American corporation from bribing a foreign official as a means to secure or promote business for itself. The act prohibits any American corporation—whether registered or not under the 1934 legislation—from bribing foreign officials. The 1977 act also imposes accounting, recordkeeping, and internal control provisions on corporations registered under the 1934 act so that they maintain accountability for the control of their assets, whether they engage in international trade or not.

Accounting, Recordkeeping, and Internal Control Provisions

The 1977 act requires covered companies to make and keep books, records, and accounts that in reasonable detail accurately and fairly reflect the transactions and disposition of assets of the issuer. The corporation must also devise and maintain internal accounting controls that are sufficient to provide reasonable assurances that transactions are authorized and recorded for a proper purpose and that corporate assets are accounted for. In sum, the act prohibits keeping inaccurate books, maintaining off-the-book accounts, and engaging in related practices.

To reinforce the obligation of corporations, the act requires them to disclose in their reports to SEC any illegal or questionable corporate practices related to corrupting foreign officials. The SEC has responsibility to enforce the accounting, recordkeeping, and internal control provisions.

Corporate officers, directors, accountants, insiders, and any other person can be subject to the civil and criminal penalties of the SEA of 1934 if their fraudulent conduct would constitute a violation of the provisions of the Foreign Corrupt Practices Act and associated SEC rules regarding accounting, recordkeeping, and internal control requirements.

Antibribery Provisions

It is unlawful for any corporation, whether or not registered under the 1934 act, or any of its directors, employees, shareholders, or agents to commit foreign bribery. Violation of this provision can result in fines of up to $1,000,000 for companies. Individuals may be fined up to $10,000 and imprisoned up to five years, or both. The company cannot pay, directly or indirectly, any fine imposed upon its directors, employees, agents, or shareholders. The SEC may also sue violators civilly for violation of the antibribery provisions.

7

Dissolution and Liquidation

Dissolution
  Voluntary Dissolution
  Involuntary Dissolution
Liquidation

The legal existence of a corporation may be terminated in a number of ways. The common term for the termination of the corporation when its legal existence ceases is *dissolution*. *Liquidation* is part of the dissolution process and refers to bringing the business to an orderly end through the sale of assets, payment of debts, and the distribution of assets to shareholders.

Termination can occur by agreement of shareholders, expiration of the corporate charter, insolvency, bankruptcy, reorganization, forfeiture or revocation of its charter, by law, or court decree. These various kinds of termination of the corporation can also be classified as *voluntary dissolution* or *involuntary dissolution*.

DISSOLUTION

Voluntary Dissolution

The termination of the corporation can be brought about by the corporation itself. This is called voluntary dissolution. Since the voluntary termination of the corporation is not compelled by a court proceeding, it is also referred to as nonjudicial dissolution. Likewise, an involuntary dissolution, which is brought about through a court proceeding, is sometimes referred to as an involuntary judicial dissolution.

At the incorporation stage, if the business never gets off the ground, it can be voluntarily dissolved by the incorporators or the initial board of directors. This can only be done if the corporation has not engaged in any business and no shares have been issued.

After incorporation, the corporation can be dissolved at the initiative of the board of directors. The directors can pass a resolution for termination of the corporation. The vote required for shareholder approval of the dissolution varies from state to state, ranging from a simple majority to four-fifths of the shareholders (voting and nonvoting). Under the Model Act, a majority of all the shareholders must approve the dissolution. Approval by two-thirds of the shareholders is the most common requirement.

The shareholders can bring about the voluntary dissolution of the corporation. One way is for major shareholders, either on or off the board, to convince the board to pass a resolution for dissolution to be voted on at a meeting of the shareholders. Another way is for the shareholders to unanimously consent *in writing* to dissolution (bypassing, or in place of, a board-initiated dissolution) if the creditors' rights are covered.

In all the foregoing kinds of voluntary dissolution—initiated by shareholders or directors—appropriate documents are prepared and statutory procedures are followed. *Notice of dissolution* must be provided for creditors, *articles of dissolution* must be filed with the state, and a *certificate of dissolution* must be received from the state.

A corporation is automatically terminated at the expiration of the period stated for the life of the corporation in its charter or at the time of accomplishment of the purpose specified as the purpose of the corporation in the charter. A merger or consolidation automatically terminates the existence of the corporation.

Involuntary Dissolution

In some circumstances a corporation can be terminated automatically by law or by a judicial proceeding instituted by the state, shareholders, or the creditors. In these cases dissolution is involuntary.

In some states, a corporation's certificate is automatically revoked for not filing an annual report. State laws often provide for *suspension* of corporate existence for nonpayment of taxes. A suspended corporation loses the right to do business and to sue while suspended. Insolvency does not in itself terminate the corporate existence. Straight bankruptcy (liquidation) in which the corporation's assets are sold does not end the legal existence of the corporation but does end the corporation's practical existence since it is without assets with which to do business (unless there is a surplus above the debt obligations to pay the debts to allow the company to continue in business). A reorganization under federal bankruptcy law does call for the termination of the corporation. Under some states' laws, however, reorganization proceedings generally result in the formation of a new corporation.

Dissolution of the corporation may be obtained in a court proceeding brought by the state (acting through the attorney general in most cases) upon the following grounds: failure to file annual report with the secretary of state; failure to pay annual franchise tax; failure to appoint or maintain a registered agent; fraud or fraudulent concealment in procuring a charter; violation of state (not federal) antitrust laws; ultra vires acts by the corporation, expiration of the corporate charter, or nonuse or dormancy of corporate business (corporation fails to organize, start the business, or undertake its duties within a given period or ceases to function during a long period). The suit brought by a state attorney general to dissolve a corporation is called a *quo warranto* action.

A corporation can be dissolved by petition of a shareholder to a court. State laws generally require a certain percentage of stockholders, usually one-third, to initiate a petition that a court will consider. The petition must show the dissolution is in the best interest of the corporation. The grounds on which a shareholder petition is usually brought include gross mismanagement of corporate affairs that wastes or misapplies corporate assets; deadlock of shareholders or directors that is unbreakable and threatens or causes irreparable injury to the corporation; failure of the corporation to earn a profit or at least to do business; oppression of minority shareholders by controlling shareholders or directors acting on their behalf; and illegal or fraudulent acts by directors or those in control of the corporation.

LIQUIDATION

Dissolution refers to the termination of a corporation's existence as a legal entity. *Liquidation* is part of the dissolution process and refers to the process of bringing the business to an orderly end through the sale of assets, payment of debts, and distribution of assets to shareholders. Liquidation is also commonly known as *winding up*.

Upon dissolution of a corporation the assets are liquidated and used to first pay the expenses of liquidation and its creditors according to their respective rights. Any remainder is distributed to the shareholders pro rata according to stock preferences.

When voluntary dissolution occurs, the corporation's directors become *trustees* who hold corporate assets for the benefit of creditors and shareholders. They are usually allowed to windup the corporation's affairs without court supervision. During the winding up the directors have the duty not to undertake any new business, to make a reasonable attempt to collect the debts owed to the corporation, pay creditors first, and distribute any remaining funds to the shareholders. The directors are held personally liable for breach of these duties. If they are unwilling to serve as trustees for liquidation, a *receiver* will be appointed and supervised by the court to conduct the winding up. Creditors and shareholders can also obtain a court appointed receiver if they show good reason why the directors should not perform the winding up function. When the dissolution is involuntary, the winding up activities must be performed by a court-appointed receiver.

Shareholder rights must be preserved in a dissolution. Upon dissolution, shareholders receive corporate assets after the debts of the corporation have been paid. Shareholders having a liquidation preference are paid first. They are entitled to be paid in cash unless they waive the right by consenting to a plan of liquidation calling for a property distribution. The courts will overturn an unfair plan of distribution of assets, such as giving cash to minority shareholders and the business assets to the majority so the latter can carry on the business free from the minority.

Creditors also have clear rights during a dissolution. They must be notified of a pending dissolution. They are entitled to payment, according to their priorities, from the corporate assets prior to distribution of assets to shareholders. If corporate assets are distributed to shareholders before paying creditors, the creditors can follow them into the hands of the shareholders and sue the shareholders for recovery of the assets. The directors are personally liable to creditors if they distribute corporate assets without proper provision for the creditors.

PART II

Partnerships

8

Partnerships: Nature and Formation

NATURE OF PARTNERSHIPS

Sources of Law

Modern partnership law shows traces of roman law, the law merchant, and the common law of England; American law developed in the courts over the years on a case-by-case basis. The National Conference of Commissioners of Uniform State Laws drafted the Uniform Partnership Act (UPA) in 1914. The purpose of the UPA was to modify and modernize the common law, court decisions, and other strands of partnership law from the past into a workable statutory framework that would be adopted by the states for uniformity in partnership law throughout the nation. The UPA has been adopted (with variations) by forty-eight states (excluding Georgia and Louisiana) and is in force in the District of Columbia, Guam, and the Virgin Islands. In the jurisdictions where it has been adopted the UPA is the prevailing law for partnerships and has in most, but not all, respects displaced common law. The UPA establishes rules to govern virtually every aspect of partnership operation from creation to termination, in the absence of a formal agreement or when certain areas are not covered in the agreement.

Definition

The UPA provides the standard definition for partnership: ''A partnership is an association of two or more persons to carry on as co-owners a business for profit.''

The definition contains several elements that are required before there can be a partnership.

Elements

Agreement. The partnership must be an association of two or more persons. ''Association'' implies there is some form of agreement among the parties involved in the partnership. There is no particular form which a partnership agreement must take. It may either be oral or written or it may be implied from the parties' actions. The parties need not call or consider themselves partners or a partnership or actually be aware they formed what the law considers a partnership.

Two or More Persons. The association must consist of two or more persons. The UPA broadly defines a person to include ''individuals, partnerships, corporations, and other associations,'' and any of them may combine to form a partnership.

Co-owners. Persons must carry on a business as co-owners. Co-ownership means more than two or more persons working together but each must have some rights associated with ownership. The UPA indicates ownership involves the following three rights or duties in the business:

1. Right to share profits.
2. Duty share losses.
3. Right to manage and control the business.

It is not necessary that these three elements of ownership be shared equally among the co-owners, since they can agree to divide management responsibilities and profits and losses unequally. These three elements are, as described later, key determinants in ascertaining in disputes whether a partnership or some other relationship exists among parties in a business.

Not in every situation are parties partners merely because they own property together or earn money from its use or sale. Forms of joint ownership that do not possess the other requirements constituting a partnership should not be confused with a partnership. Forms of joint ownership of property that do not in themselves establish partnerships (regardless of whether or not co-owners share profits), include joint tenancy, tenancy in common, tenancy by entirety, community property, condominium, or part ownership.

Business. A business is defined by the UPA as any trade, occupation, or profession.

Profit. The business must be for profit. This rules out many organizations that have been established for religious, charitable, educational, and other not-for-profit purposes.

The sharing of profits is many times the most crucial element determining the existence of a partnership. The UPA provides that a person receiving a share of profits of a business is *prima facie* evidence of a partnership and raises the rebuttable presumption that he is a partner. Prima facie evidence is evidence that is strong enough to allow a judge in a jury trial to let the partnership issue go to the jury without additional evidence. The presumption is that sharing profits is not absolute proof of partnership, and thus the alleged partner may prove no partnership existed by showing the absence of other elements of partnership. Nevertheless, the UPA provides this valuable inference is not raised if the purpose of receiving profits is to pay for other purposes:

1. Debt installments.

2. Wages.

3. Rent.

4. Services rendered.

5. Interest on a loan.

6. Annuity to a surviving spouse or representative of partner.

7. Consideration to a seller of a business for its goodwill or for other property by installment.

Types of Partners

General Partner

This partner has unlimited liability for partnership debts, full management powers, the authority to bind the partnership to contracts, and the right to share in profits and losses.

Limited Partner

This partner is a member of a properly formed limited partnership who is liable for the firm's indebtedness only to the extent of his investment (capital contribution) in the firm.

Real Partner

This partner is an actual partner as co-owner of the business. A real partner may be active or inactive, silent or secret.

Silent Partner

This real partner may be known to the public but has no voice and takes no part in the partnership business.

Secret Partner

This is a real partner who can take an active part in management of the firm but who is not disclosed to the public.

Dormant Partner (Silent and Secret)

This partner is a real partner who is both a silent and secret partner. In other words, he takes no active part in transacting business and remains unknown to the public.

Ostensible Partner

This person holds himself out as a partner or permits himself to be considered such by others, although he is not in fact an actual partner. To prevent injustice to third persons, this person may be held liable much like a partner, existing in a relationship called partnership by estoppel.

Retiring or Withdrawing Partner

This partner is a general partner when he leaves the partnership.

Incoming Partner

This is a new partner coming into the firm.

Continuing Partner

A continuing partner is a party who continues in the partnership after some partner(s) departs from the enterprise.

Types of Partnerships

General Partnerships

The general partnership is the most common form of partnership. The UPA is directed at providing the principles and rules governing general partnerships. The distinctive feature of the general partnership is that its members are equally and personally liable to third persons for the partnership debts. A general partnership is a partnership in which all the partners have unlimited liability for partnership debts. General partners have the right to manage and, unless otherwise agreed, to share in profits and losses. The general partnership is formed by an agreement, express or implied, among co-owners.

Limited Partnership

In the limited partnership at least one person is a general partner and at least one or more is a limited partner. The general partners have unlimited liability, and the limited partners have limited liability. The limited partner's liability is limited to no more than the amount of his investment (capital contribution) in the firm. The limited partnership must have at least one general partner. The general partner(s) manage the business and share profits and losses. The limited partners merely invest in the business and have no right, without an agreement to the contrary, to manage and share losses and profits. In order for a partnership to come into existence, there must be a statute allowing and governing the creation of the limited partnership. All states but Louisiana have adopted the Uniform Limited Partnership Act (ULPA) or the Revised Uniform Limited Partnership Act (RULPA) to make possible the creation of the limited partnership. The formation of the limited partnership requires substantial compliance with the ULPA or RULPA. As with a general partnership, a mere agreement for a partnership is not enough. There must be a certificate of limited partnership containing certain information or other forms required by the state, and they must be filed in a public office as required by the ULPA, which in most states is the secretary of state. Limited partners are supposed to be passive in the management of the limited partnership business. The more active the limited partner becomes in management decisions, the greater the risk that he will be considered a general partner and acquire unlimited liability.

Joint Venture

The joint venture is similar to a partnership in that it also involves two or more persons who are engaged in some business activity. The courts have traditionally treated joint ventures like partnerships. Joint ventures resemble partnerships in every respect except two—purpose and duration. First, joint ventures are created to accomplish a single purpose. Second, they do not involve an ongoing business but have a limited duration. For example, a joint venture might involve two oil companies that agree to jointly explore an offshore area or two persons who invest together to buy an apartment building for resale. A partnership is created to carry on a business for an indefinite period of time and is dissolved by the death or resignation of one of the partners. Despite the major distinction of a joint venture being that of a single activity versus the multiple, ongoing activities of a partnership, the general principle of partnership law applies to the joint venture (i.e., chiefly unlimited liability and fiduciary relationship among the owners).

Trading Partnership

A trading partnership is one engaged in the business of buying, selling, or leasing goods, real estate, or other property.

Nontrading Partnership

A nontrading partnership provides services as its business for profit, such as law, accounting, or physician partnerships.

Partnership by Estoppel

This is not an actual partnership voluntarily formed by an agreement of the parties. It is an equitable doctrine by which the court holds persons who are in fact not partners to be accountable to third persons as though they were partners. This occurs when a person's behavior leads a third party to think he is a partner. The principles applied by the courts are essentially the same as those applied when they find promissory estoppel in contracts or apparent agency. The person who presents himself as a partner when he is not is termed an apparent or ostensible partner. The ostensible partner is liable to the third party to whom the misrepresentation of partnership has been made when the third party detrimentally relies on the misrepresentation. A common instance of partnership by estoppel occurs when a person to whom the misrepresentation is made acts on it by giving credit to the actual or apparent partnership. For example, X, in attempting to secure a loan from a bank, represents that Y, his best friend and a wealthy businessman, is a partner in his business. Y knows of X's misrepresentation but does nothing about it. If the bank relies upon the financial creditworthiness of Y and X defaults on the loan, Y is an apparent partner and under the doctrine of partnership by estoppel is liable to the bank for repayment of the loan. Y will be "estopped" from maintaining he is not a partner of X to the extent of the loan.

FORMATION OF PARTNERSHIPS

Agreement

The formation of a partnership can be relatively simple and may be done consciously or unconsciously. It is a voluntary association by two or more persons who as co-owners are carrying on a business for profit. For a partnership to exist there must be an agreement between the parties to form such an association. There is no particular form that a partnership agreement must take. The agreement may be oral or written or it may be implied from the parties' actions. It is not necessary that the parties label themselves as partners or their relationship as a partnership. Likewise, they may not know that they have agreed to form what is legally known as a partnership. In other words, they may not have intentionally wished to form the partnership that the law determines they did. Conversely, they may believe they have agreed to have formed a partnership, but a partnership does not arise if they lack the elements of a partnership. That is, the parties' intent in creating a partnership is important but not determining. If they wanted to create a partnership but failed to comply with one of the requirements for its formation, no partnership is formed. The law of partnership is concerned with what is done in substance rather than what is done in form or name.

Express Agreement (Oral or Written)

A partnership agreement may be an express one. An express agreement may be either oral or written. A written agreement creating a partnership is sometimes referred to as *articles of partnership*. As a general rule an express agreement need not be in writing. A mere handshake can create a partnership. However, a written agreement, while unnecessary, is usually highly desirable to avoid subsequent controversies and misunderstandings as to the mutual rights and duties of the partners, better delineate the businesses' objectives, and even prove whether a partnership exists among the parties. As one commentator has put it, what begins as a handshake may end with shaking fists.

Contents of Partnership Agreement

The following is a list of some matters a written partnership should cover:

1. Partnership's name.
2. Partner's names.
3. Partnership's purpose.
4. Location of the partnership.
5. Start-up date and duration of the partnership.
6. Capital contributions of each partner—in amount and form (money, real estate, etc.).
7. Property of a partner used in the business that is to be considered partnership property—i.e., a clear delineation of partnership assets as opposed to each partner's personal assets.
8. Each partner's proportional share of net profits while the business is operating and upon dissolution.
9. Parties' duties and time owed to the partnership.
10. Procedures to add and eliminate partners.
11. Formula for division of profits and losses.
12. Rights (if any) to salaries and advances or draws on profits.
13. Procedures for settling disputes among partners.
14. Restrictions, if any, on partners.
15. Bookkeeping and accounting methods to be used.
16. Access to books and records.
17. Manner for handling partnership affairs if a partner dies, is dissolved, becomes incompetent, or bankrupt.
18. Manner of terminating the partnership.
19. Selection of which partner, if any, will be in charge of winding up the business upon dissolution.

20. Provision for continuation of the business by remaining partners, if desired, in the event of the death of a partner or other dissolution causing event, and the method or formula for appraisal and payment of the interest of the deceased or former partner.

21. Requirements and procedures for notice to partners and partnership creditors in case of dissolution.

Secret Agreements

General partnership agreements can be made secret. They do not have to be filed in any public office to be valid. Only partners have the right to see them, unless the partnership interests are considered "securities" requiring registration by statute.

Statute of Frauds

The Statute of Frauds requires certain kinds of contracts to be in writing in order to be enforceable. The Statute of Frauds does not specifically apply to a contract for the formation of a partnership, and therefore no writing is required to actually create the relationship.

However, the Statute of Frauds requires written agreements for any contract which cannot be performed within one year. If the parties intend the partnership to last more than one year, e.g., ten years, the agreement would have to be in writing. By contrast, if the partnership is meant to be of indefinite duration, a written document is not required because conceivably the agreement would be performed within a year. In sum, an oral agreement to create a partnership is enforceable, provided it does not bind the partners for more than one year.

The Statute of Frauds also applies to contracts for the transfer of land, goods over $500, or miscellaneous intangibles over $5,000. The courts do not require a written document for the formation of a partnership to engage in the business of buying and selling land or such goods. A contract to form a partnership engaged in a business conducting activities covered by the Statute of Frauds is distinguishable from contracts entered into by the partnerships for these activities. Thus, the transfer of real estate, goods over $500, or miscellaneous intangibles over $5,000 to or by a partnership is governed by the Statute of Frauds and requires a writing to be enforceable.

Implied Agreement

The agreement that is essential to the formation of a partnership may be implied by the conduct of the parties, rather than arising out of an express oral or written agreement. If two or more persons conduct a business which meets all the elements that constitute a partnership, the existence of a partnership is implied even though the parties might not have intended to form what in the eyes of the law is considered a partnership. For example, assume A owns a vacant lot and a friend, B, grows flowers. The two decide to operate a flower stand in which A will do all the work of selling flowers, and the both will divide the profits.

Although A and B might not consider themselves partners, they have formed a partnership and are subject to all the rights and obligations demanded by partnership law. The implication that a partnership is formed exists when parties engage in a business which is conducted in a manner that satisfies the elements defining a partnership, e.g., sharing profits and joint management.

Who May Be Partners—Capacity

Any "person" who has the legal capacity to enter into contracts may enter into a partnership. The UPA broadly defines person to encompass both natural and artificial persons and includes an individual, partnership, corporation, or any other association. Certain individuals—minors and insane persons—have the right to escape partnership agreements because they are deemed to lack legal capacity to enter into a partnership.

Minors

Minors do not have full contractual capacity, but they can enter into contracts. What distinguishes minors is that they can, while still a minor, disaffirm (get out of) the contract. This right to disaffirm and withdraw from the contract or carry it out means the contract is voidable. While the minor partner can withdraw from the contract from his side, the partnership itself is still bound by the contract and must continue in the relationship if the minor insists. And the partnership is still bound by the business contracts it entered into with others while the withdrawing minor was a partner. A withdrawing minor partner is entitled to return of his investment and his share of profits but only after the creditors of the partnership are paid. The right of a minor partner to disaffirm only exists before attaining the age of adulthood. If the right has not been exercised before reaching adulthood, it cannot be exercised afterward, and the person has all the liabilities and responsibilities of a partner. When a minor continues in the partnership relationship he has the same rights as other partners, such as the right to share profits, engage in management, and incur debts for the partnership. While a partner the minor is liable to co-partners and partnership creditors. If the agreement is disaffirmed during minority, the minor's status as a partner is deemed to have been repudiated not from the moment it is actually made but back to the date the partnership was joined. Hence the minor is freed from personal liability for breach of the partnership agreement, to any former co-partners, and partnership creditors.

Insane Partners

A person is considered insane for purposes of contract law when due to insufficient mental capacity he cannot understand the nature and effect of the contract from its inception. Contracts by a person legally adjudged to be mentally incompetent at the time the contract was entered into are void; that is, they are unenforceable whether the insane person wants the contract to be enforced or not. Prior to adjudication of mental incompetency, like a minor, the mentally incompetent's contracts are merely voidable. In other words, an insane person can be a partner until adjudged to be insane or incompetent by a court. If a court does declare a partner mentally incompetent, then any other partner can dissolve the partnership.

Proving the Existence of the Partnership

When parties establish a partnership through a written agreement, there is little difficulty in determining whether a partnership exists. But when the parties do not clearly or explicitly express their intention to establish a partnership, it is not clear whether a partnership has been formed. This is when problems arise, because it may be to the advantage of some partners to show the existence of a partnership and to the advantage of others to show it does not exist. The question of whether or not a partnership has been created is important in these situations because it will resolve the rights and obligations of partners among each other and in respect to outside third parties. For instance, a creditor hoping to take advantage of the individual liability of partners may seek to hold several persons liable for the debts of a business on the grounds that they are partners. In another instance, a person may claim he and another are partners and that the other must pay damages because the other breached the fiduciary duty characteristic of a partnership.

The burden of proving the existence of a partnership is on the person who claims it exists. It should first be noted that while the intention of the parties in creating a partnership is important, it is not conclusive and controlling. As described earlier, the parties may have intended to create a partnership, but if one of the essential elements is missing then no partnership has been formed. Conversely, the parties may not have intended to create a partnership and yet their business relationship may result in a partnership if all the elements for its existence are present.

When faced with a dispute about the existence of a partnership, the courts look at a number of factors surrounding the business relationship. There are three factors that have come to be seen as the most important and thus are used as tests as to whether a partnership exists. These three tests are, in order of importance: (1) sharing of profits, (2) joint control and management, and (3) joint ownership of property. All these tests are directed toward satisfying an all-encompassing requirement, that there must be co-ownership of the business.

Sharing of Profits

Sharing profits is widely considered the most important test of a partnership. As discussed earlier, the receiving or sharing of profits is prima facie evidence in court and raises the rebuttable presumption that a partnership exists, shifting the burden of proof from the person claiming the partnership exists to the person disputing it.

The sharing of profits, which is of major importance in proving the partnership, should be distinguished from the sharing of gross revenues or returns, which is slight, if any, evidence of partnership. Gross returns are the income of an enterprise before expenses are deducted to arrive at a profit figure.

As described earlier, there are instances when a person receives a payment from profits and this does not raise the inference he is a partner. The payments from the profits can be for a debt, wages, rent, service rendered, an annuity to a deceased partner's surviving spouse or representative, interest on a loan, or payment for the goodwill (or property) in the purchase of a business.

Parties may share profits from jointly held property and still not be considered partners. As noted before, the joint ownership of property and the consequent sharing of its income do not necessarily mean the co-owners are partners. Neither does joint ownership preclude them from being partners. Joint ownership is simply a neutral factor in determining the partnership's existence.

Courts also consider the intent of the parties to share profits, but the intent is not conclusive. If the parties intend to share profits or even go a step farther and do in fact share profits, a partnership still does not exist if the other elements needed to form a partnership are not present.

Joint Control and Management

The right to share in the management of the business is one of the basic rights of a partner, and thus the presence or absence of control in a business is significant in determining whether a person is a partner. Evidence of participation in the management or control of a business, standing alone, is not conclusive proof of a partnership. Employees, for example, may have a voice in management. Conversely, a person who is actually a partner may decide not to take an active part in the affairs of the business or may agree not to exercise any management or control functions. Compelling evidence of a partnership occurs when there is both the exercise of control or management responsibilities combined with the sharing of profits; together they create a strong presumption of partnership.

Joint Ownership of Property

Of the three basic tests of a partnership, co-ownership of property or assets is the least important. It is helpful evidence but evidence to be taken into consideration along with the other tests of a partnership. A basic part of co-ownership of property is the sharing of profits or income. Consequently, the dual existence of co-ownership of property and the sharing of profits do not necessarily establish a partnership. Moreover, the presumption of a partnership is not necessarily created by the fact that co-owners of property share the profits generated from its use. On the other hand, the inference of partnership is warranted if the jointly owned property is part of a larger enterprise and the parties share the profits from the entire enterprise as well. For example, two persons may jointly own an office building and share the rental income. This alone does not make them partners since it does not show they are running the office building as a business for profit. However, if they use part of the building as the office premises for a going enterprise of some type, sharing the rent from the building along with the profits and management of the enterprise, these endeavors are likely to render them partners.

9

Partnerships: Property of Partnership and Partners

PARTNERSHIP PROPERTY

Partnership property consists of all the real or personal property contributed by the partners, property acquired for the firm or with its funds, and property created or manufactured by the partnership business. Legal title to partnership property owned by the partnership need not be in the name of the partnership but may be held in the name of one or more of the partners. Hence, "paper title" does not determine, nor is it conclusive evidence of, ownership. Moreover, the fact that a partnership uses or possesses property does not necessarily mean that the property is partnership property.

Consequences of Property Ownership by Partners versus Partnership

The distinction between partnership property owned by the partnership (partnership property) and property owned personally by an individual partner is important for many reasons.

1. Creditors of the partnership have priority over the personal creditors and any partner in regard to partnership property.

2. Creditors of the partnership must resort to partnership property for satisfaction of their claims before they can take the property of individual partners.

3. Creditors of a partner have priority over the partnership creditors in property personally owned by the partner, that is, non-partnership property.

4. Creditors of the partner have no right to attach or execute against property owned by the partnership.

5. Neither the partnership nor the partners' personal creditors have any right in property possessed by the partnership but owned by a third person.

6. Taxes on the property are owed by its true owner, not by whoever has paper title or possession.

7. At the death of a partner, all partnership property remains part of the firm's property and does not pass as part of his estate (although the value of his interest in the partnership property must be paid to his estate).

8. A partner has no right to sell or transfer partnership property without authority of the other partners, unless the sale or transfer is in the ordinary course of business.

9. At dissolution of the partnership, only partnership property is distributed to the former partners or creditors, while nonpartnership property leaves with its individual owner.

10. Partnership property is for the common partnership use, and no one partner can be deprived of it without his consent.

Determining Ownership of Property

Ownership of property is determined by the intention of the parties as indicated by agreement or conduct of the partners. This includes money, personal property, land, intangibles, right to services, and so forth. Disputes or doubts about ownership of property can be avoided if the dedication of the property appears in the written partnership agreement or articles of partnership. It is helpful if the partnership maintains clear records concerning the partnership dealings with property. Unfortunately, partners often do not clearly indicate their intentions in agreements or recordkeeping as to whether property is owned by the firm or by one or more individuals.

In the absence of a clear agreement as to ownership, written or otherwise, the courts attempt to uncover the parties' intent. Where the intent of the parties cannot be uncovered by an agreement, whether express or implied from conduct, the court looks deeper at several pertinent factors. These factors or tests used by the courts to determine whether an item of property was intended to be owned by the partnership include the following:

1. It is carried on the books as partnership property.

2. It was purchased by partnership funds.

3. It is used for partnership purposes.

4. Title was taken in the partnership name.
5. The partnership pays taxes levied upon it.
6. Partnership funds are used to maintain, improve, and/or repair the property.
7. The partners declare the property to be partnership property.
8. Income generated from the property is received by the partnership.

No one single factor is conclusive evidence of the parties' intention to dedicate property for partnership ownership. To the extent relevant, some or all factors are considered together, with the cumulative calculation by the court helping it to come to a decision. The first four factors have special significance.

The first, if the property is carried on the partnership books as an asset of the business, is strong evidence it is meant to be partnership property. Even stronger evidence is the unpaid balance on the property being carried in the records as a partnership liability—the second factor. The UPA establishes that any item of property purchased with partnership funds is presumed to be partnership property. Because of this presumption, proof that partnership funds were used to buy the property is sufficient to establish the partnership as the owner even if this is the only evidence presented. However, the presumption is not absolute. It can be rebutted by contrary evidence of use and intention. Nevertheless, a great deal of contrary evidence is required to overcome the presumption. Use by the partnership of the property, the third factor, is considered by the courts as evidence of partnership ownership. Standing alone, however, such use is not sufficient to establish partnership ownership, particularly when the property is held in the name of the individual partner. It is not unusual for an individual partner to allow use by the partnership of his property without any intention to surrender ownership of it. Where there is no clear agreement as to ownership, the strongest evidence of property ownership is the fourth factor, the party who has legal title (i.e., in whose name the property is held). Almost invariably the courts will hold property to be partnership property if the partnership has title to it. However, the fact that a title certificate shows ownership in a name other than that of the firm does not forego the possibility that the partnership has actual ownership. That is why the various aforementioned factors are assessed and calculated together by the courts to determine the intention of the parties.

Transfer of Title to Partnership Property

The partnership can hold and transfer personal property in the firm name. Partnership property is frequently titled, that is, held in the name of one or more partners rather than that of the partnership. Usually when the partnership property appears of record to be owned by a partner, he owned the property prior to the formation of the partnership and never went through the formality of transferring title to the partnership, or a partner of an existing firm used partnership funds to purchase the property and failed to put its title in the name of the partnership.

In either case, the partner holding title is considered by the law as a *trustee* holding the property for the benefit and use of the partnership, which is regarded as the actual owner.

Transferees of partnership real property have different rights, depending upon whether the property was held in the name of the partnership or in the name of a partner. Ordinarily, the buyer of partnership real property has obtained legal title when (1) the transfer has been made by a partner or agent of the partnership with authority to make the transfer and (2) the transfer was made by the holder of paper title, whether a partner or the partnership. Title to partnership property held in the name of one or more partners ordinarily cannot be transferred without proper authority, that is, when a partner transfers partnership property titled in his name to another person without authority from the partnership, the partnership can recover the property from the person to whom it was conveyed. There is an exception for innocent purchasers, what the law calls *bona fide purchasers for value*. A bona fide purchaser for value takes title in exchange for value and does so without knowledge or notice of the partner's lack of authority. This innocent purchaser may keep the partnership property titled in the partner's name even though it was not the partner's to sell. There is no similar protection for a bona fide purchaser for value of partnership property held in the name of the partnership. Here the partnership may recover the property from the innocent purchaser who bought the real property from the partner who lacked actual authority. However, if the transfer of real property is authorized but title was conveyed in the name of a partner rather than the true owners—the partnership—the transferee has the right to a proper instrument of conveyance executed by the partnership.

PARTNER'S RIGHTS IN PROPERTY AND PARTNERSHIP

Individual Partners' Property Rights in the Partnership

The UPA names three property rights of individual partners.

1. *Rights in specific partnership property* is the right to possess and use partnership property for partnership purposes. The partners interest in the partnership's property is known as a *tenancy in partnership*. Individual partners do not have the right to mortgage, sell, or give by will particular pieces of partnership property. Tenancy in partnership is a form of co-ownership.

2. *Partner's "interest" in the partnership* refers to the partner's right to share profits, surplus and goodwill, right to repayment of loans, and the right to return of capital contributions. The partner has the right to assign any particular aspect, or all aspects, of his interest in the partnership.

3. *Right to participate in management.* (see Chapter 10.)

Rights in Specific Partnership Property—Tenancy in Partnership

A partner does not actually own, as an individual, any particular piece of partnership property. The partner is a co-owner of the property along with the other partners. But the partner, as a co-owner, does have rights in partnership property. A partner's interest in the partnership property as a whole is a specific type of joint ownership known as *tenancy in partnership*, which means the partner has the right to use all partnership property but has no rights, superior or inferior, in specific items. Each partner's common ownership interest in any specific item of partnership property makes him a *tenant in partnership*. Tenancy in partnership is a legal interest created by the UPA, which is similar to another form of co-ownership of property recognized in common law—joint tenancy. Tenancy in partnership has the following four characteristics:

1. *Each partner has the equal right to possess and use property for partnership purposes.* This right to use and possess the property is only for partnership purposes. The partner has no right to make personal use of any specific item of partnership property unless the other partners first give their consent. For instance, the partners may agree a particular partner has the right to use for sales calls an automobile owned by the partnership. However, the partner has no right, without the consent of the other partners, to use the automobile to take his family on vacation.

2. *The partner has no right to sell, assign, or mortgage any particular piece of partnership property without authority from the other partners.* The authority of a partner to sell, assign, or mortgage a specific item of property is obtained in two ways: a) all the partners' consent is given or b) the transfer is part of carrying on the partnership business.

3. *A creditor of a partner cannot proceed against any specific items of partnership property.* Any partnership property, despite the partner's rights of co-ownership in it, is immune from attachment or execution by the personal creditors of the individual partner. Only the partnership's creditors can seize, attach, or execute against the partnership property. A partner's personal creditor can, however, proceed against the partner's interest in the partnership through what is called a "charging order". Also a partner may assign his "partnership interest" to pay a creditor.

4. *On the death of a partner, his right in specific partnership property does not become part of his estate, but vests in the surviving partners as a right of survivorship.* In other words, the deceased partner's previous right in partnership property is not inheritable by will or interstate succession. When a partner dies, all the partnership property remains as part of the firm's assets and does not, for example, pass to his surviving spouse. However the estate of the deceased partner does have a right in the *value* of his ownership interest in the partnership, as distinguished from a right in any particular item of partnership property. At the death of a partner, the remaining partners must account and pay to the deceased's estate the value of his partnership interest, which consists of his share of profits and capital contribution.

Partner's Interest in the Partnership

A partner's rights in the partnership is different from his interest in the partnership. The latter is defined as his share of profits earned by the business, and when the business ends, is defined as his right to a share of surplus and goodwill, repayment of loans, and return of his capital contributions. Stated another way, the partner has an ownership interest in the business enterprise as a whole, not in any of its individual assets. This ownership interest is the personal property of the partner, even if the firm only owns real estate. The partner's interest in the partnership is his ownership share of the partnership and in the net worth of its assets. The characteristic of a partner's rights in partnership property (tenancy in partnership) versus his interest (share) in the partnership are complete opposites. As stated previously, partnership property is not subject to the claims of an individual partner's creditors, not transfferable by a partner to a third party without consent of the other partners, and not inherited by the partner's estate. In contrast, the partner's interest is subject to claims of his personal creditors, assignable to others without need to gain consent of the other partners, and does pass to his estate at his death.

Creditor's Rights Against Partner's Interest

Creditors of a partner cannot seize (attach or execute against) partnership property for the repayment of his personal debts. However, these creditors can reach his partnership interest to enforce payment of the debt, and this is done by obtaining a *charging order* from the court, a type of attachment or judicial lien against the partner's personal property interest in the partnership. A creditor who has charged the interest of a partner with a judgment debt may apply for the appointment of a receiver. The receiver can take the partner's profits in the partnership and distribute them to his attaching creditors. The creditors may foreclose the charging order through a process resulting in the judicial sale of the partner's interest. Any time before the sale, the partner, or any of his co-partners, can redeem (buy back) the partnership interest by repaying the debt. The receiver or the person buying a foreclosed partnership interest does not become a partner by virtue of receiving the partner's share of profits and therefore has no rights to participate in the management of the partnership. The partner remains a partner, merely being deprived of his share of profits which are diverted to creditors.

Assignment of Interest in Partnership

The partner can sell or assign his interest in the partnership to a third party. This act is different from the principle that a partner's right to possess and control partnership property cannot be assigned or sold without the consent of the partners. The assignability of a partner's interest allows him to sell or dispose of it to the partnership itself, to another partner, or to a third party. The partners can agree they will have the right, either collectively or individually, to buy any partnership interest offered for sale before sale to an outside party—*right of first refusal*. A partner also may assign his partnership interest to pay a creditor.

A third party (assignee) who has received the assigning partner's interest does not become a partner and has none of the important rights of a partner such as the right to participate in management decisions or inspect the books of the partnership. The assignee is merely entitled to receive the share of profits the assigning partner would have received during the continuation of the business and whatever share of the surplus that would have come to the assigning partner when the partnership is dissolved. The assigning partner remains a partner with all the other usual rights and duties. Moreover, the assignment of a partner's interest does not in itself cause dissolution of the partnership.

Heirs Rights in Partner's Interest

When a partner dies, his interest in the partnership, because it is personal property, becomes part of his estate. The interest is inherited according to the provisions of the deceased partner's will or, if he dies without a valid will, according to the inheritance laws of the state. It is especially important to distinguish between the ownership of specific partnership property and ownership of an interest in the partnership. The partner's rights in specific partnership property ceases at his death. The interest passing to the estate is the *value* of the decedent's interest in the partnership, which consists of his share of profits and capital. In contrast, title to firm property stays in the firm for the surviving partners. For instance, the estate has no rights to the desk the decedent partner had occupied.

When the transfer of the partnership property in the firm name was not authorized, the partnership can recover it from the transferee even if that purchaser was a bona fide purchaser for value, i.e., paid for the property in good faith without knowledge of the partner's lack of authority.

10

Partnerships: Rights, Duties, and Liabilities of Partners

RIGHTS AMONG PARTNERS

Partners' Rights

The rights and duties among the partners are governed by the partnership agreement. If the partnership agreement is silent as to the rights and duties, the following principles and rules from the UPA and case law govern.

Right to Participate in Management

In a general partnership, unless there is a specific agreement to the contrary, each partner has an equal right to take part in the management activities and decisions in that partnership. This equal voice in management exists regardless of the partner's relative contribution of capital or services to the firm. The equal right to share in management can be varied by the partnership agreement.

The majority generally governs on all matters concerning the ordinary business affairs such as establishing prices and production schedules, entering into leases, setting up levels of inventory, and so forth. If there are an even number of partners, they must have an understanding as how to break a stalemated vote since the courts will generally not hear a suit between partners concerning ordinary business matters. The principle of the equal right to share in management may be altered by the partnership agreement.

As a practical matter, it is not uncommon for partners to agree that day-to-day decisions do not require a majority vote and to delegate these decisions to a *managing partner*. This partner will act as the general manager of the business.

Certain types of decisions require unanimous action or vote unless the partnership agreement specifically provides otherwise. Such decisions include amending the original articles of partnership, admitting a new partner, engaging in a new business activity, changing the division of profits, confessing judgment against the partnership or submitting claims to arbitration, disposing of all the partnership personal property, assigning partnership assets for the benefit of creditors, moving the partnership office, taking any action that would make the further conduct of business impossible, and attending to any other matter that is not in the ordinary course of business. Finally, if any matter is forbidden by or contrary to the original partnership agreement, a unanimous decision is required. The partners may provide in the partnership's agreement for the bypassing of the requirement for a unanimous vote for any or all of the above matters and may require only a majority vote, a two-thirds vote, or any other proportion beyond a majority.

Right to Information and Inspection of the Books

Every partner always has the right to inspect and copy the records and books of the partnership. This absolute right to inspect is available to active and inactive partners. The right may be exercised by a duly authorized attorney or accountant on behalf of a partner. The personal representative of a deceased partner also has this right. The records and books must be kept and maintained at the partnership's place of business, unless the partners agree on some other location. Finally, each partner has a general right to be informed about the particular details of the partnership's operations.

Right to Share Profits

Each partner is entitled to a share of the partnership profits. The partners may agree to establish a formula for sharing profits, with the distribution, if they so wish, in unequal proportions. If there is no agreement, express or implied, as to the sharing of profits, then the law presumes the partners are entitled to equal shares of the profits. This presumption applies without regard to the amount of capital contributed to or services performed for the partnership. Furthermore, if there is no specific agreement, the partners share losses in the same proportion as profits. Consequently, if nothing is said about or agreed to concerning profits and losses, they are shared equally. With an agreement, the partners may provide for the bearing of losses in a different proportion than the sharing of profits.

No Right to Compensation

The UPA provides that partners have no right to salaries or any other compensation for their services, unless otherwise agreed. The prohibition against compensation, short of an agreement otherwise, applies even if the services performed are unusual or more difficult or extensive than the services performed by other partners. The law presumes the partner's rightful remuneration is his right to a share of the profits, if there is no agreement for compensation or salaries for services rendered. This presumption is based on the common law perspective that what a partner does for the partnership he does for himself, since he co-owns the partnership. Consequently, if salaries or other rewards are to be paid, there must be a specific agreement for this purpose.

It is common for an agreement among partners to provide salaries and to vary this and other forms of compensation according to each partner's share of work or extent of management responsibility. It is normal for the partners to receive regular salaries, with distribution of profits occurring at the end of the year. It is also possible that a partner may, under the agreement of the partners, receive a salary to be deducted from his share of profits, receive a salary in lieu of profits, or receive an increased share of profits in lieu of salary.

Right to Return of Capital Contributions

A partner is entitled to the repayment of his *capital contribution* (investment) to the partnership at its termination, unless there is an agreement to the contrary.

Partners do not have a right to interest on their capital contributions, unless otherwise agreed. The repayment of capital contributions is a liability of the partnership.

The property and money contributed by a partner and dedicated to permanent use in the business are his capital contribution. The sum total of these contributions by the partners is the *partnership capital*. Each partner is entitled to the return of his capital contribution upon the dissolution of the partnership but only after the partnership assets have been applied to partnership debts, including loans to the partners. Before a dissolution, the partner may not withdraw his capital contribution without agreement of the other partners, and the withdrawal requires a new partnership agreement and hence creates a new partnership. If a partner contributes more than his required share, the excess amount is considered a loan for which he is entitled interest.

Right to Repayment of Loans

A partner is entitled to return of any money advanced or loaned to the partnership. The partner has a right to interest on any loan to the partnership, unless otherwise agreed upon. Loans have priority over the capital contributions of the partners upon the dissolution of the partnership. Since the loans are entitled to interest an capital contributions are not, withdrawal of capital requires a new partnership agreement and the repayment of a loan does not. Furthermore, since loans have priority over capital contributions, it is important for a partner to make sure the money is documented as a loan. A partner's payment of money to a partnership is presumed to be a capital contribution rather than a loan unless specified otherwise.

Right to Reimbursement, Contribution, and Indemnification

A partner has the right to be reimbursed for payments made on behalf of the partnership. A partner who pays more than his share of partnership expenses, debts, or other obligations is entitled to payment, called *contribution*, from other partners. For example, if one partner loses a lawsuit brought by an injured party for the negligence of an employee while acting in the scope of partnership employment and pays damages to the injured party, the partner may enforce contribution from the other partners.

The partnership must indemnify, and individual partners are required to provide contribution to any partner for payments made and personal liabilities reasonably incurred in the ordinary and proper conduct of the business or in order to preserve its business or property. But the right to indemnification or contribution is not allowed if the partner (1) acts in bad faith; (2) negligently causes the necessity for payment; or (3) previously agreed to bear the expense, loan, or obligation.

Right to Choose Fellow Partners

No partner can be forced to accept another person as a partner. The unanimous consent of the partners is required to admit a new partner, unless there is another agreed procedure for choosing partners. If a partner sells his interest to another, the buyer does not become a partner with all the rights inherent in a partner.

Right to An Accounting

A person is entitled to a legal proceeding called an *accounting* of partnership property and monies (1) whenever he is wrongfully excluded from the partnership business or possession of its property by other partners, (2) whenever one or some of the other partners have derived a personal benefit from a transaction without the consent of the partner, or (3) otherwise whenever such a proceeding is just and reasonable. The accounting is a suit in equity that requires all records of the partnership to be produced and all balances to be computed under court supervision. A partner may demand an accounting without dissolution of the partnership. However, an accounting is most commonly demanded as part of the dissolution of the partnership. If a dissolution takes place, it must be accompanied by an accounting.

Rights in Specific Partnership Property

Each partner has an equal right to possess and to use partnership property for partnership purposes because each partner is a co-owner of all partnership property and any specific partnership property. This form of co-ownership by partners is called a *tenancy in partnership*. The partner cannot assign his right to another in specific partnership property—that is, transfer to another of the right to use and possess the property. The partner can, however, assign his right to share in profits. A partner's right to use and possess specific partnership property is not subject to attachment or execution by the partner's creditors. Upon the death of a partner, the partner's remaining rights in the partnership pass to the surviving partner or partners. These remaining partners, in other words, have what is called survivorship rights in partnership property. On the other side of the coin, it means the partner's right in any specific partnership property is not inheritable. For instance, his office furnishings at the partnership place of business do not pass to his estate when he dies because they are partnership property. However the deceased partner's share of profits and capital do pass to his estate.

Partner's Suits to Enforce Rights

The ability of a partner to sue his co-partners to enforce his rights in the partnership is limited. The general principle is that a partner cannot sue co-partners to enforce the partnership agreement or resolve disagreements between partners. If there is a dispute within the partnership, the partners cannot go to court to resolve it. They must either settle the matter among themselves or dissolve the partnership.

The prohibition against partners suing each other applies to actions at law, but there is one equitable action, an *accounting*, in which partners can sue each other. An accounting enforces a partner's rights to his share of the profits or to inspect the partnership books. An accounting also may be sought in connection with a suit brought by a partner for dissolution of the firm. An accounting is a normal part of a dissolution, which a court will enforce under the following circumstances: (1) a partner has been wrongly excluded from the partnership business or possession of its property by other partners; (2) the right exists under the agreement; (3) the partner is accountable as a trustee or fiduciary; or (4) any other circumstances that render an accounting just and reasonable.

DUTIES AMONG PARTNERS

Partners owe each other the duty of loyalty and good faith (a fiduciary duty), a duty of care, a duty of obedience, a duty to account, a duty to communicate, and a duty to share in partnership losses.

Basic Fiduciary Duty

A fiduciary duty by one person to another is a duty to act with the highest degree of good faith, loyalty, and honesty. It is a duty of trust and confidence. The party owes his fellow partners and the partnership this fiduciary duty. The fiduciary duty owed by a fellow partner is similar to that owned by an agent to a principal. Features of this duty of good faith and loyalty require that a partner not profit secretly at the expense of the partnership and not compete with the partnership.

To profit secretly means secretly using partnership property or funds for personal benefit or the payment of personal debts. If a partner misuses partnership property or money, the UPA requires him to account to the partnership for any benefit received and repay any profit made through the use of the property.

A partner can engage in other businesses outside the partnership, so long as the activity is not prohibited by the partnership agreement and does not cause the partner to neglect partnership duties. In any case, a partner cannot compete against the partnership, that is, not engaging in another enterprise that is in the same business, and not seizing an economic opportunity that would be to the disadvantage or adverse interest of the partnership. For instance, when approaching the time of expiration of the lease for the building that the partnership occupies as its place of business, one partner cannot renew the lease in his name alone but must renew in the partnership name. In this instance the law imposes the responsibility on the partner to be a trustee who is regarded as holding the lease for the firm because his failure to renew in the name of the partnership breaches his fiduciary responsibilities of good faith and loyalty to the firm. In the same vein, if a partner learns of a favorable price for an item of property that would be beneficial to the partnership, he cannot purchase the "good deal" without giving the partnership the opportunity to buy first.

Duty of Obedience

Partners must obey the partnership agreement, and the business decisions must be properly made by the partnership. If a majority decision has been made by the partnership, a dissenting partner must comply with it. A disobeying partner is liable for any loss he creates. For example, if the partnership directs that no credit be extended to a particular customer, and he extends credit anyway, the disobeying partner is liable to the other partners if the customer does not pay his bill.

Duty of Care

Each partner must exercise reasonable care in conducting the partnership—he must refrain from negligence. A partner who negligently carries out partnership duties is liable to the other partners for any losses. The partner does not breach the duty of care and is thus not liable for honest errors of judgment in carrying out his business activities. These concepts constitute the business judgment rule.

Duty to Communicate

A partner has the duty to inform the partnership about any matters that may affect the business. If one partner asks another partner a question on a matter, he is entitled to receive true and full information. While there is the duty to inform, there is also the duty not to disclose confidential information to third parties.

Duty to Account

A partner has a duty to account to co-partners for any partnership funds or property within his control or possession. The partner must turn over business records to any other partner or his representative. If one partner has been delegated the responsibility to keep the partnership books and accounts, they must be kept properly. The partner keeping the records is liable if the records contain mistakes.

Duty to Share Losses

Partners must share partnership losses. Unless established differently by the partnership agreement, the share of the loss of each partner is the same as his partnership share.

RELATIONS BETWEEN PARTNERS AND THIRD PARTIES

The law of agency governs the partnership's relationship with third parties. The partnership is the principal, and each partner is an agent of the partnership and for every other partner. As in agency law, the partnership can be liable for and bound by a contract entered into by a partner who has the authority to bind the partnership to contracts with third persons. Partners are jointly liable for such contracts. It is not uncommon for the partnership to have an agreement among themselves that limits the authority of a partner to act for the firm. Each partner is an agent of the partnership able to bind it to contracts, therefore, a third party who has no notice of such internal restrictions among the partners themselves is not bound by the restriction on the partnership authority. This restriction will not relieve liability to the third party. As in agency law, the partnership and its partners are jointly and severally liable for torts committed by an employee or one of the partners in the scope of the partnership business. Because of the law's reluctance to impose vicarious criminal liability, partners are not liable for crimes committed by other partners unless they themselves participated, planned, aided, authorized, or acquiesced in the commission of the crime.

Contractual Liability

Partners, like agents, can bind the partnership and other partners to a contract if they have authority. There are four means by which the partner can acquire authority to bind the partnership to contracts with a third person: (1) express authority; (2) implied authority (implied-in-fact); (3) apparent authority; and (4) ratification.

Express (Actual) Authority

Express authority is authority actually granted to a partner to act on behalf of the partnership with third persons. The authority may be granted in the partnership agreement or a collateral agreement and may be written or oral. Because each partner is an agent for the partnership, an agreement among partners denying any particular partner express authority is not binding upon third parties who do not know about the restriction.

Implied Authority

Even without express grant or denial of authority, the law understands that in certain instances partners have the implied authority to do what is reasonably necessary to carry out the business of the partnership in a usual way.

Implied authority is associated with transactions that are of a usual and customary nature for conducting the kind of business in which the partnership is engaged. Implied authority can be reasonably deduced from the nature of the partnership, terms of the partnership agreement, or the relations of the partners. It is also called *implied-in-fact* authority because it can be implied from the surrounding facts and circumstances of the partnership, that is, its conduct and activities. Examples of implied authority discussed below include entering into contracts, hiring and firing employees, selling partnership property, purchasing property for the partnership, borrowing money, receiving and enforcing obligations, settling claims against the partnership, and insuring partnership property.

A partner may enter into any contract related to the operation of the partnership business. A partner has the authority to hire agents and employees whose services are reasonably necessary for carrying on the partnership business, to make reasonable arrangements for their compensation, and to dismiss them. A partner may sell goods, real estate, or any other property that is in the regular course of the business, e.g., all or part of the inventory. If the partnership consists of selling sporting goods, a partner can sell the entire stock of baseball gloves. But since the partnership is not engaged in the buying and selling of real estate, he does not have implied authority to sell the business's store building owned by the partnership. And even if the partnership is in the business of selling a certain type of goods, a partner does not have implied authority to sell most or all of the items in inventory if this would lead to a cessation of business.

A partner usually has the implied authority to purchase any kind of property reasonably necessary to the operation of the partnership's business. The purchases may be cash or credit.

A partner has the authority to borrow money and execute a mortgage on behalf of the partnership but only if such actions are for the purpose of carrying on the partnership in a usual fashion. The UPA does not distinguish between the authority of a partner in a trading partnership and that of one in a nontrading partnership, but the majority of courts have used this distinction in determining implied authority. Trading partnerships engage in the buying and selling of goods and real estate, while nontrading partnerships, such as lawyers, doctors, and accountants provide services. The courts generally hold there is implied authority for a partner to bind the partnership in securing loans and executing mortgages and promissory notes exists for trading partnerships but not ordinarily for nontrading ones.

A partner has implied authority to insure firm property, cancel an insurance policy, submit claims to the insurer, and accept settlements for losses.

The partner has the implied authority to adjust, receive payment, and release debts and other claims of the partnership. He has the authority to compromise, adjust, and pay bona fide claims against the partnership.

Another type of implied authority allows a partner in an emergency to enter into contracts necessary to protect the partnership business or property. This authority for emergencies is implied by the law not by facts and is called *implied-in-law* authority.

Actual implied authority gives a third party the impression that the partner has the authority to enter into a contractual arrangement on behalf of the firm. But the partners may have agreed to restrict or limit the particular partner's authority. As noted before, agreements among the partners limiting their powers are not binding on third parties unaware of these internal restrictions.

Apparent Authority

Apparent authority exists when a partner is held out to a third person to have authority to act for the partnership by the words or conduct of other partners. For instance, the partnership may have an agreement conferring exclusive authority on one partner to secure loans. Partner X, on whom the exclusive authority is conferred to obtain loans, is incapacitated by an illness. Partner Y attempts to secure a loan from Bank Z for the partnership, believing, wrongly, it is in need of new capital. The bank, used to dealing with Partner X, telephones him and asks whether Partner Y has authority to obtain the loan, and Partner X says he does, but without receiving permission of the other partners, who would probably oppose Y's negotiating a loan for the business. Led to believe by one partner that another partner has permission to bind the partnership, allows the bank to enforce the loan agreement against the entire partnership, even though the partner lacked actual authority.

Limitations on Implied and Apparent Authority

There are certain actions that are considered so out of the ordinary course of business that a third person should view with suspicion any partner undertaking such actions on behalf of the partnership. In these instances when the partner's apparent or implied authority is suspect, the burden is on the third party to prove implied or apparent authority exists.

These types of extraordinary partnership activities for which a partner's apparent or implied authority is limited include

1. *Assignment of partnership property for the benefit of creditors.* This kind of transaction involves placing partnership property—real, personal, and funds—in trust for the partnership's creditors and is used as one way an insolvent business can settle with its creditors without formal bankruptcy proceedings.
2. *Confession of Judgment Against the Partnership.* A confession of judgment is an agreement by a party to a lawsuit with the opposing party to allow the latter to have a judgment entered in his favor without contest. For instance, a partner might confess judgment for the partnership in a lawsuit by a creditor alleging the partnership owes him on a debt or by an accident victim who sues the partnership for injuring him.

A partner, in a lawsuit against the partnership, may not make any written admission of liability on the partnership's behalf.

3. *Disposing of the partnership's goodwill.* The goodwill of a business is the reputation for honesty, efficiency, and fairness that it has built up. An example of a transfer of goodwill is when the partnership agrees to a covenant not to compete as one of the terms of a sale by the partnership of part of its business. Another more obvious example is the sale of the rights to the firm's logo, an action a single partner does not have the implied or apparent authority to carry out.

4. *Submitting a partnership claim or dispute to arbitration.* While arbitration is a common method to settle commercial disputes, no partner has the authority—without the unanimous consent of the co-partners—to submit a partnership claim or dispute to arbitration.

5. *Execution of contracts of guaranty or suretyship in the firm name for nonfirm business.* A partner lacks authority to solely agree that the partnership will act as a surety, that is, perform the promise that a second person (usually a debtor) owes to a third person (usually a creditor) if the second party fails to perform. A surety, which in the broadest sense includes any guaranty that serves to fulfill the obligations of another, encompasses an obligation to pay, answer for, or satisfy the debt, default in performance, or wrong of another person, association, or entity. Examples include construction bonds, fidelity bonds, assumption of and agreement to pay an existing mortgage by a purchaser of real estate, and an unqualified endorsement on a draft or promissory note. The restriction that a partner does not have the implied authority to assume in the name of the partnership, liability for the debt of another, only applies if such a guaranty is not related to the firm's business. A partner may have implied authority if the nature of the partnership business includes this type of transaction. For instance, the partnership may be in the business of providing construction bonds, or it may be a stock brokerage and commonly guarantees some types of securities it sells.

6. *Any act that would make it impossible to carry on the ordinary business of the partnership.* This is a catchall that restricts implied or apparent authority. An example is an agreement made by a partner to cancel the lease of the building where the partnership conducts its business, an act that would clearly make it impossible to continue the business.

7. *Charitable activities.* A partnership is formed for the purpose of making a profit. Hence, it is not in the usual and customary course of a business for a partner to involve the partnership in charitable activities or to give away partnership property. Exceptions are allowed where it actually is customary for the business to provide certain free services to its customers for promotional purposes.

8. *Purchases of corporate stock.* Unless the partnership is in the business of buying and selling corporate stock, a partner does not have the implied authority to buy stock in a corporation for the partnership.

Joint Liability of Partners on Contracts

The UPA establishes that partners are *jointly* liable on all debts and contracts of the partnership. All the partners must be liable, or none are. Under joint liability, if all the partners are sued on a contract and one partner is dismissed from the suit for want of liability, the suit against all the partners can be dismissed. The effect of joint liability is to require a suit to be against all the partners and against the partnership; it does not suffice to sue one or some of the partners and not all of them together. A court judgment based on this joint obligation for the debt or contract is not effective unless it is rendered against all the partners in one suit at once. This contrasts with *joint and several liability* for the torts of the partnership (described below), whereby not all the partners need be joined in a lawsuit by the injured party, and one or some can be sued for the entire amount of damages.

Liability of Incoming Partners

A new partner admitted to an existing partnership has limited liability for all the partnership debts and obligations arising before his admission. The incoming partner's liability for preexisting debts and obligations is only to the extent of his capital contribution (investment) to the firm. The new partner's liability for the prior debts can be satisfied only out of partnership property, not his personal property. However, the new partner may assume liability for the prior obligations through assumption of novation agreements. An assumption agreement entails the incoming partner agreeing to be responsible for some portion of all of the preexisting partnership debts, while a novation is an agreement between the incoming partner, an outgoing partner, and the partnership's creditor in which the creditor agrees to substitute the incoming partner for the outgoing partner and to hold the former liable for the debt.

A new partner has unlimited liability for partnership debts and obligations arising after his admission to the partnership.

Liability of Outgoing Partners

A partner who withdraws from the partnership (such as a retiring partner or one who sells his interest to the partnership) continues to be personally liable for debts incurred before his departure, unless the creditors expressly release the partner or until the claims against the firm are satisfied. The withdrawing partner's liability for debts incurred before his departure continues even if the remaining partners agree to pay his debts.

A withdrawing partner is personally liable for debts incurred after his departure unless he gives actual notice to creditors and constructive notice to all others who do business with the firm. Constructive notice is achieved by placing a notice of his departure in an appropriate newspaper. The outgoing partner is not liable to creditors who actually know of his withdrawal, even if they were not given actual notice.

Liability Through Estoppel

Partnership by estoppel is not an actual partnership voluntarily formed by an agreement of the parties. It is an equitable doctrine in which the court holds persons who are in fact not partners to be accountable to third persons as though they were partners. This occurs when a person's behavior leads a third party to think he is a partner. The person making the representation becomes a partner by estoppel because he is "estopped" (prohibited) by equitable principles from denying that he was an actual partner in a suit brought by a third party.

Partnership by estoppel does not make the ostensible partner a member of the partnership when in fact there is no partnership. Partnership by estoppel is only for the purpose of imposing liability on the apparent partner and does not impose liability on the partnership or its partners. However, by holding himself to be a partner, that person becomes an agent of any actual partner who expressly or implicitly consents to the representation; thus, any consenting actual partner is liable as well to the third person to whom the representation is made. Actual partners who do not consent are not liable.

The person who presents himself as a partner is termed an apparent or ostensible partner. The ostensible partner is liable to the third party to whom the misrepresentation of partnership has been made when the third party detrimentally relies on the misrepresentation. A common instance of partnership by estoppel occurs when a person to whom the misrepresentation is made acts on it by giving credit to the actual or apparent partnership. For example, X, in attempting to secure a loan from a bank, represents that Y, his best friend and a wealthy businessman, is a partner in his business. Y knows of X's misrepresentation but does nothing about it. If the bank relies upon the financial creditworthiness of Y and X defaults on the loan, Y is an apparent partner and under the doctrine of partnership by estoppel is liable to the bank for repayment of the loan. Y will be "estopped" from maintaining he is not a partner of X to the extent of the loan.

Ratification

Sometimes a partnership may consent to an unauthorized act after the act has occurred. This consent, which may be express or implied, is called ratification and will bind the partnership to the previous contract or obligation.

Liability by Knowledge or Notice and Admission

As a general rule all partners are charged with knowledge of any matter concerning partnership affairs that comes to the attention of any of its members. For instance, if one partner knows that a product the partnership manufactures is defective and may cause injury to consumers, all members of the partnership are assumed to have knowledge of the danger. This principle does not apply to attribute knowledge and liability to the other partners when the partner acts adversely to the partnership. Hence, if a partner embezzles partnership money, the co-partners are not presumed to have knowledge of the theft.

Partners are also charged with knowledge of any *notice* received by a partner regarding partnership affairs. For example, if one partner receives a summons to appear in court for a lawsuit brought against the partnership, the notice is effective against the partnership and the other partners even if the partner ignores the summons and does not take any action or fails to inform his co-partners of the lawsuit. A default judgment entered against the partnership for its failure to appear in the lawsuit is valid in this situation, although the other partners who were not informed of the lawsuit have the right to be indemnified by the partner who did receive notice and failed to inform them.

Tort Liability

Each and every partner is liable for torts committed by any other partner or an employee of the partnership in the course of partnership business. Torts include such wrongs, among others, as negligence, fraud, trespass, assault, battery, and so forth. In order to make the partnership in its entirety liable, the tort must be committed in the course, or within the scope of, partnership business. Whether a tort has been committed in the course or scope of partnership business is similar to the liability of a principle for the torts of his agent. The partnership is not liable for a tort a partner or employee commits that has no relation to the partnership business. However, even if a partner's tort did not involve partnership business, any other partner participating in, directing, or authorizing the tort is personally liable along with the partner or employee who actually committed the tort.

A partnership's tort liability is *joint and several*; the third person who is harmed can sue each partner separately, several partners, the partnership as an entity, and one or more partners for the entire amount of the damages sought. Under joint and several liability one can sue any partner for the entire amount, even if a partner not sued caused the harm. A judgment against any partner does not bind the others to directly pay the injured third person, although the partners collected from have the right of contribution for the damages they pay from their co-partners and the partnership not sued. The partner who caused the harm has the duty to indemnify the partnership and any partner who must pay the award of a lawsuit. A judgment against any partner does not bar subsequent suits against the others until the entire amount of damages has been satisfied. A release from liability of one jointly and severally liable partner does not release any other partners.

A partner's tort liability is personal, that is, the victim of the tort can not only collect from out of the partnership property but also, if that collection is not adequate, seize for payment the personal property of the individual partner.

Criminal Liability

As a general rule, a partner is not liable for a crime committed by other partners, even if the crime is committed during the course of activities on behalf of the partnership. Partners are criminally liable for co-partners' crimes only in instances where they themselves participated, planned, aided, or acquiesced in the crime. This criminal liability is not attributed to the partnership or co-partners but is simply personal culpability anyone incurs when involved with a crime with another.

While a partnership cannot generally be held criminally accountable for the acts of any partner, a partnership will be held criminally liable for violations of certain regulatory statutes that hold a business association accountable for crimes. These regulatory statutes dispense with proof of criminal intent as a requirement for a conviction and instead base criminal culpability on strict liability. Strict liability crimes do not require intent, only that a party commit a prohibited act, and if they do, they are held strictly liable for it. Examples of regulatory crimes for which partnerships can be held strictly liable include illegally selling liquor to minors, mislabeling goods, adulterating products, transporting in an unsafe manner explosives, or violating antitrust laws. In such cases the partnership can be fined, and the partnership assets are vulnerable to pay the fine. The conviction of the partnership does not necessarily mean that the individual partners will be jailed or fined.

11

Partnerships: Termination

OVERVIEW

A partnership may come to an end. There are three steps leading to the end of a partnership: (1) *dissolution*, (2) *liquidation* (*winding up*), and (3) *termination*. These three steps represent the successive process leading to the extinguishment of the partnership. Dissolution ends the right of the partnership to carry on as it is presently constituted. Winding up is the process of settling the affairs of the partnership after dissolution if the dissolution does not allow remaining partners to carry on the same business. At the conclusion of the winding up process the partnership is terminated, that is, it no longer legally exists.

    The dissolution, the first step, does not by itself bring the partnership to a finish but is instead the "beginning of the end" of the partnership. Dissolution is the moment in time when the normal operation of the partnership ends and the object of the partners changes from continuing the partnership in its current form to discontinuing it. When a partnership is dissolved it is not at that time ended, that is, terminated. The UPA describes dissolution as the change in the relation of the partners caused by any partner ceasing to be associated with the carrying on of the business. This change may be either voluntary or involuntary. There are twelve ways dissolution may occur:

1. Partners agreeing to expressly dissolve the partnership.
2. Terms or conditions of the partnership agreement, such as expiration of time provided in the agreement or accomplishment of the purpose for which the partnership was formed.
3. A partner's expulsion.
4. Withdrawal or addition of a partner.
5. Death of a partner.
6. Bankruptcy of a partner.
7. Subsequent illegality of partnership business.
8. Partner being judicially determined to be insane.
9. Partner's incapacity preventing him from functioning as a partner.
10. Partner's misconduct that is prejudicial to the business or persistently breaches the partnership agreement.
11. A business impracticality.
12. Other circumstances making it inequitable for the partnership to continue.

The first four types of dissolution occur by the partner's acts, the second three by operation of law, and the remainder by court order. All will be discussed below in detail.

Certain acts or events are not considered causes for dissolution. The voluntary sale or transfer of a partner's interest or involuntary sale for the benefit of his creditors does not cause dissolution of the partnership, nor does the transferee of the partnership interest, such as a creditor, become a partner or displace the liability of the assigning partner. The creditor, along with any other party to whom a partnership interest is assigned, merely obtains the partner's right to profits, surplus, goodwill, repayment of loans, and return of capital upon dissolution. An accounting sought by a partner does not cause a dissolution.

Dissolution may trigger the next step, the winding up process. Winding up is the process of settling up the affairs of the business following the events of dissolution. During the winding up process the partnership is still legally in force and can continue the business. However, the firm cannot enter into any new transaction unrelated to closing down the business. For example, a grocery owned by a partnership that is winding up its affairs may sell the items on its shelves but may not order more stock. In the winding up process existing contracts are performed, the partnership assets are sold, creditors are paid off, and the remaining property is distributed to the partners. Winding up can also be called liquidation of the business.

Dissolution changes the legal status of both the partnership and its individual partners. Dissolution ends the authority of each partner to act on behalf of the partnership, except for the authority to wind up the affairs of the partnership and complete unfinished business.

A dissolution does not have to result in the termination of the partnership business; thus, a formal winding up that entirely liquidates the business is not needed since the business will not be ended. A dissolution without a winding up occurs when certain partners wish to continue the business even though the partnership as it is currently constituted is dissolved. In these cases,the termination of the partnership consists primarily of purchasing the interests of non-continuing partners and appropriate bookkeeping entries. Then the business is carried on either by a remaining partner as its sole proprietor or by a new partnership consisting of the remaining partners and perhaps new partners.

Only when the process of winding up has been completed is the partnership terminated. At termination the partnership ceases all business activity, and it legally ends.

DISSOLUTION

A dissolution by acts of the partners may or may not be in violation of the agreement. A partner has the *power* to leave and dissolve a partnership, but whether he has the *right* to do so is determined by the partnership agreement. A partner who withdraws from the partnership in violation of the partnership agreement is liable to the remaining partners for breach of the agreement for damages. The partnership agreement may provide for dissolution without breach or violation of the agreement.

A partnership may be rightfully dissolved by the act of the partners if there is (1) agreement for a dissolution by all the partners, (2) expiration of the term of the partnership or accomplishment of the purpose for which it was formed, (3) expulsion of a partner in accordance with the power to expel in the partnership agreement, or (4) withdrawal or addition of a partner.

Dissolution by Act of the Partners

Agreement of the Partners

The partners may agree among themselves to end the partnership. Since the partnership is a voluntary association it can be dissolved by a voluntary agreement. This kind of voluntary dissolution usually requires unanimous agreement, unless the partnership agreement specifies less than a unanimous vote. The dissolution does not necessarily mean that the partnership business will come to an end.

Terms of the Partnership Agreement

The partnership agreement can specify when the partnership ends. The articles may stipulate the partnership is for a definite duration or undertaking. At the end of the partnership duration, the partnership ends. This is called dissolution by expiration. If the stated purpose is accomplished or can no longer be undertaken, dissolution occurs.

Expulsion of a Partner

The partnership agreement may provide for the expulsion of a partner who violates the agreement. In this case the partnership has the right to expel the partner without violating the agreement. Any time parties are lost from the partnership it is dissolved because, according to the UPA, dissolution is any change in the relations of the partners caused by any partner ceasing to be associated with the conduct of the business. Dissolution by an expulsion of a partner does not necessarily cause the partnership business to end. The remaining parties may reorganize themselves into a new partnership or some other form of business organization.

The expulsion must be for a bona fide cause specified by the agreement, otherwise it is wrongful. A properly expelled partner does not lose the value of his investment in the firm. The expelled partner has a right to receive the value of his partnership interest, which is either determined in a manner specified by the agreement for expelled partners or, if no such method has been established, by an accounting of the worth of the partner's interest minus any debts the partner owes the firm. The expelled partner essentially receives the net worth, if any, of his portion of the partnership's book value. The expelled partner does not escape liability for any partnership debts incurred by the partnership while he was a partner.

Withdrawal or Addition of a Partner

A partnership dissolves whenever its membership changes. A partner has the power to withdraw at any time, but he does not have the right if the withdrawal is in the violation of the partnership agreement. For a wrongful withdrawal—one in violation of the agreement—the withdrawing partner will be liable to the remaining partners for damages for breach of the partnership agreement. The partnership agreement may provide that a partner may leave at any time, thus creating a *partnership at will*; any partner can withdraw at any time without incurring liability to the other partners. A partnership at will is also created when the partnership agreement says nothing about its duration, and consequently any partner can elect to leave and thus dissolve it without incurring liability for violating the agreement.

As noted before the partnership is dissolved whenever the membership of the partnership changes, and this includes adding partners.

As a practical matter, partnership agreements often contain a business continuation provision (a buy and sale agreement) that allows the partnership to continue operating after dissolution caused by the death, retirement, departure, or withdrawal of a partner. In other words, the addition or departure of a partner causes the former partnership to dissolve, but the business may continue without liquidation of the affairs and assets of the previous partnership. The continuation clause will usually contain a buy-out provision, which allows the remaining partners to buy out the departing or dead partner's share. These continuation clauses often permit the partnership to continue under the firm's original name even when the partner whose name the firm bears has died or left. Even without such a provision in the articles of partnership, the partners often immediately reorganize and continue the business when a partner leaves. In the case of a withdrawing partner, a buy-out provision in the partnership agreement financially settles the interest of the withdrawing partner without liquidating the business. For a new partner, the agreement will provide for a "sale" to him of a place in the partnership, that is, the capital contribution expected of the new partner for entry into the firm.

Dissolution by Operation of Law

A partnership is automatically dissolved by operation of law upon (1) the death of a partner, (2) the bankruptcy of a partner or the partnership, or (3) the subsequent illegality of the partnership.

Partner's Death

The death of a partner automatically, that is, by operation of law, causes the dissolution of the partnership. A business continuation agreement, or buy-out provision, in the partnership articles, allows the surviving partners to buy the deceased partner's interest and lets the remaining partners continue the business without winding up. Dissolution still occurs, but the agreement allows for the continuation and reorganization instead of liquidation.

Bankruptcy of a Partner or the Partnership

Dissolution automatically follows the bankruptcy of any partner or the partnership entity. Bankruptcy is a proceeding under federal law that may be initiated voluntarily by a debtor or brought by a creditor and may result in either the reorganization of the firm's debts or the liquidation of the firm's assets. Mere insolvency does not by itself cause dissolution.

Subsequent Illegality of the Business

The partnership is automatically dissolved by any event that makes it unlawful for the business of the partnership to be carried on or for one of its members to engage in business. The commonest situations of dissolution by subsequent illegality occur when a partner loses his occupational license or the business in which the partnership is engaged becomes prohibited by a statute. Examples include a partner losing his real estate brokerage license in a partnership formed to buy and sell real estate, a gambling partnership having its gambling permit revoked, a partner becoming a judge in a state in which it is unlawful for a judge to practice law, a partner in a law firm being disbarred, or a partnership formed to sell an insecticide being subsequently banned by the Environmental Protection Agency (EPA).

Dissolution by Court Decree

In five cases, a partner can seek and obtain a court order for dissolution of the partnership without violating the partnership agreement. In all these instances the partnership is dissolved involuntarily for the partners against whom the decree is sought. The partnership is not dissolved automatically by operation of law as in the cases described above but instead requires a court order. A partner may obtain a decree of dissolution for any of the following reasons:

Insanity of a Partner

A partner is judicially determined to be insane or of unsound mind.

Incapacity of a Partner

A partner is permanently (not temporarily) incapacitated so that he is incapable of performing the terms of the partnership agreement. The incapacity can be physical or mental.

Misconduct of a Partner

One of the partners has been guilty of serious misconduct that is substantially prejudicial to the business, is a willful and persistent breach of the partnership agreement, or makes it difficult for the partners to function together in business. Examples include habitual drunkenness, misappropriation of partnership funds, serious neglect of partnership affairs, erratic and upsetting behavior that sours the working relationship in the firm, treatment of customers in a manner that permanently injures the partnership business, or any other conduct that causes the firm to earn public disrepute or ridicule. The misconduct must be serious, not trifling. An honest mistake of judgment or an occasional loss of temper by a partner is not sufficient misconduct to justify a dissolution decree.

Business Impracticality (Lack of Success)

When the business can be carried on only at a loss, it is impractical and futile to continue, and a court order for dissolution is warranted. In other words, if the business is a failure, then judicial dissolution is possible.

Equitable Causes

The courts may dissolve a partnership for other equitable reasons; that is, where circumstances make it unfair for the partnership to continue in business.

An example would be constant disagreements and irreconcilable differences among the partners which jeopardize partnership profitability.

Dissolution Liability

Dissolution affects the rights of partners vis-à-vis each other and the rights of third parties with whom the partnership has business dealings, particularly creditors.

Dissolution and Partners' Liability to Each Other

A withdrawing partner must provide notice to the remaining partners that he is no longer a member of the firm in order to be freed from liability to the remaining partners for their actions following his withdrawal (other than for winding up). When the firm is dissolved by an act of a partner, notice need not be given to the other partners if they actually know of the act to withdraw to dissolve the firm or if they should know (constructive notice) because the acts in question showed an intent to withdraw from or dissolve the firm. However, as between the partners, the UPA requires knowledge or notice for dissolution by death or bankruptcy. If knowledge or notice is not present when required, the partner withdrawing or causing the dissolution is liable to his co-partners for his share of any liability created by another partner acting for the partnership—just as though the partnership had not been dissolved.

Dissolution Liability to Third Parties

Dissolution terminates the actual authority of partners to act on behalf of the firm, except when winding up the affairs of the firm, when completing transactions begun during the life of the partnership, and when lacking actual or constructive notice of a dissolution caused by an act of another partner or by an agreement by the other partners.

Dissolution does not discharge the existing liabilities of the individual partners and the partnership. The dissolved partnership and its individual partners continue to be liable to creditors of the partnership. The partners and partnership must still complete performance on existing contracts, for example. However, in some limited instances the cause of dissolution may result in discharging an executory contract (a contract unperformed on both sides). For example, if a contract requires the personal services of one of the partners, his death will discharge the contract as well as causing the automatic dissolution of the firm.

When the partnership continues with remaining partners, a retiring or rightfully withdrawn partner normally is liable for partnership debts incurred during the time he was a partner. However, the departing partner may escape liability through a novation agreement in which the departing partner, remaining partners, and a creditor agree that the remaining partners will accept full liability in place of the departing partner.

Although actual authority ends upon dissolution, the partnership and partners may be liable by estoppel or apparent authority unless proper notice of dissolution occurs.

Dissolutions are usually private affairs, and so the liability of the firm to third parties is determined by notice or knowledge of dissolution. Generally, if a third party has neither knowledge nor legal notice of dissolution, he may hold the partnership liable for business transactions or credit extended during dissolution. When dissolution is caused by an act of a partner or the agreement of the partners, notice must be given to third parties, to creditors in particular. A party who has previously extended credit to the partnership or engaged in business transactions may hold the partnership liable for any additional credit extended to or contractual obligations entered into with the partnership during dissolution unless they had knowledge or received *actual* notice of the dissolution. Actual notice requires either a spoken statement to the third party or actual delivery of a written statement declaring dissolution, that is, as a practical matter all creditors and others with whom the partnership had been doing business must be notified immediately of dissolution. Constructive notice is sufficient notice to creditors and businesses who knew of the partnership's existence but who have had no previous dealings with the partnership. Constructive notice may be carried out by publishing in a newspaper of general circulation, posting a placard in a public place, or using some other similar method directed to the public. In sum, actual notice of dissolution is required for third parties who have had previous dealings with the partnership, and constructive notice is sufficient for those third parties without such previous dealings. Where dissolution is automatically caused by operation of law, notice to third persons, actual or constructive, is not generally required.

Continuation of the Partnership

Dissolution usually does not lead to a formal winding up of the affairs of the partnership and its termination. In the case of the death or withdrawal of a partner, the remaining partners may wish to continue the business. A true termination of the business is preceded by a formal winding up of the affairs, that is, a physical liquidation consisting of selling the partnership assets, paying all the debts, and distributing the remainder. Remaining partners wishing to continue the business rather than winding up the affairs of the firm through liquidation undertake an accounting of assets and liabilities of the partnership and pay the departing partner's share to him or his estate and then carry on the business. These remaining partners continue the business through a reconstituted partnership without the departed partner. Any time there is a change in partnership membership there is a dissolution, but when it is not followed by a true winding up it is called a "technical dissolution." Often the partnership agreement contains a continuation statement, which applies in case of a dissolution, under which the remaining partners may elect to make any settlements necessary and continue the business or to terminate and wind up the enterprise. If the business continues, either with remaining partners or with some of them and additional partners, it is nevertheless a new partnership.

When a partnership is dissolved because a partner has wrongfully withdrawn from the firm or has been expelled pursuant to the partnership agreement, the remaining partners have the choice to either liquidate the partnership and recover damages from the breach of the partnership agreement or to continue the partnership by buying out the withdrawn or expelled partner. The departing partner has no say in the decision.

When the partnership agreement provides for continuing the business after dissolution, it dictates the procedures to be followed. When there is no continuation statement, the rights of the withdrawing partner depend on whether the withdrawal was proper or wrongful. If the partner rightfully withdraws (that is, not having breached the partnership agreement in doing so), the remaining partners must pay him or his estate the fair market value of his partnership interest. The value of his interest includes his share of the value of the partnership's goodwill. Goodwill is the difference between the business's fair market value and its book value as shown by its balance sheet. But if a partner wrongfully withdraws and, by doing so causes dissolution, he is not entitled to his share of the business's goodwill value. In other words, his share of the enterprise's goodwill value is deducted from his share, which amounts to his share of the lesser book value of the business. This amounts to a penalty for the wrongfully withdrawing partner for in effect "walking away" from the partnership. Moreover, damages caused by the wrongful dissolution are deducted from the total amount paid to the departing partner. The remaining partners retain the business's goodwill value, on the principle that the wrongful partner, having caused the dissolution of the partnership, should not profit with a full share of the enterprise's value. A partner who wrongfully withdraws is liable to the partnership for damages it suffers as a result of the withdrawal.

The remaining partners may elect to postpone a settlement to the wrongfully withdrawn partner until the expiration of an agreed term or undertaking. But if they do continue the enterprise over the partner's objection they must provide a bond to guarantee the future payment of the wrongfully withdrawn partner's share. Furthermore, the remaining partners, if they wish, may sue the capital contributions of the wrongdoing partner for the unexpired term of the partnership agreement, although this investment must be returned at the time of settlement minus the wrongfully withdrawing partner's share of the partnership debts.

The creditors of an old partnership have claims against the reconstituted partnership of the remaining partners.

When the remaining partners agree to continue the business without the physical liquidation of a formal winding up, the departing partner or the representative of a deceased partner's estate is entitled to receive in cash his share of the value of the partnership. However, the departing partner or estate's representative may elect to leave the share of the partnership in the business as an investment instead of receiving its cash value. If the partnership share is left in the firm then a choice must be made at that time to receive interest on the share or to receive whatever profits in the continuing business the share earns.

LIQUIDATION (WINDING UP)

As described earlier, *winding up* is the final step after dissolution and leads to the termination of the partnership. A formal winding up is the physical liquidation of the business. The winding up process consists of selling the partnership assets, collecting any outstanding accounts, paying off creditors, returning capital contributions of the partners, completing unfinished business, taking inventory, auditing partnership books, and then distributing whatever assets remain. The purpose of winding up is to sell the partnership assets for as much money as possible in order to pay off partnership debts as fully as possible and maximize the final distribution of cash to the partners.

Right to Wind Up

The right to wind up is valuable, and the winding up is conducted by all the partners (with certain exceptions). Participation in winding up is denied to partners who wrongfully withdrew from the partnership and thereby caused its dissolution and to any partner whose bankruptcy caused the dissolution.

When the firm is dissolved by the death of a partner, the partnership property vests in the surviving partners, and they have responsibility for winding up. The administrator or executor of the deceased partner's estate is generally denied the right to wind up, with one exception. In some states, if the dissolution occurs because a partner dies and the surviving partners have decided not to continue the business, the winding up *must* be performed by the executor or legal representative of the deceased partner's estate.

When no provision has been made for winding up the partnership affairs in the partnership agreement and the partners disagree about operation of the winding up process, any partner may ask a court to appoint a receiver to conduct the winding up. A partner may also ask the court to appoint a receiver if there is waste, fraud, mental incompetence, refusal to render an accounting, refusal to allow the right to inspect records, or misconduct or any other breach of duty by a partner connected with the winding up process. The appointment of a receiver is discretionary with the court. When a receiver is appointed, all the partners are excluded from conducting the winding up. Finally, an absolute rule is this: Persons who are not partners cannot participate in the winding up process.

While all partners who have not acted wrongfully to bring about the partnership's dissolution are entitled to participate in the winding up, they usually appoint one of the partners to perform or lead the task.

Partners are generally not entitled to compensation for their winding up services unless the partners agree that pay is to be allowed. They are entitled to receive reimbursement for their expenses incurred as a result of the winding up process. There is one situation in which a partner or the partners are entitled to be paid—when the dissolution is due to the death of a partner. A court-appointed receiver who conducts a winding up is also entitled to compensation.

Duties Among Partners in Winding Up

The fiduciary duty and duty of care that one partner owes another during the existence of the partnership continue for any partner who conducts a winding up. The most common fiduciary problems during winding up involve (1) improper exercise of winding up duties, (2) improper purchase by a partner of partnership property, and (3) seizure of partnership rights or opportunities for personal gain.

In the first situation, the best efforts of a winding up partner are required to protect partnership assets, collect funds due the partnership without personal gain, settle the debts of the partnership, and properly distribute profits following reduction of the assets to cash. The winding up partner who improperly exercises his duties is liable to the other partners for any damage in an action for an accounting.

It is natural and commonplace for a partner to want to buy partnership property during the winding up. Any partner who wishes to purchase partnership property during the winding up must deal fairly with his co-partners, revealing any information he knows relating to its value. The sale of property to a partner is void if he fails to disclose all the facts available to him or fails to reveal that he is the purchaser and instead uses a sham intermediary to buy the property, thereby concealing his real identity. The penalty for any wrongful usurpation by a partner of partnership rights or opportunities is the accounting for their value in the final computation of money owed to or by the partners.

The duty of care requires any partner engaged in winding up to perform his duties in a prudent manner; to enter into only those contracts that are necessary for winding up; and to follow any applicable rules of distribution, whether established by the partnership agreement or not; and to follow the rules of the UPA. When the winding up is carried out by the surviving partners of a partnership dissolved by the death of one of them, they must make an accounting to the representative of the deceased partner's estate with reasonable promptness following the collection of assets and payment of debts.

Distribution of Assets

After the partnership assets have been collected and reduced to cash, they are distributed to the creditors and partners. There are two possible situations in which the distribution occurs: first, when the partnership is solvent (assets exceed liabilities), in which case the order of distribution is not critical, and second, when the partnership is insolvent (liabilities exceed assets), the order of distribution being critical. The UPA provides rules for the order or priority of distribution of assets for both the solvent and insolvent partnership. When the partnership is solvent the order of distribution is not particularly significant, since all the creditors will be paid. When the partnership is insolvent the order becomes extremely important, since not all the creditors will be paid, and the payment is according to an order of priority.

Distribution of a Solvent Partnership

The UPA established the order of priority for the payment of liabilities of the solvent partnership owed to various classes of parties. The obligations of each class must be fully paid before the next group can be paid, and so forth. Once outside creditors are paid, the remaining partnership assets are distributed. The order of priority for payments is as follows:

1. *Outside creditors*, that is, creditors other than the partners.

    a. Creditors of the partnership (partnership creditors) have first priority regarding partnership assets, and creditors of individual partners (nonpartnership creditors) share in any remaining assets.

    b. Individual (nonpartnership) creditors have priority for the personal assets of their debtor-partners and a subordinate right (to that of the partnership creditors) to participate in partnership assets to the extent of the interest therein of the individual debtor-partners.

    c. Secured creditors have priority over unsecured creditors in regard to property subject to the security interest. Unsecured creditors have an equal claim to unsecured property.

2. *Inside creditors*. Loans (advances) and interest on them owing to individual partners (other than capital and profits).

3. *Capital contributions*. The individual partner's investment in the firm and any agreed upon interest.

4. *Profits*, if any, of the partnership.

The profits are shared equally by the partners unless there is an agreement among them for a different allocation. The partners may by agreement alter the order (2, 3, and 4 above) of payoff among themselves but not that of outside creditors.

Distribution of an Insolvent Partnership

The same general formula is followed for the distribution of an insolvent partnership as for a solvent partnership, and so the order of preference is to pay creditors first, then pay loans from partners, and finally pay each partner's capital contributions. However, there are no profits but rather losses when the firm is insolvent. If there are insufficient firm assets, the partners are personally liable for the firm's debts. The losses are shared in the same equal manner as profits are unless an agreement exists among them to share in some other proportion.

If one or more of the partners is insolvent, bankrupt, or by virtue of being out of the court's jurisdiction, refuses to contribute, the other partners are required to pay the additional amount necessary to pay the firm's liabilities in the relative proportions in which they share the profits. If any partner has paid more than his proper share of losses, he has the right of contribution against the other partners who have not paid their share.

Marshalling Assets and Bankruptcy

Under the distribution formula, when outside creditors are paid, the partnership assets first go to pay partnership creditors and each partner's personal assets first go to pay their personal debts. This procedure is called marshaling of assets or the "jingle rule." Any surplus in individual assets goes to pay partnership creditors, and any surplus in partnership assets goes to pay the individual partner's creditors. This marshaling of assets, which treats individual partner and partnership creditors as separate groups, applies only in equity courts.

The federal Bankruptcy Act rejects the marshaling principle when the partnership is in bankruptcy. The Bankruptcy Act allows the partnership creditors to take nonbankrupt individual partner's assets to pay partnership debts rather than wait behind their personal creditors. The marshaling rule is eliminated only in bankruptcy cases. It still applies in nonbankruptcy partnership matters.

12

Limited Partnerships

NATURE AND FORMATION

Definition

A limited partnership is formed pursuant to a statute and consists of at least one general partner, jointly and severally liable as an ordinary partner and by whom the business is conducted, and one or more limited partners who contribute capital but who have no right to manage the firm's business and who are liable for the firm's debts only to the extent of their capital contribution.

There are three distinguishing characteristics in a limited partnership. First, there must be a statute providing for the formation of limited partnerships. By comparison, a general partnership does not need statutory authorization and compliance but can be formed merely by an agreement by two or more parties. All states except Louisiana have adopted such statutes, based on the ULPA or RULPA. Second, the limited partnership must comply completely with the requirements of the limited partnership statute. Third, the purpose of the limited partnership is to allow certain partners to have limited liability for the debts and other liabilities of the partnership, in contrast to the unlimited liability, which characterizes the general partnership. While the limited partner gains the benefit of limited liability lacking for the general partner, he is denied the right to engage in management of partnership business that is available to the general partner.

Formation

The ULPA or RULPA dictates the procedures for the creation of a limited partnership and the rights and duties of the partners.

Filing and Contents of Certificate

A limited partnership certificate must be prepared, signed, and sworn by all the general and limited partners, filed with the state having jurisdiction, and recorded in the recorder's or clerk's office of the county in which the business is located. The certificate must state the name of the partnership; the address of its principal place of business; names and addresses of general and limited partners; nature of the firm's business, duration of the partnership; share of profits or other income each limited partner is to receive; method for determining changes of personnel and continuance of the business in the event of the departure, death of a general partner, or other instance of dissolution; and the amount, nature, and description of each limited partner's capital contribution.

Failure of the parties purporting to form a limited partnership to file a certificate and fully comply with the content requirements for a certificate results in a limited partnership not being formed at all. Instead, the parties are all regarded as general partners and personally liable for the debts and obligations of the business. However, a person who has contributed capital to the business while believing he has become a limited partner in a limited partnership is not liable as a general partner if upon learning of the mistake he promptly renounces his interest in the business.

A limited partnership terminates at the date specified in its certificate. If partners wish to continue the business beyond the termination date, they may, before that date arrives, file an amended certificate establishing a new termination date.

Name of a Limited Partnership

The name of the limited partnership must include in full without abbreviation the words "limited partnership." "Ltd." is not sufficient. The name of a limited partner cannot be used in the firm name unless it is the same name as one of the general partners. A violation of this rule makes the limited partner liable as a general partner to any creditor who did not know he was a limited partner. The name of the limited partnership cannot be deceptively similar to any other corporation or limited partnership. If a general partner's name is part of the name of the limited partnership and he leaves a firm that will continue to exist, the partnership can retain the same name if the partnership agreement so provides.

Contributions of Capital to Limited Partnership

The capital contributions of limited partners can be in the form of cash or property but not services. There is no similar limitation on the capital contributions of the general partners in the business. A limited partner is liable to the partnership for the difference between his real contribution to the firm and a higher amount stated in the certification as his contribution. If the limited partner fails to make a promised contribution of capital, the partnership can take legal action to compel the partner (or his estate, if he has died) to pay the value of the promised contribution in cash. When a partner fails to meet his obligation for the promised contribution, the limited partnership can, with the unanimous agreement of the other partners, reduce his obligation. Since the contributions of limited partners are described in the certificate of limited partnerships, creditors are aware of their extent and may grant credit based on the contributions specified in the certificate. If a creditor does rely on the certificate in terms of the extent of a limited partner's contribution, that partner is liable to the contribution stated in the certificate even though his real contribution is less.

Foreign Limited Partnerships

A limited partnership is a "foreign" limited partnership in any state other than the one in which it was formed. In order to do business in another state, the foreign limited partnership must register with the secretary of state of that state. A foreign limited partnership cannot bring a lawsuit in the state unless it has registered, but it can defend itself in that state's courts.

Business Activities

The limited partnership may conduct any business that a general partnership can, unless there is a statutory restriction against any such business. Many states do not permit a limited partnership to engage in banking or insurance businesses.

Limited Partnership Agreement

The crucial instrument needed for the valid formation of a limited partnership is the certificate. If the statutory requirements for the contents and filing of a certificate of limited partnership are satisfied, a limited partnership is formed and ready to engage in business. A written agreement, or articles of partnership, is not required to form a limited partnership. Nevertheless, the parties would be well advised to draft articles of partnership to provide for details not considered in the limited partnership certificate. A partnership agreement is especially important to limited partners who might wish to use it to limit the powers of the general partners, for instance, to buy and sell partnership property. The ULPA or RULPA do not impose requirements on the form or content of a limited partnership agreement. In general, the limited partnership agreement covers matters concerning the affairs of the limited partnership, the conduct of its business, and the relationship of the partners to the firm.

Rights and Liabilities of General Partners

There must be at least one general partner, who is liable as a general partner, in a limited partnership. Of course, there may be more general partners. Any legal person can be a general partner in a limited partnership and can include individuals, partnerships, corporations, and other associations. The general partner, in addition to making contributions in that capacity, may also make contributions (investments) as a limited partner. A person can be both a general partner and a limited partner in the same partnership. Such status gives the person the powers and duties of a general partner along with the rights of a limited partner.

The general partner has all the rights and powers of, and is subject to the same duties and liabilities as, a partner in a general partnership. The most noteworthy power of general partners in a limited partnership is exclusive control and management in the enterprise. The limited partners have no power to be managers. Limited partners are, in sum, merely investors in the enterprise. Because of the absolute control exercised by a general partner in conducting the business of the partnership, the general partner can enter into any agreement or execute any instrument to carry on the partnership activities. As a result, a general partner can buy or sell partnership property without the knowledge or permission of the limited partners when such is in furtherance of partnership business and in accordance with the partnership agreement.

There are some important restrictions on general partners in conducting partnership business, and these relate to acts that are regarded as being outside of the ordinary course of the partnership business and thus beyond the authority of a general partner to engage in alone. In these cases, a general partner can act only with the written consent of all the partners, general and limited. The following acts require such unanimous consent:

1. Any act in contravention of the certificate of partnership.
2. Any act that makes it impossible to carry on the ordinary business of the partnership.
3. Confession of a judgment against the partnership.
4. Admission of a new general partner or a limited partner (unless the right to admit limited partners is allowed by the certificate of partnership).
5. Continuation of the business, using the partnership property, upon the death, retirement, or insanity of a general partner.

General partners owe a fiduciary duty to the limited partners and to each other. The fiduciary responsibility of a general partner to any limited partner includes the following: to use his best efforts in conducting partnership business, devote partnership property for the purposes for which the partnership was formed, provide any information about the finances and affairs of the firm upon request by any limited partner, comply with all laws pertaining to the partnership business, account for any personal profit made in buying and selling partnership property, refrain from seizing any business opportunity that rightfully should be obtained for the partnership, and fully disclose to any limited partner whose interest is sought to be purchased all information pertaining to the value of the interest and the consideration offered for the interest.

The liability of general partners in a limited partnership for debts and torts to third parties is the same as in a general partnership. The general partner is also fully liable to anyone who suffers a loss as a result of relying on a statement in the certificate that the general partner knows to be false. For example, if a loan by a bank is made to the partnership on the basis of an inflated financial statement in the certificate, any and all general partners are liable.

As described in previous sections, general partners in general partnerships have no automatic right to compensation, only to profits. In a general partnership, compensation for managing the affairs of the business, however, can be permitted in the partnership agreement. Likewise, compensation for the general partners can be provided in the limited partnership agreement and usually is since the general partners occupy the role of managers and the limited partners are in the restricted role of investors.

A general partner ceases to be a member of a limited partnership by withdrawal, assignment of his interest, removal according to the terms of the agreement, personal bankruptcy, incompetency, or death.

Rights of Limited Partners

Any legal person can be a limited partner in a limited partnership, and that person includes individuals, partnerships, corporations, and other associations. To admit a limited partner, written consent is required of all partners, both limited and general, unless the certificate specifically allows general partners to decide alone to admit new partners.

Limited partners have many rights, but one of the most important rights is denied them—the right to exercise control and management responsibilities for the business. If a limited partner does take an active part or interferes with the management of the business, he forfeits his limited liability and takes on the unlimited liability of a general partner. There are a number of activities not regarded as taking control of the business, activities in which a limited partner can engage without losing limited liability. These activities include (1) being a contractor for, or an agent or employee of, the limited partnership or of a general partner; (2) consulting or advising a general partner about partnership business; (3) acting as a surety for the partnership; (4) approving or disapproving an amendment to the partnership agreement; and (5) voting on the dissolution and winding up of the partnership, on the sale, encumbering or transfer of partnership assets other than in the ordinary course of business, on borrowing by the partnership other than in the ordinary course of business, on a change in the nature of the business, or on the removal of a general partner.

While a limited partner is denied the right to take an active part in the control or management of the partnership business, he can be hired as an employee and as such can receive compensation. A limited partner can also transact business with the partnership, unless prohibited by the partnership agreement or certificate.

A limited partner can also lose his limited liability and be held liable as a general partner if he permits his name to be used in the firm name. In some states, a limited partner may be liable for withdrawing his investment during the continuance of the partnership and is under the obligation, if sued by the other partners or creditors, to restore the sums withdrawn with interest.

The extent to which a limited partner shares profits is determined by the certificate, which usually provides for the limited partner to receive his share of profits before the general partners. The certificate can also provide for compensation to limited partners. Under the RULPA, profits and losses can also be allocated among partners by the partnership agreement. If the partnership agreement does contain such a provision, then the profits and losses are allocated on the basis of the value of the contributions made by each partner. A limited partner does not share in the losses beyond the amount of his capital contribution.

A partner may withdraw from the partnership only at the time and under the circumstances specified in the certificate of limited partnership and in accordance with the partnership agreement. Withdrawal from the partnership does not mean the limited partner is automatically entitled to the return of his capital contribution. A limited partner is entitled to demand the return of his capital contribution in three cases: (1) upon dissolution of the partnership; (2) on the date specified in the certificate; or (3) after six-month's written demand to the general partners if no time is specified in the certificate for return of contribution or for dissolution. In the latter instance, if there is no provision for withdrawal, any limited partner who wishes to withdraw and recover his investment must give at least six-months' written notice to each of the general partners. In each of the three cases, the limited partner's right to the return of his capital contribution is subject to the liabilities owed to third party creditors and the other limited partners to be paid in full first.

The limited partner is entitled to have the books kept at the principal place of business, to inspect the books, and to copy them. He is entitled to demand and receive a formal accounting if circumstances warrant. The partner has the right to receive his capital contribution (investment) upon withdrawal from the partnership, subject to creditors' rights. Upon just cause he can initiate a suit for dissolution of the partnership.

A limited partner can assign his interest to a third party. The assignee does not automatically become a limited partner but can be made a limited partner if all the other partners consent or if the assigning partner has the power under the certificate to give the assignee this right. The estate of a deceased limited partner has all the rights he had when living, including the power to confer upon his assignee the right to be a limited partner.

Duties and Liabilities of Limited Partners

Unlike a general partner, a limited partner does not owe the partnership and other partner a fiduciary duty. For instance, the limited partner can compete with the limited partnership in which he invested his money. Likewise, the limited partner owes no duty of care to the partnership or other partners.

A limited partner does not have the authority to bind the partnership to contracts. He is not an agent of the partnership. The limited partner is not liable for torts committed by general partners, agents, or employees of the firm.

The most distinctive and appealing feature of the limited partnership is the limited liability it offers to limited partners. The limited partner is not *personally* liable to the firm's creditors and only shares in partnership losses to the extent of his investment (capital contribution) in the firm. In other words, all he can lose is his investment in the limited partnership when it is successfully sued. However, a limited partner may lose his limited liability and assume the unlimited liability of a general partner in three instances: (1) a certificate of limited partnership is not filed; (2) the limited partner allows his surname to appear in the partnership name; or (3) the limited partner takes an active part in or interferes with the management of the partnership.

A personal creditor of a limited partner can reach the interest of a limited partner through a charging order from a court. When the charging order is foreclosed, the purchaser at the foreclosure sale becomes an assignee of the limited partner's interest but does not become a limited partner.

DISSOLUTION

Unlike a general partnership, the death, total disability, or bankruptcy of a limited partner does not cause dissolution. The ULPA grants a limited partner the right to have a partnership dissolved and a winding up whenever he rightfully but unsuccessfully demands the return of his contribution. There are other events that also result in dissolution; they are:

1. The time or event specified in the certificate of limited partnership for dissolution has arrived;
2. All the partners reach a unanimous written agreement;
3. A general partner withdraws (unless the certificate allows for the continuation of the business by any remaining general partners). If there are no general partners remaining, the limited partners have the choice, within ninety days, to agree in writing to continue the business and appoint one or more general partners.
4. A court decree is drawn up. Any general or limited partner can apply to the court to dissolve the partnership if it is no longer reasonably practicable to carry on its business.

Winding Up

Winding up a limited partnership is within the power of a general partner who has not wrongfully caused the dissolution. If there is no general partner willing or available, then winding up may be performed by one of the limited partners or by a receiver designated by a court.

Distribution of Assets

The order of distribution of assets upon dissolution and liquidation of a limited partnership is different from that of a general partnership. The distribution order proceeds as follows:

1. To secured creditors other than general partners, including loans from limited partners.
2. To unsecured creditors other than general partners, including loans from limited partners.
3. To limited partners with respect to their share of undistributed profits and other income on their capital contributions.
4. To limited partners with respect to their capital contributions.
5. To general partners with respect to their loans to the partnership.
6. To general partners with respect to profits of the partnership.
7. To general partners with respect to their capital contributions.

Part III

Agency

13

Agency: Nature and Creation

Nature of Agency
  Who Can Be A Principal or Agent
  Types of Agents
  Agency Distinguished From Other Partnerships
Creation of the Agency Relationship
  Formalities
  Methods of Creating Agency Relationships

NATURE OF AGENCY

Agency is a relationship between two parties, a *principal* and his *agent*. In this relationship there is an agreement that one party, the agent, will act to perform work or services as the representative of and under the control of the other, the principal. More simply put, the agent is someone who represents another person, called a principal.

The agency relationship is *consensual*. That is, it is created by the mutual agreement or assent of the parties. Because it is consensual, the agreement to create an agency need not meet the requirements for establishing a contract. Hence, a person may agree to be an agent for another as a gift, without the consideration necessary to create a contract.

Four elements must be present to create an agency relationship. First, there must be a manifestation by the principal that the agent will act for the principal. Second, the agent must agree to act for the principal. Third, the agent must be subject to the principal's direction and control. As will be seen later, control is crucial and distinguishes agency from other relationships similar in appearance. And finally, the parties must be legally competent to be principal and agent.

Who Can Be A Principal Or Agent

Capacity To Be A Principal

Any person who can act for himself in entering into a binding contract may be a principal and act through an agent. "Person" includes individuals, trusts, corporations, and partnerships. The principal's legal capacity to act is more important than that of his agent because when a contract is executed by the agent for the principal, it is the principal's contract not the agent's. The agent's capacity is usually immaterial.

A contract made by an agent for a principal lacking capacity is void or voidable to the same extent that it would be had the principal made the contract. For example, a minor can act through an agent but can escape the contract as voidable as any minor could if by himself. Unincorporated associations and legal incompetents such as persons adjudged insane lack the capacity to contract under any circumstances and their contracts are void, thus they cannot act as principals. One also cannot be a principal if the law specifically excludes activity in a particular area. For example, a corporation formed for the purpose of providing insurance and limited to such an activity by its corporate charter cannot appoint agents to sell real estate or engage in any other acts outside the authority of the corporate charter or the applicable law.

Capacity To Be An Agent

Since the act of the agent is the act of the principal, it is usually immaterial whether the agent has legal capacity to make a contract for himself. Consequently, it is permissible to appoint as an agent persons who are aliens or minors or others who lack the capacity to make contracts in their own right. Hence a valid and enforceable contract can be made between the principal and the third person who dealt with an agent who might lack the capacity to make contracts for himself. However, in a contract between an agent and the principal, the capacity of the agent is relevant, and the contract of agency may be voidable or void.

The principle that the mental capacity of the agent is irrelevant to bind the principal in a contract with a third party is not absolute. Under certain situations minors of tender years, lunatics, and imbeciles may be adjudged by a court to be incompetent to act even as agents. This category includes persons who have been adjudicated incompetents and require conservators or legal guardians.

Types of Agents

Actual Agent or Ostensible Agent

All agents are either actual or ostensible. An actual agent has been given express or implied authority to act on behalf of another. An ostensible agent (apparent authority) (agent by estoppel) is not an actual agent but is represented by the principal or justifiably regarded by a third party as having authority to act on the behalf of the principal. Agents, whether actual or ostensible, can be further classified into different types, as described below.

General Agents

A general agent is given broad authority to represent a principal. A general agent is authorized by the principal to transact all business for a particular enterprise or to transact all business at a particular place. Examples are a person hired to manage a hardware store or a business manager for a professional athlete who does not conduct his own business.

Special Agents

A special agent is given limited authority to represent a principal. A special agent is appointed to perform a specific transaction or single task or a series or group of related transactions or tasks. For instance, a person may be employed to sell the principal's automobile or to buy a house for the principal.

Universal Agents

A universal agent is authorized to transact any and all manner of things to carry out the affairs of a principal. They possess a "blanket power of attorney." For example, a seriously ill person facing a long, indefinite hospital stay may confer such a blanket power of attorney on another.

Del Credere Agents

Del credere agents are sales agents who can sell someone else's goods on credit and promise to pay the principal if the buyer defaults on payment. The del credere agent in effect guarantees the accounts of his customers.

Gratuitous Agents

A gratuitous agent receives no compensation for his services. Hence, a person may unwittingly take on liability as a principal for a friendly act of a neighbor or relative that the friend or neighbor has been authorized to carry out. For example, if a friend is asked by a car owner to take his car to the service station for gas, the owner of the care may be liable to any victim of a car accident caused by the friend's reckless or negligent driving.

Attorneys at law

An attorney at law is qualified by admission to the bar to represent other persons in legal matters.

Attorneys in fact

The attorney in fact is usually not a licensed attorney and can act for another under a written *power or letter of attorney.*

Auctioneers

Auctioneers are agents for the seller until the fall of the gavel and thereafter an agent for both parties.

Factors or Commission Merchants

A factor is a commercial agent hired by the principal to sell or dispose of goods. The compensation for this type of agent is called *factorage* or *commission*. The factor is usually entrusted with the possession of the goods but does not have legal title, which remains with the principal. The factor thus is a type of bailee.

Exclusive Agents

An exclusive agent has an agreement with the owner of real or personal property that the owner will not sell the property to a buyer procured by any other agent. In an *exclusive sale* agreement the agent is given exclusive rights to act for the sale of his property during the duration of the agency, with no right to sale remaining even with the owner.

Agency Coupled With An Interest

Within this kind of agency, the agent has a property or security interest in the thing disposed of or managed under the power created by the agency. This kind of agency is irrevocable, that is, the principal cannot terminate it. There are two types—the agent may have an *interest in the authority* or an *interest in the subject matter*. An agent has an interest in the authority when he has given consideration (he usually has paid) for the right to exercise a particular kind of authority. For instance, a bank, in return for a loan, may be given authority to collect rents due the borrower as security for the loan. An agent has an interest in the subject matter when for consideration he is given an interest in the property with which he is dealing. For example, the agent may purchase the right to sell the property of the principal and bargains for a lien in the property as security for any commission or fee the principal has agreed to give the agent.

Subagents

A subagent derives his authority from an agent, not from the principal. As a general rule an agent or employee has not authority to delegate the work to others without the employer's or principal's permission. When an employee gets another person to perform his work, the latter person is also known as a *subservant*. If a servant or agent without permission from his superior hires another to undertake his responsibilities, the servant or agent becomes the master or principal of the subservant or subagent. Hence the servant or agent takes on a master's or principal's responsibility for any wrongful act the subservant or subagent may commit in the course of his work. If, however, the servant or agent was authorized to take subagents or subservants, the master or principal is liable for torts committed by them.

The authority of an agent to appoint a subagent does not necessarily have to be expressly authorized. The subagent may be implicitly authorized as well. Implicit authorization might be a result of the conduct of the principal, character of the business, usages or prior conduct of the parties, necessity of responding to an emergency, or the relative insignificance of the acts committed to the subagent.

Agency Distinguished From Other Relationships

Every agent is an employee in the sense that he works for a principal. But not all employees are agents. There are two other employment relationships closely related to, but yet distinguished from, agency, and they are employer to ordinary employee (master to servant) and employer to independent contractor.

As will be described in later sections, the employer-employee classifications are important because the employer has more legal liability to third parties when employees are agents or servants than when they are independent contractors. This liability of employers to third parties is called *vicarious liability*—if one person does something, another is legally responsible. The Latin legal term for vicarious liability is *respondeat superior*. Control is the reason employers have more legal liability for agents and servants than independent contractors, and the employer's control is a key factor in distinguishing these relationships. As a general rule employers and principals are liable to third parties for the torts committed by their agents and servants while in the scope of their employment or agency. An employer is not ordinarily liable in respondeat superior for the torts committed by an independent contractor. And finally, an ordinary employee or independent contractor, in contrast to an agent, cannot bind its employer to contracts negotiated with third parties on his behalf.

Principal-Agent

There are three defining characteristics of the agency relationship. First, one person, the principal, engages another, the agent, to enter business relations, usually contracts, with third persons. In other words, the purpose of the principal-agent relationship is to establish legal relations with others. Second, the agent owes an inescapable fiduciary duty to the principal. And third, the agent must be subject to at least some minimum degree of control or right to control by the principal for the performance of services for the principal.

The term "agent" is sometimes used to describe a relationship which is not that of principal and agent. The major example is "real estate agent," which is meant to describe a party hired to find a buyer or seller of property. The more apt and an interchangeable term is real estate "broker." A real estate broker is not usually an agent with the authority to make a contract with a third person that will bind the broker's client. Usually when a third person and the broker sign a "contract," it is generally only an offer by the third person that the broker transmits to the client. The contract does not become one until the client has accepted it.

Master-Servant (Employer-Employee)

At common law, employees without management discretion were called *servants*, and their employers, *masters*. Most courts today use the word "employees" rather than servants. This relationship is distinguished by the control the employer has over the physical conduct of the employee and the nature of the work performed by the employee. In the employment relationship the employer has the right to control the physical conduct of the employee. Evidence of the existence of control an employer exercises over an employee includes the employer paying wages, the employee working on the employer's premises, the employee using the employer's tools or equipment, or the employer directing the methods used by the employee in performing a job. A person can be an employee even though he receives no compensation so long as he is subject to a high degree of control or the right to control held by the employer. An ordinary employee usually is allowed to make decisions within the scope of his duties but has no authority to enter into contracts on behalf of the employer.

The distinction as to whether one is hired as an agent or servant is usually important only in determining whether the employer is obligated for the contracts of the employee. If the issue is the employer's liability, it is unimportant whether the employee is an agent or servant, since in either case the employer is vicariously liable for the employee's acts.

The ordinary employee, unlike the agent, is not hired to represent the employer in dealings with third persons. However, the same person can be both an agent and an employee. For example, the driver of a beer delivery truck is an employee, but he is also an agent in making contracts between the beer distributor and its customers.

Employer-Independent Contract

The distinction between the master-servant (ordinary employee) and the agent relationship on the one hand and independent contractor relationship on the other rests on the degree of control the employer retains over the conduct of the person performing the service and the end result of the job. The principal or master in the agent or servant relationship has the right to control both the means and manner of performing the work and the object or result of the job. In contrast, the employer seeks results only from the independent contractor, and the independent contractor controls the manner and methods of performing the job. Thus, a construction contractor hired to build a house is usually an independent contractor, while a secretary hired to type is usually a servant. An independent contractor, like a servant, ordinarily does not have the power to contract on an employer's behalf like an agent. The employer's right to inspect and determine if work is done properly does not constitute sufficient control to make a contractor an ordinary employee.

A person may be an independent contractor generally but an agent for a particular transaction. For example, a homeowner may hire a painting contractor to paint his house and give him the authority to charge for paint supplies at the local hardware store.

The main importance of the independent contractor status is that the employer is not generally vicariously liable for the torts committed by the independent contractor, whereas he is liable for the torts of servants and agents.

There are five well-recognized exceptions to the nonliability rule for contracts and torts of independent contractors. First, to clear title to real estate when selling it, landowners must pay off mechanic liens obtained by independent contractors who performed improvements on the property because they have not been paid. Second, the employer is vicariously liable for torts if extra hazardous activities have been conducted by the independent contractor. Examples of extra hazardous activities include razing buildings, clearing land by fire, blasting, spraying of poisons, and constructing dams and reservoirs. In these cases where the employer is responsible to third parties for the harm done by the dangerous work of the independent contractor, the tort liability is based on strict liability. Third, tort liability is imposed on the employer for harm done to a third party by the contractor. The employer's duty is nondelegable. Nondelegable duties are those owed the public that the courts feel are of such significance that responsibility for their harmful consequences cannot be passed off. Examples include (1) statutory duties, such as the statutory duty of a railroad to keep crossings safe; (2) duty of a city to maintain safe streets; (3) duty of a landlord who assumes responsibility to make repairs to ensure they are done safely when undertaken by a contractor; and (4) the duty of a business owner to keep his premises reasonably safe for members of the public who are customers. Fourth, the employer is liable for the torts of an independent contractor when he has failed to exercise sufficient care in selecting the contractor. Fifth, even if the employer might have been careful in selection he is liable if he exercised excessive control over an otherwise independent contractor, creating as a result a master-servant relationship.

CREATION OF THE AGENCY RELATIONSHIP

Formalities

There is no demand for formalities, such as consideration or a written agreement, to create an agency relationship. Oral authority is usually sufficient to establish an agency relationship. However, in some cases, those where the Statute of Frauds applies, the writing requirement is imposed on agency contracts just like other contracts. As an exception to the general rule that oral contracts are enforceable, the Statute of Frauds requires certain kinds of contracts to be in writing in order to be enforceable. Under the Statute any contract incapable of being performed within one year must be in writing. Consequently, any agreement for agency that is meant for a definite period beyond a year must be in writing in order to be enforceable, for example eighteen months. A written contract is not required for agents hired for an indefinite period, since the contract may be completed or terminated in less than a year.

The most common agency contract that must be in writing is one which authorizes an agent to sell real estate for the principal, since the Statute requires contracts involving the transfer of land to be in writing in order to be enforceable.

A party resisting a suit that alleges he orally agreed to be a principal or agent can use the Statute of Frauds as a defense. A third party usually cannot use the lack of a writing between a principal and an agent as a defense.

Although a written agreement is not required to create an agency relationship, it is usually best to delineate in writing the agent's authority and any other relevant matters. The formal written authorization given by a principal to an agent is often called a *power of attorney*.

Methods of Creating Agency Relationships

An agency may arise by express appointment (express agency), by conduct (implied agency), by estoppel, or by ratification, each of which is described in detail below.

Express Agency

The most common method of creating an agency is by express authorization. The principal tells the agent to perform a certain act, and the agent thereby obtains express authority to do it. The agent has actual express authority to represent the principal from his words. In an express agency the principal's appointment of an agent is accomplished by clear language, either oral or written. In an express agency the principal gives the agent actual authority to act on his behalf. Express agency requires an agreement between the principal and the agent whereby the latter will do work for the former. As noted previously, there are no formal requirements for an agreement establishing agency by express authority. In most cases the law does not require a written contract of agency, and even if there is a written agreement, it need not be supported by consideration as is necessary to create a valid contract.

When the appointment of an agent is authorized in a written form it is called a *power of attorney*. In a power of attorney, whatever the principal cannot do, he cannot delegate the agent to do. For example, since a minor has the power to disaffirm a contract because of lack of capacity, he cannot delegate to an agent the authority to make a contract for him. An agent who receives authorization by a power of attorney is called an *attorney in fact*.

An exception to the general rule that a writing is not required to create an express agency occurs when the agreement to create the agency is covered by the Statute of Frauds. The Statute of Frauds requires certain contracts to be in writing in order to be enforceable between the parties. And this applies to agency contracts as it does to other contracts. Under the Statute, any agreement that by its terms is incapable of being performed within one year must be in writing to be enforceable in court. Consequently, any agreement for agency that exceeds a definite period beyond a year must be in writing in order to be enforceable, for example eighteen months. A written contract is not required for agents hired for an indefinite period, since the contract may be completed or terminated in less than a year.

Another exception to the general rule that an oral appointment of an agent is enforceable, involves the Statute of Frauds in an indirect way through what are called *equal dignity statutes*, which exist in most states. These laws require the agency agreement to be written if the Statute of Frauds requires the contract the agent makes with a third party on the principal's behalf to be in writing. For instance, the Statute requires contract for the transfer of land to be in writing. Hence, the equal dignity statutes require the appointment of an agent to sell the principal's land to be in writing in order to be enforceable by either agent or principal against each other.

Agency is not created by the mere fact of co-ownership of property or of the relationship of the parties. For instance, when a check is made payable to the order of a husband and wife, each must endorse the check since there is no agency.

Implied Agency

This kind of agency is not created by the express or explicit words of the parties, as in an express agency, but is inferred from the words or conduct manifested to the agent from the principal. In this case the agent has actual implied authority rather than actual express authority. Another term for this form of authority is *implied in fact authority*.

Sometimes implied authority arises from express authority. This is called *incidental authority* and is a form of actual implied authority. Another term for incidental authority is *general authority*. Authority expressly granted to an agent to accomplish a particular purpose necessarily includes the authority to use the means reasonably required to accomplish it. For instance, the principal may tell his agent to hire a truck driver. The principal's command is express. The agent has the implied authority to put an advertisement in the newspaper, conduct interviews, and offer a reasonable salary, with all the expenses incurred for these actions to be paid by the principal. The implied authority is limited by the express authority. The agent cannot hire two truck drivers, only one.

The implied agency that arises out of an express agency is often a matter of what would be customary for the express agent to do to carry out his agency. This form of incidental or implied authority is called *customary authority*.

General or incidental authority to manage or operate a business for the principal implicitly confers, unless otherwise agreed, authority for the agent to buy and sell property for the principal; to make contracts reasonably necessary to conduct the business; to acquire equipment and supplies; to make repairs; to hire, supervise, and fire employees; to receive payments due the principal; to pay debts the principal owes; and to direct the ordinary operations of the business. In sum, all these activities are customarily part of an express agency to manage a business.

Another form of implied agency arises *by operation of law*, whereby the law implies authority for the agent to act for the principal regardless of the express or implied intentions of the parties. This kind of authority is called *implied-in-law* authority. Another way of explaining this agency is to say the authority of the agent to act for the principal is implied in law. There are circumstances that give rise to an agency relationship by operation of law: (1) in emergencies; (2) when spouses or unemancipated minors purchase necessaries; (3) under the family purpose doctrine; and (4) under nonresident motorist statutes.

Implied-in-law authority arising from emergencies includes any unexpected event requiring immediate attention from the agent to protect the principal's interest when the agent is unable to contact the principal, the principal did not inform the agent beforehand as to how to act in such a situation, and the agent acted reasonably to protect the interests of his principal. For example, a truck driver might hire a helper to guard his employer's truck and its contents after a mechanical breakdown. While the driver in ordinary circumstances would have no authority to hire, the employer is required to pay the helper hired by the driver, who has implied authority to act as an agent in emergency circumstances.

An unemancipated minor is considered the agent of his parent for the purchases of necessaries by the child when the parent does not supply them. Necessaries include food, clothing, shelter, and medical care. For example, a child, while his parents are away, gets into an accident, is taken to an emergency room with a life-threatening injury, and is treated. The parents are liable for the cost of his care. A spouse is an agent for the other for the purchase of necessaries.

The agency implied-by-law for the necessaries of spouses and children and when an emergency arises is also called *agency by necessity*.

The *family purpose doctrine* has been adopted by many states as part of their statutory law. Under this doctrine an agency relationship for tort liability arises whenever an automobile registered in the parent's name is used, with parental consent, for a family purpose by members of the family. For instance, if a child with the parent's consent borrows the family car to go to the supermarket and injures a pedestrian on the way, the parent is liable.

The final instance of implied agency created by operation of law is for nonresident motorist statutes that appoint the secretary of state as the agent of a nonresident motorist involved in an accident or in a traffic violation for the purpose of serving legal process.

Agency by Estoppel

Agency by estoppel is created by operation of law and arises when the principal's words or acts lead a third person to believe the agent has authority. Here the principal did not give the alleged agent actual express or implied authority to undertake an action, but will be held liable because he created the appearance that the alleged agent has authority. The alleged agent appears to be authorized from the point of view of a reasonable third party and regarded to have apparent authority. If it is unreasonable for the third party to believe there is authority, then apparent authority is not available. The appearance of agency makes the agent an apparent agent. The principal is estopped, (that is, he may not deny that the individual acted for him).

Estoppel traditionally was restricted to situations where the third party, relying on the apparent authority, detrimentally changes his position. That is, he does something he otherwise would not have done. Apparent agency does not require a detrimental change in position of the third party, but rather modern law applies estoppel in court if his reliance on the apparent authority was reasonable. The appearance of authority must come from some act or omission by the principal, not the agent. Sometimes apparent authority arises out of acquiescence of the principal. For example a janitor at an auto dealership, in order to impress his boss and gain a long awaited chance to be promoted to the sales staff, poses as a salesman to a customer and sells a car. The owner of the dealership is watching all along but does not interfere in the sale. The owner's failure to stop the janitor creates the appearance to the customer that the janitor has apparent authority to sell cars. And, in the interest of justice, the owner is estopped from reneging on the sale on the grounds that the janitor was not authorized to engage in sales.

Apparent authority may occur when secret restrictions on authority are communicated to an agent but not to third parties. It may occur when actual authority is terminated, as when the agent is fired, but third parties are not notified. Apparent authority often arises when an existing employee or agent exceeds actual authority, but a reasonable third party is unaware that the actual authority has been exceeded. Apparent authority not only includes actual employees or agents who exceed their authority but also a third person who is unconnected to the alleged principal and never had actual authority. In this event many courts label the authority the individual possesses as *ostensible authority*. For instance, a young man hopes to impress a large company and obtain employment from them as a salesman. He solicits orders for the company's products and plans to bring them to the company to show how good a salesman he is. The company learns of his activities but does nothing to stop him, adopting the attitude that it will take advantage of any orders he brings in but will not hire him. The company is estopped from reneging on any agreements for orders the young man has negotiated.

Secret limitations on an agent's express authority are not binding on third persons who properly believe the agent has apparent authority to bind the principal. For instance, a storeowner may have an agreement with his manager, who is his agent in most respects, that only the storeowner has the authority to purchase inventory. Nevertheless, a supplier provides goods to the store ordered by the manager without knowledge of the restriction on his express authority. The storeowner is bound to pay the supplier despite the restriction on the manager's express authority.

Agency by Ratification

It is possible for a principal to confer authority on a person for an act *after* it is done. (This retroactive grant of authorization is called ratification.) As a result, a previously unauthorized act can be approved by a person who thereby becomes a principal. This approval may be of an unauthorized act done by an agent or an act done by a person who was not an agent.

Ratification hinges upon the question of intention. Frequently there is a dispute over whether the principal intended to ratify the action of the unauthorized agent. There are two methods of ratification, two methods by which the intention to ratify are manifested—*express* and *implied*. In express ratification the principal manifests his intention to ratify by expressly communicating his intention to do so to the agent, the third party, or someone else. Express ratification is directly communicated in words. In implied ratification, the conduct or words of the principal reasonably indicate his intention to ratify. For example, the principal pays for the goods of the agent, previously unauthorized to order them.

In addition to the intent (expressed or implied) to ratify, the following requirements must be satisfied in order for the intention to take effect as ratification:

1. The act must have been purported to have been done in the name and on the behalf of the person ratifying.
2. The act ratified was legal.
3. The entire act must be ratified, that is, the principal cannot ratify in part and reject in part.
4. The principal must have been legally competent to authorize the act when it was done and at the time it was ratified.
5. The principal had full knowledge of the material facts at the time he approved the act.
6. If any formalities, such as a writing, would have been required for an original authorization, no less than the same formalities must be satisfied in ratifying the transaction.
7. The principal must ratify the act before the third person withdraws.

Ratification has the effect of releasing the agent from contractual liability to both the principal and third person for exceeding the agent's authority. Ratification does not have to be communicated to anyone to be effective. However, communication is usually necessary in order to prove ratification.

14

Agency: Duties and Liabilities

DUTIES OF AGENT AND PRINCIPAL TO EACH OTHER

Agent's Duties to the Principal

Agents owe their principals an assortment of duties. These obligations include the duty of loyalty, duty of obedience, duty to account, duty to inform, duty to use reasonable care, duty to perform personally, and duty to indemnify. The duty to be loyal, obedient, and to account to the principal arise from the basic foundation that the agency relationship is a *fiduciary relationship*. (The term fiduciary is a Latin word that has as its roots *fides*, meaning "trust" or "confidence.") The agency relationship is based on the trust and confidence the principal places in the agent in conferring on him the power to handle the principal's affairs. Hence, the agent is said to owe a fiduciary duty to his principal.

Duty of Loyalty

Probably the most important duty the agent owes the principal is that of utmost loyalty, accountability, and good faith. This duty of loyalty means the principal's interests come first, even before that of the agent himself, concerning matters within the scope of his work as an agent. The duty of loyalty lasts beyond the life of the agency, that is, it continues even after termination of the agency. In sum, it is the duty of the agent not to act adversely to the principal.

The duty of loyalty means the agent cannot serve two principals or masters without the consent of both. The agent cannot further the interest of a third party in his dealings with the principal, nor can he act as an agent for two parties in a transaction, known as *dual agency*, unless both of them know of the dual agency and agree to it. Dual agency or representation does not occur in situations where the agent stands in the middle between two potential contracting parties. In these cases the agent speaks for neither party in establishing price or terms. A real estate agent is a common example of a person who, depending upon the situation, can either be subject to the obligations of an agent or be in the position of standing in the middle. If both principals did not know and consent to the agent's double status, they can, upon learning about it, either refuse to pay the agent or else secure return of any compensation that has been paid, and then rescind any agreement negotiated by the agent, recover damages from the agent, and terminate the agency. In the simplest terms, agents representing both parties to a transaction are not entitled to payment from either. When one of the principals knew of the double agency then only the nonconsenting principal can avail himself of the above-mentioned remedies, and additionally he can sue the duplicitous principal for damages. However, if both parties are aware of the dual agency and approve it, the agent has the right to dual payment.

The agent cannot take advantage of business or economic opportunities rightfully belonging to the principal. A business or economic opportunity is the chance to capitalize on a transaction for which there is a potential profit or benefit for the employer. Suppose, for example, that an employee is a geologist for an oil company. In the course of his geological surveying he uncovers a huge oil deposit but keeps it to himself with the intention of biding his time for several years, quitting the oil company, and forming his own outfit to develop the oil discovery. The geologist in this case seized the economic opportunity rightfully belonging to his employer. This is also an example of the duty of loyalty lasting after the end of the agency relationship. The remedies available to a principal include a court order to require the agent to turn the opportunity over to the principal, an injunction to restrain the agent from competing with the principal, and a court order requiring the agent to turn over profits made by the agent.

The agent cannot keep any secret benefits from a principal in connection with the agency, usually in the form of secret profits or secret gifts or commissions. The principal is entitled to sue the agent for these secret benefits. An example would be that of an agent authorized to sell certain property for his principal for one price and finding a buyer who pays a higher price and pocketing the excess without telling the principal. The agent must not only turn over the secret profit to the principal, but he must also turn over any commission to which he otherwise would have been entitled had he not breached his duty of loyalty. A purchasing agent who receives a kickback to purchase from a particular supplier of the principal is another example. The kickback received by the agent belongs to the principal.

Unless given permission by the principal, the agent has the obligation not to personally use or disclose confidential information obtained in the course of the agency, e.g., customer lists, trade secrets, manufacturing processes, marketing techniques, or future marketing plans. This duty not to disclose confidential information exists not only during the duration of the agency but also after the agent has left the employment of the principal. The fiduciary relationship does not end simply because the employment has terminated. Whether or not a departed employee is using trade secrets or customer lists is a frequent source of litigation and usually revolves around the issue of whether the former employer can make a legitimate claim that the information used by the former employee is a trade secret or customer list. A trade secret is any information that gives a firm an advantage over its competitors and for which the firm takes reasonable precautions to keep secret from the public and competitors. Trade secrets usually involve industrial processes. If an industrial process is not kept confidential, then it is not a trade secret and knowledge of it can be used by the former employee in his new business or with his new employer. Trade secrets should not be confused with the skills, experience, and know-how the employee acquired during his former employment. Because trade secrets are confidential he cannot use them in his new employment, but he can use what he has learned on the job to the extent it is not confidential and crucial to his former employer. A customer list is a compilation of the names and addresses of potential purchasers of the goods or services of the former employer. It need not be written, but can be retained in the memory of the former employee. Because the customer list has been developed through the expenditure of time, money, and marketing efforts it is considered property of the business. The courts generally permit the former employee to do business with the customers of his former employer who are openly engaged in business or whose names can be discovered through readily available sources of information, such as business directories or the yellow pages of the telephone book. In cases where a former employee is using trade secrets or customer lists for the new employer, the principal is entitled to an injunction to prevent either or both of them from using the information.

An employee or agent has a qualified right to use the fruits of his employment, such as inventions that were developed while working for the employer. However, the employer also has rights in the invention under the *shop rights privilege* or *doctrine*. The shop rights doctrine is a facet of the agent's duty to pass along to the employer all information relevant to the agency. The shop right interest of the employer means the employee owns the invention, but the employer has the right to use it without paying royalties or fees to the inventor. The shop right doctrine only applies when the employee's duties did not include research or invention but he used the employer's facilities, materials, or equipment to conceive and perfect the invention. If the employee has research or invention duties on the job, then any product of his labors belongs to the employer alone, and the employee is not entitled to patent the product or to receive royalties if there is no agreement allowing this.

An agent is under a duty not to compete with the principal. For instance, on his off-duty hours the agent cannot try to sell a rival brand of products to the principal's potential customers. In the absence of a covenant not to compete, the former agent can work, perform, and compete against his former employer. The former agent cannot, as indicated above, use confidential information in his new employment or business.

The agent employed to purchase for the principal cannot sell his own property to the principal without first disclosing his ownership to the principal. The principal has the right to rescind such a transaction even when the principal does not suffer a financial loss. The principal also has the option to abide by the transaction and sue the agent for any secret profit he might have gained.

When the agent is employed to sell for the principal and the price of an item is negotiated by an agent, he cannot buy from the principal without first disclosing he is a buyer. Likewise, the sales agent cannot surreptitiously buy from the principal through a relative, friend, or sham buyer. There is no restriction on the ability of the agent to buy from the principal when he has had no role in establishing the price.

Duty to Obey

The agent has the duty to act only as authorized by the principal and to obey any and all reasonable and legal instructions and directions of the principal. The agent must follow the instructions of the principal even if he believes them to be foolish or stupid. Deviation from clear and legal instructions is justified only on rare occasions, the most common being an emergency during which it would be unreasonable, even dangerous, to follow the instructions. The agent is under no duty to follow an order to commit a tort or a crime. If an agent does not obey a legal instruction, he is liable to the principal for damages.

Duty to Account

The agent is under a duty to keep accurate records and render an account for money and property received from the principal or a third party for the principal. The duty to account is ancillary to the duty to be loyal and is an effective means to corroborate loyalty. The term "accounting" means either a demand by the principal for the return of money or property or for an accurate disclosure and rendering of all receipts and expenditures by the agent. An agent must turn over the principal's money or property when he demands it. If the agent does not do so he commits the tort of conversion, and the principal can bring suit for recovery. When the principal asks for a rendering of the account, the agent must provide one within a reasonable time. The agency agreement may provide for periodic accounting at specified times. The burden is on the agent to provide an accurate account to the principal's satisfaction. The agent must not mix or "commingle" the principal's funds with his own. If any loss occurs as the result of the commingling, the agent is strictly liable for it.

Duty to Inform

The agent must notify the principal of all information they know is relevant to the agency. Information is relevant if it does or could materially affect the principal's interests. The relevant information must be told to the principal as soon as possible after it is learned. This presumes that an agent has given the principal all notices and information pertinent to the agency. In other words, the principal is presumed to know what the agent knows. Thus if the agent is served with a summons and complaint for a lawsuit against the principal and fails to inform the principal with the result (that a default judgment is rendered against the principal), the judgment is binding on the principal. Of course, the agent is liable to the plaintiff for any award against the plaintiff in the lawsuit. There are two exceptions to the presumption that the principal has received notice and information from the agent. First, the principal is not presumed to know about information the agent acquires in confidence. For example, if the agent is an attorney and receives information from another client in confidence, he cannot reveal it to his other client-principal. Second, the principal is not presumed to have knowledge that the agent is embezzling from the principal.

Duty to Use Reasonable Care and Skill

The agent is normally required to exercise the degree of care and skill in carrying out his duties that are reasonable under the circumstances and in the line of business in which he is engaged. Simply, the employee or agent cannot be negligent in the performance of services. The agent satisfies his duty by using the standard of care that is ordinary or average in the occupation or line of work he is undertaking for the principal. Thus if the agent is a salesperson, he is required to exercise the diligence of an "average" salesman in the same field. Sometimes more than average or ordinary care is required when the agent is employed or appointed for special skills or expertise he possesses, for example as a broker or attorney. Any such expert must use not just ordinary care and diligence but must perform in accordance with the higher skill and diligence expected of an expert. Whether expert or nonexpert, the agent does not guarantee the success of his undertaking or that he will make no mistakes in the work, unless he expressly guarantees the result by express contract.

Duty to Perform Personally

As a general rule the agent or employer is under a duty to perform the work personally for the principal. He cannot delegate the work to others unless the principal or employer expressly or implicitly consents. This rule that the agent cannot make a delegation or substitution is expressed in the Latin aphorism, *Delegatus non potent delgare*, which means "a delegate cannot delegate." The rule is based on the premise that the agency relationship is one of trust and confidence and thus necessitates personal performance of the work by the agent. There are certain circumstances when delegation of responsibilities is allowed, however. Unless there is a specific agreement, the agent may delegate when the nature of the business requires it, where known and established custom permits, or when delegation involves purely clerical or mechanical acts. In general an act is not delegable by an agent to a subagent when it involves discretion and requires the judgment and decision of the agent himself.

Duty to Indemnify

If the agent acts negligently and causes damage to the principal's interests, he has a duty to pay the principal for his losses. Principals may waive the indemnification right against their agents or employees.

Principal's Duties to Agent

The principal or master owes several duties to his agents and servants, but he does not owe a fiduciary duty to them. Seven major duties the principal owes the agent are primarily contractual: (1) the duty to compensate, (2) to reimburse, (3) to indemnify, (4) to keep accounts, (5) to perform the agency contract, (6) to not unreasonably interfere, and (7) to provide work tools or means to the extent necessary. Often these seven matters are not provided for in an express agreement, and in such a case these duties are implied. The principal also has a tort responsibility to the agent, and that is the duty to provide a safe workplace.

Duty to Compensate Agent

Compensation is not a test or requirement for an agency to exist, rather, authorization to act is the test. If the agent agrees not to work for compensation, he is acting gratuitously, that is, his agent's status is a gift. Unless an agent has agreed to serve gratuitously, the principal has the duty to pay the agent even if the employment or agency contract does not specifically mention payment. If the rate of compensation is not specified, then the agent is entitled to the fair value of his services. If a person acts without authority, the principal has no duty to pay, but if the principal later ratifies the unauthorized act, the principal must pay the agent fair compensation.

If the compensation depends upon achievement of a certain result, the agent earns what is commonly referred to as a "commission," "fee," or "bonus." If the result is not achieved regardless of how much time or money was spent by the agent, then no compensation or reimbursement is due. For transactions based on commissions, if the transaction is canceled by the third party without influence or fault from the principal, then likewise the agent is not owed compensation.

Some agents on commission receive advances for their performance to cover their living and work expenses until commissions begin to flow. Agents have no automatic right to advances unless the agency contract provides for it. When the amount of the advance exceeds the commissions earned, the issue becomes one of whether the principal has the right to recover the overpayment. In the absence of an express agreement or custom to the contrary, advances generally are treated as minimum salary and the principal is not entitled to their return. In other words the contract should clearly give the employer the right to recover overpayments, otherwise he cannot obtain their return.

In many kinds of businesses, such as insurance, the agent who made the original contract with a third party is entitled to compensation or commission for all subsequent renewal or additional contracts. For the agent or his estate to continue to receive payments for repeating transactions either after termination of his employment or after his death, the right must be specifically provided in the agency contract.

Certain acts by the agent excuse the principal's duty to pay. These acts are fraud or conversion against the principal, waiver of right of payment, substantial failure to do the job, an illegal act, and a breach of his fiduciary duty. Moreover, the agent is not entitled to compensation from either principal in the case of dual agency.

Duty to Perform Contract with the Agent

The principal must continue the agency for the duration agreed upon. The agency may exist for a fixed period, in which case it is an *agency for a term*; it may have no fixed period, in which case it is *at will* and can be terminated at any time; or it may exist for the accomplishment of a stated purpose.

Duty Not to Interfere

While the principal has the right to control the means and methods of the agent's services, he cannot unduly interfere with the agent's activities so as to make them meaningless, particularly when the agent has paid for the privilege of representing the principal. Furthermore, the extent to which the principal can interfere with the agent's activities is controlled by the agency agreement, which can limit or prohibit such interference. Part of the duty not to undermine the effectiveness of the agent is the duty not to harm the agent's reputation. If the agent is to effectively represent the principal his reputation is important.

Duty to Reimburse Agent

The principal owes the duty to reimburse his agent, even when the agent has agreed to act gratuitously (i.e., without compensation). Reimbursement must be made for reasonable and necessary expenses of the agent; however, the acts for which the agent is reimbursed must be authorized. Fines and penalties are not considered ordinary and necessary and thus the principal does not have to reimburse the agent for them.

Duty to Indemnify Agent

The principal must indemnify the agent for losses and liabilities while performing agency duties, so long as the agent is not at fault. In order to be entitled to indemnification, the agent must be carrying out the principal's instructions and the act must not be illegal. The agent is not owed indemnification if he breaches his duty to the principal, such as committing a tort against a third party.

Duty to Keep and Render Accounts

The principal must maintain and render an accurate account to the agent of money and other things due the agent. An agent can bring an action for accounting if the principal fails to keep or render proper accounts.

Duty to Provide Means to Accomplish the Work

The principal is normally under no duty to provide tools or other instruments of work for a nonservant agent. He usually does have a duty to provide such tools and instruments for his servant-type employees. And he has the duty to provide them with safe tools.

Duty to Provide Safe Workplace

This is one of the tort duties the principal owes the agent. The employer or principal must provide his servant with reasonably safe conditions of employment and warn him of any unreasonable risk involved in the employment. The employer is liable to his agent or employee for injury caused by the negligence of other employees or agents working for him.

Remedies for Breach of Duties

Principals and agents have a variety of legal remedies available to each, depending upon the circumstances, to enforce the duties each owes the other.

For breach of obligations by an agent, the principal may fire him, withhold compensation, recover secret profits, recover wrongfully withheld property, enjoin the agent, recover damages for breach of the agency, obtain indemnification, or rescind the agency agreement. For breach of obligations by a principal, an agent may quit the employment, sue for reinstatement at work, recover damages for breach of employment, recover compensation, sue for an accounting, sue for reimbursement, and obtain indemnification.

LIABILITY OF PRINCIPAL AND AGENT TO OTHER PERSONS

Contract Liability of Principal

Third Party's Duty to Ascertain Agent's Authority

A third party is under a duty to determine whether an agent is being dealt with, and if so, the extent of the agent's authority. Although the third party can bind a principal when his agent is authorized to act on his behalf, he nevertheless has the duty to determine the validity and extent of the authority of a person claiming or appearing to represent another. First, the person must determine whether the person is in fact an agent. And, secondly, if the person is an agent, must determine the limits of the agent's authority.

The third party's duty to inquire is implicitly guided by a reasonableness requirement. This means that in certain cases a third party does not need to make such an inquiry. For instance, an inquiry does not need to be made if the agent pays cash for a sale. But if the sale is on credit, the seller acts at his peril in that the agent is purchasing for another who will supposedly provide payment. After the existence and limits of an agent's authority have been determined by a third party, the seller can presume the agent's authority continues until he is notified or learns otherwise (the authority has been terminated).

When the authority of an agent is conditioned upon the occurrence of some event, the third party cannot ordinarily rely upon the representation of the agent that the event has occurred. An exception to this rule is made when the occurrence of the event is virtually limited to the knowledge of the agent and cannot be readily determined by the third party dealing with the agent.

A third party is presumed to know the normal scope of the agent's authority if the agent is the kind with whom he usually deals. There are certain cases when the agent's assertion of authority out of the ordinary should prompt the third party's duty to inquire. One such instance is when the agent's acts are clearly adverse to the interest of the principal.

The third party cannot disregard his knowledge of any limitation of the agent's authority. For instance, if the third person knows that the authority of the agent is contingent upon the principal obtaining financing, the principal is not bound by the acts of the agent if that financing is not obtained. If the third person is unaware of secret limitations the principal has imposed on the agent's authority and it is reasonable to assume the agent has authority which he in fact lacks, the third party is not bound by the secret limitations.

Transactions with sales personnel do not necessarily involve the salesperson being an agent and binding his employer under contract for an order from a third person. A salesperson is ordinarily regarded as a *soliciting agent* whose authority is limited to soliciting orders from third persons and transmitting them to the principal for acceptance or rejection. A soliciting agent lacks authority to make a contract that will bind the principal to a third party, and the employer of the salesperson is not bound by the contract until the employer accepts the order. In short, the customer's giving a salesperson an order does not ordinarily become a contract with the salesperson's employer until the employer approves the order. The customer can withdraw from the sale any time before this approval.

A salesperson is more than a soliciting agent, he is a contracting agent when he has the authority to make binding contracts. The employer's approval is not required nor waited for. Once the customer has made an order, he cannot withdraw. A contract of sale has been made. Here the employer, as principal, is as equally bound by the order as is the customer.

Disclosed and Undisclosed Principal

While third parties have a duty to ask whether a person is an agent of another, agents do not have a duty to disclose their principals. The agent may even be forbidden by his contract with the principal to reveal the agency or the identity of the principal.

The existence of a principal may be disclosed, partially undisclosed, or undisclosed to third parties. Normally, the principal is liable for a contract made by his agent whether or not the principal has been disclosed. Some exceptions to this rule are described below, but disclosure or nondisclosure generally makes no difference in regard to the principal's liability. In contrast, the liability of an agent to a third party on a contract he made for a principal is greatly affected by whether the principal was disclosed or not disclosed.

A principal is disclosed when both the existence of the agency and the identity of the principal are known to the third party with whom the agent contracted. If the third party knows he is dealing with an agent of a principal but does not know the identity of the principal, that principal is partially disclosed. An agent acts for an undisclosed principal when he appears to be acting only in his own behalf, and the third person with whom he is dealing does not know the agent is acting as an agent. In other words, the third party believes the agent is the principal.

A dispute commonly arises over the liability of the disclosed principal for false representations made by his agent to a third party during the negotiation of a contract. If the false representations are within the kind of representations normally made in the principal's business, then the principal is bound. This is so even if the agent made the representations without the principal's knowledge or authorization. So long as the representations are within the agent's apparent or incidental authority, the principal is liable. In contrast, the disclosed principal is not liable for a misrepresentation that the third party knows or should know the agent is not in a position to make.

The disclosed principal may attempt to limit his liability to third parties through the use of an *exculpatory clause* in a written contract. The clause will declare the agent has no authority to expand the representations in the written contract. Courts have tended to disfavor and not enforce exculpatory clauses when the salesperson has made extensive representations or buried such clauses in form contracts so the buyer would not notice them.

The principal may intentionally or unintentionally be undisclosed by an agent. The principal's agreement with the agent may forbid the agent to disclose that he is representing another. If the principal is undisclosed, he is virtually always liable for the contracts his agent makes for him. However there are exceptions, one being when the contract has been fully performed by the agent, another is when the contract is a negotiable instrument—checks and promissory notes. If an agent signs a note for the undisclosed principal, the third party cannot hold the principal liable, and his only recourse is against the agent. And finally, the undisclosed principal is not liable if the contract between the agent and the third party specifically excluded an undisclosed principal or if personal performance of the agent is important.

Normally, as will be discussed in a later section, a third party cannot sue the agent and hold him personally liable for a contract negotiated for a principal. However, an agent is liable for the contracts of an undisclosed principal. The third party will often go ahead and sue the agent, never knowing there is a principal who can be sued. Upon the discovery of the existence of the undisclosed principal, the third party can elect to hold either, but not both, the agent or undisclosed principal liable. If the third party obtains a judgment against the agent, he cannot sue and obtain a judgment against the undisclosed principal and vice versa. While the third party can hold either the undisclosed principal or agent liable, he may obtain only one satisfaction. Assume that after the third party has learned of the identity of the principal but elected to sue the agent and received a judgment, he learns that the agent is insolvent. Because a judgment has been obtained, the agent is barred from suing the principal and recovering from him.

The partially disclosed principal is generally treated the same as an undisclosed principal. However, there are two exceptions. First, the undisclosed principal cannot ratify the unauthorized contracts of his agent, while the partially disclosed principal can. Second, the rule about the election of lawsuits against either the undisclosed principal and agent does not apply when the principal is partially disclosed. The third person has the right to sue both the partially disclosed principal and the agent and therefore can obtain a judgment against either without discharging the other.

Contract Liability of Agent

Generally an agent is not liable for a contract that the agent negotiated with a third party on behalf of the principal.

There are important exceptions to the nonliability of agents to third parties. The agent is personally liable to a third person in the following situations:

1. There is a nonexistent or incompetent principal.

2. There is a partially disclosed or undisclosed principal.

3. Agent exceeds authority and lacks apparent authority.

4. Breach of warranty of authority by the agent, he acts without authority or exceeds the scope of his authority.

5. Agent perpetrates a fraud.

6. Agent personally assumes liability for a particular transaction.

7. Agent signs contract or note without indication of representative capacity.

8. Agent's agreement with third person to be jointly liable.

Nonexistent or Incompetent Principal

The agent is seen as representing a nonexistent principal when the agent does not know the principal's exact name and makes a mistake in signing it to a contract. For instance, the agent mistakenly signs "Acme Corporation" instead of "Acme, Inc." When corporate promoters sign preincorporation contracts it would seem they are acting as agents for the corporation they are attempting to establish, but since it has not yet been formed it cannot be regarded as a legal entity and thus is nonexistent. In such cases the agent is personally liable even if the third party knows of the nonexistence, unless the contract specifically exempts the agent from personal liability.

The agent is also liable on a contract made for a legally incompetent principal. The common situations in which the principal lacks the legal capacity to be bound by a contract include when he is a minor or when he has been adjudicated incompetent by a court on the basis of insanity or habitual intoxication.

Partially Disclosed or Undisclosed Principal

The agent is liable on a contract he makes for a partially disclosed principal. As described earlier, if the principal is partially disclosed, the agent makes known that he is representing another but does not reveal the principal's identity. The third person can elect to hold either the agent or the principal, but not both, to the contract. The agent can avoid liability if the contract specifically exempts him from personal liability.

An agent acts for an undisclosed principal when he appears to be acting only on his own behalf and does not reveal to the third party he is representing another. In this case, the agent is personally liable to the third party. The third person can hold the agent liable for the contract; or, once he learns of the agency and the principal's identity, he can elect to hold either, but not both, the principal or agent liable.

Agent Exceeding or Lacking Authority

The agent is not liable to a third party if the agent lacks actual authority, but the principal is liable due to the apparent authority of the agent. However, if the agent lacks both actual and apparent authority, he is liable to the third party.

Breach of Warranty of Authority

A person who makes a contract in the capacity of an agent implicitly warrants that he is authorized to act as an agent and make such a contract. Sometimes the agent is mistaken in his belief that he has authority to make a contract. In these cases, when the agent does not have authority to bind the principal, the agent can be held liable by the third party for breach of warranty of authority. There are three ways even the unauthorized agent can avoid liability for breach of warranty of authority: First, the contract expressly disclaims the agent is responsible for any lack of authority; second, the third party had actual or implied knowledge that the agent lacked authority or was acting for an incompetent principal; or third, the principal subsequently ratifies the previously unauthorized contract by the agent.

Agent's Fraud

A person commits fraud if he falsely represents to a third person that he has authority to make a contract for a purported principal. He is liable to the third party in a tort action for deceit for any damages incurred as a result of the misrepresentation. The tort of deceit has also occurred when the agent fraudu lently misrepresented or concealed the principal's lack of capacity to be bound to a contract.

Assumption of Liability

The agent is liable on a contract made for a principal if he agrees to guarantee the performance of the contract. In other words, the agent agrees to act as a surety for the principal. An agent acting as a surety usually pledges his personal credit on the contract.

Obscured Capacity

An agent is personally liable when his signature on a contract does not clearly indicate he is signing in a representative capacity. This most commonly occurs when the agent's name appears on a promissory, check, draft, or other contract; and the principal's name does not. The agent is liable on it, and the principal is not. For instance, the agent John Doe might sign, "John Doe." He would not be liable if his signature indicated his representative capacity, such as "Acme Corporation, by John Doe, agent" or "Acme Corporation, John Doe, Treasurer."

Joint Liability with Principal

An agent for a principal may also expressly agree to be jointly liable on the contract with the principal. For instance, the agent cosigns a promissory note for the principal in addition to signing for the principal in a representative capacity.

Principal's Tort Liability

The depiction of the principal's tort liability that follows applies only to the principal-agent and pure employer-employee (master-servant) relationships in which the principal controls or has the right to control the performance of the agents' or employees' duties. In general the principal, because of this control, is liable for the torts committed by employees and agents, herein grouped together as "agents." The employer is not ordinarily liable for the torts of an independent contractor because, while the employer or principal bargains for an end result to be performed by the independent contractor, the means and method of reaching that result are under the control of the contractor rather than the principal or employer.

Direct Liability

Every person is liable for his own torts. The superior is directly liable if he commanded or intended the commission of a tort to be carried out by his subordinate or agent. The commonly occurring primary liability for a principal for negligence or recklessness result from giving improper or ambiguous orders, using improper persons or means, or providing inadequate supervision.

The employer or principal is directly liable if he expressly directs or intends the employee or agent to commit an act that is a tort. For instance, the principal authorizes the agent to fraudulently misrepresent his product to a third party. The employer or principal is liable if he carelessly allows the agent or employee to operate potentially dangerous equipment; for example, the employer permits an employee driver with a bad driving record to drive a company delivery truck and a third person is injured when the employee drives over him. Allowing an employee or agent to operate equipment for which he is unqualified or incapable of safely handling is called *negligent entrustment*. An employer or principal is liable for negligently failing to supervise a subordinate. The employer is also liable for negligence in hiring an unqualified or unsuitable employee.

Vicarious Liability

If an employee or agent commits a tort, he is liable for it. When a subordinate commits a tort, the additional question arises whether his superior is also liable. If the superior did not direct or intend the commission of a tort he is not directly liable. However, the tort liability of the employer or agent does not end when it is not direct liability. Even if the employer or principal has committed no tort himself, the third person may also be able to hold him liable for the wrongs of his employees or agents. This kind of derivative liability is called *vicarious liability*. When a third person is injured by a subordinate, vicarious liability is usually looked for since direct liability is not as commonly found and the superior has "deeper pockets" than the subordinate, either having greater personal wealth or being insured.

When the law finds a superior vicariously liable for the acts of a subordinate it does so under the well-worn doctrine of *respondeat superior*, meaning "let the master respond." Under respondeat superior, the principal or employer is without fault but nevertheless held liable for his subordinate's acts. It is a form of strict liability, which does not require fault. Respondeat superior does not make the principal or employer responsible for every tort committed by an employee. The fundamental requirement of respondeat superior is that the tort be committed by the employee while acting within the "scope of the agency or employment." If the employee or agent was not so acting, there is no vicarious liability.

There is no question as to whether an agent's act is within the scope of his employment when he is performing acts he is expressly authorized or directed to perform. The question becomes disputed when the principal claims or can prove the agent's acts were not authorized. An act of an agent may be within the scope of employment even when not expressly authorized or even when committed in violation of the employer's instructions, so long as it is reasonably related or incidental to the activities the agent is authorized to perform.

An act can be within the scope of employment not only when the employee exceeds his authority but also when he acts in flagrant disobedience of the employer's instructions. There are limits on the extent to which a deviation from authority by an employee is considered within the scope of employment. When the employee exceeds these limits and goes beyond the scope of authority, he is seen by the law as "on a frolic of his own" and the employer is not vicariously liable. A *frolic* is a substantial departure from or abandonment of the employer's business during which the employee does what he wants.

There is no single definition that can be used to prove scope of employment when a third party cannot prove the act of the agent was directly or expressly authorized. Determining whether the act is within the scope of employment in these cases depends largely on conforming with certain sensible factors that lead to the reasonable conclusion that the agent was performing an act that was reasonably incidental to his authority. In general an act of an employee or agent is considered within the scope of employment if it satisfies three factors: (1) it is of the same general nature as the acts he is authorized to perform, (2) it has a reasonable connection in time and place with his work, and (3) the purpose of the acts performed was to serve the superior. In other words, the employee's act is within the scope of employment if it serves the same purpose as the authorized work and has a reasonable connection in time and place with that work.

The three requirements that determine whether an act is within the scope of employment are best understood with illustrations that follow.

An employee or agent is acting within the general nature of his work when performing an act that is related to the work he is authorized to perform, even though the particular act that constituted the tort was expressly authorized by the employer. For instance, a bill collector who uses abusive language and threats to intimidate a debtor into paying a bill might be acting against the written policy of his bill collection employment company, but his action might be regarded as reasonably incidental to the work or foreseeable by the employer. The failure of an employee to act might also be regarded as within the scope of employment because it is foreseeable. For example, at a construction site an employee leaving work for the day might fail to put up a protective barrier to prevent passersby from falling into an excavation. This failure is reasonably foreseeable and thus within the scope of employment for which the employer is liable.

The second requirement for respondeat superior is that the employee's act that constituted the tort had a reasonable connection in time and place with his employment duties. Commonly time and place are important concerns when the employee's tort occurred going to or coming from work or during his lunch hour. As a general rule, the tort of an employee that occurred when commuting to and from work is not within the scope of employment—the "going and coming rule." There are exceptions to this rule; for example, the employer asks the employee to deliver a parcel on his way home from work, and the employee has an auto collision with a third party before the package is delivered. Here the employee's act was authorized and served the purposes of the employer and is thus within the scope of his employment. Furthermore, the "dual purpose" or "dual enterprise" rule applies. A dual enterprise is the mixing of an employee's personal activities with the work of the employer. A tort committed during a dual enterprise is considered within the scope of employment. Another exception to the rule that commuting to and from work is not within the scope of employment is when the employee uses a company vehicle for work and nonwork purposes and is "on call" during nonworking hours. The lunch hour rule is similar to the going and coming rule, in that torts committed during the employee's free time generally are not considered imputable to the employer. However, if the lunch or coffee break of the employee occurs on the employer's premises, then the employee continues to be within the scope of his employment.

Dispute about scope of employment frequently occurs when the employee, for personal purposes or reasons, departs from the time or place of employment and then returns. When the deviation from authority for personal purposes or reasons is great or represents a substantial departure or abandonment of the employer's work, the employee is regarded as on a frolic and the employer is not liable. But not every departure or deviation from work is regarded as a frolic that will allow the employer to avert liability. Another kind of deviation from work for which the employer might be considered vicariously liable is a *detour*, in which the employee makes a brief digression or departure from his duties and expects to return to them. Thus when the deviation is slight the employee is only on a detour, and the employer is liable; when it is great it is considered a frolic, and the employer is not liable. For instance, on his way back from an errand for the employer, the employee goes a couple of blocks out of his way to buy a birthday card for his daughter. If an accident occurs during the detour, the employer would likely be considered liable, since the employee has primarily been engaged in the employer's business. Unfortunately, there is no clear rule that determines where a detour ends and a frolic begins.

Another problem is determining when the frolic ends. When the frolic ends and the employee then commits a tort, the tort has occurred within the scope of employment, and the employer is liable. The courts have adopted three viewpoints to determine when the frolic ends and each revolves around a determination as to when the employee reentered the employment relationship. First, when the deviation from work is slight, reentry into the scope of employment is seen as occurring only when the employee *actually returned to the authorized route or activity*. Second, reentry occurs the moment the employee, with intent to serve his employer's business, *begins to turn back toward work*. Third, (the most common viewpoint), reentry is that moment when the employee, with intent to serve the employer's business, *has turned back toward and come reasonably close to the point of deviation*.

The final requirement of respondeat superior is that the employee's or agent's act was undertaken with the intent, at least in part, to serve his employer or principal or that the tort was connected with his employment. The converse of this requirement is that when an employee or agent acts solely for his own purposes or interests, with not the slightest intent to serve the employer or principal, then the latter is not liable. Normally an employee's negligent acts are considered within the scope of employment when done during work hours at the workplace, while driving along an authorized route, or while complying with the employer's directions. Even under these circumstances, however, the employer is not liable for the negligent acts of the employee when the tort is committed solely to satisfy the employee's own purposes. For instance, an employee leaves his office where smoking is not allowed and goes to the restroom to take a smoking break. He negligently allows a bar of soap to remain where he dropped it, and a few moments after he leaves a visitor to the business slips on the bar of soap in the restroom and injures himself. The employer might likely not be considered liable because the employee's trip to the restroom was solely for his own purposes.

Most cases of respondeat superior are concerned with the negligent acts of an employee or agent. An employee's or agent's intentional torts, such as assault and battery, libel, slander, fraud, trespass and so on can also be included in respondeat superior. However, intentional torts by an employee are generally *not* covered by respondeat superior, and the employee is not liable because an intentional tort is usually motivated by personal reasons rather than by employer needs. On the other hand, if the intentional tort is motivated in any part to serve an employer's interest or purpose, although it is not authorized or even if it is in disobedience of the employer's instructions, it is considered within the scope of employment.

An unusual form of respondeat superior involves the *borrowed servant* or *borrowed employee*. In these cases the regular employer (the *general employer*) temporarily loans or furnishes his employee to another employer (the *special employer*). The question arises as to which employer is liable under respondeat superior if the borrowed employee commits a tort while working for the special employer. Some courts hold only the borrowing employer liable since his immediate interests were being served by the borrowed employee. Many courts, however, do not automatically hold the borrowing employer liable but start from the premise the loaned employee remains in the service of the lending employer while undertaking duties for which he was loaned. In this view, liability under respondeat superior passes to the borrowing employer only when he alone exercises control over the employee and the interests of the lending employer are not being served by the employee's activities.

Principal's Criminal Liability

An agent is liable for all of his crimes, whether authorized or unauthorized, directed or undirected by the principal. If a superior tells a subordinate to commit crimes in his work, these instructions are not a defense for the employee. It is also no defense that the employer threatened to fire the employee if he did not do an act that the law regards as criminal.

A principal is not ordinarily liable for the unauthorized criminal acts of his agents. The commission of a crime usually requires intent. If the employer has not planned, directed, ordered, acquiesced, or participated in the commission of the crime, he lacks the necessary criminal intent. In other words, the principal is not vicariously or derivatively culpable for his agent's criminal acts. The principal is liable if he directed or authorized the crime, but this liability is not derivative since the principal is seen as having direct criminal responsibility as a perpetrator, solicitor, accessory, or co-conspirator, depending upon the circumstances.

There are no exceptions to the general rule that an employer or principal is not liable for the unauthorized criminal acts of his employee or agent. These exceptions fall into two categories: (1) a limited respondeat superior rule in corporate criminal matters; and (2) violations by employees of strict liability criminal statutes.

A small number of courts, but only a small number, have applied the respondeat superior rule to make a corporate employer liable for employee crimes committed within the scope of the employee's job and for the employer's benefit. See, for example, *United States v. Gibson Products Co., Inc.*, 426 F. Supp. 768 (1976). Under this view, even if the criminal acts of the employee are unauthorized or in disregard of company rules or orders, the business is responsible for the employee's crimes done while on duty that benefit the enterprise and are within the scope of his employment. This view does not apply to off-duty crimes. Since a corporation cannot be jailed and its officers cannot be imprisoned when the criminal responsibility is imputed to the corporation as a legal entity, the criminal punishment is usually a fine to be paid by the corporation.

A widely accepted exception to the general rule that an employer is not criminally responsible for the acts of his employee concerns the employee's violations of strict liability statutes that are meant to regulate the kind of business in which the employer is engaged. Strict liability crimes do not require intent for a violation. Rather, "strict adherence" of the statute is required, and any violation, intentional or unintentional, results in automatic criminal liability. The kinds of strict liability statutes under which an employer is responsible for the crimes of his employee, even if not known to the employer and in direct disobedience of his orders, include liquor sales laws, pure food laws, antitrust laws, laws regulating prices, and environmental laws. Many of these strict liability laws directed at corporations limit criminal liability to crimes committed by high-level employees. This is called the *superior agent rule*. It is also common that these strict liability laws limit corporate liability for employee crimes to acts that were within the scope of employment and for the corporation's benefit. Generally, corporation officers and directors are not criminally liable for employee on-the-job violations of strict liability criminal statutes done on the corporation's behalf but of which these officials were unaware, even though the corporation itself is liable and might be subject to criminal fines.

Agent's Tort and Criminal Liability

Agents, servants, and independent contractors are personally liable for their own torts, that is, wrongful acts that injure or damage third persons. The agent is liable whether or not the principal may also be liable and also whether or not the acts were within his scope of authority, were directed by the principal, or were done in good faith or unaware of wrongfulness. The law holds persons liable for the wrongs they themselves commit.

The liability of an agent is both joint and several. This means the third party can sue both the agent and principal (joint liability) in the same action or sue each in separate lawsuits (several liability). However, only one satisfaction is permitted. If the principal must pay, he can seek indemnification from his agent, although this is usually impractical.

A limited defense is available to an employee to escape direct liability in suits against him for fraud. If the employer fails to inform the employee of a crucial fact and the employee in good faith makes a false representation, he can use this fact as a defense. For instance, assume that John agrees to sell Mary's car for her. She tells him that the car runs perfectly but knows it has a defective transmission. If John does not know about the car's defect when he sells it, he would be liable for a false representation but not for fraud in the inducement.

A person is liable for the crimes he commits, and it is irrelevant if he was acting as an agent or to advance the interest of the principal. "Just carrying out the orders of the employer" is no defense.

15

Agency: Termination

Termination by Acts of the Parties
Termination by Operation of Law
Notice of Termination

An agency can end either because of something done by the parties or by operation of law (events or change of circumstances that are outside the control of the parties). Through an act of the parties, the agency may end by mutual agreement of principal and agent, revocation by the principal, renunciation by the agent, occurrence of the agency's purpose or a specified event, or expiration of the agency agreement. The events by which the operation of law terminates the agency include death, insanity or bankruptcy of either principal or agent, unusual change in business conditions, impossibility of performance due to loss or destruction of subject matter, subsequent illegality of the agency's object, change in business conditions, breach of agency relationship by agent or principal, or physical or legal incapacitation of the agent.

Termination by Acts of the Parties

Mutual Agreement of the Parties

The agent and principal may agree to end their relationship, even when the agency agreement originally specified the relationship would continue longer.

Occurrence of Agency Purpose or Specified Event

When the stipulated objective of the agency has been fulfilled and nothing remains to be done, the agency is automatically terminated. Similarly, the agency terminates on the occurrence of a specified event, the happening of which the parties originally agreed would end their relationship.

Expiration of Agency Agreement

The agency agreement may be its terms expire after a stated period or at a particular date. When the stated period ends or date arrives, the agency relationship automatically ends. When no duration is specified in the agency agreement, the agency continues for a reasonable time and may be terminated at the will of either the principal or the agent.

Revocation by Principal

The principal has the *power* to terminate the agency at any time, although he might not necessarily have the *right* if the agency agreement specifically provides he cannot revoke it. If the agreement provides the principal cannot revoke the agency until the occurrence of some event or for an agreed period of time, the principal lacks the right to revoke unless the agent has committed some wrong. A principal who wrongfully terminates the agency is liable for breach of contract and the agent may recover damages. Damages are the only remedy available to the agent. The law will not grant specific performance, that is, compel the principal to continue the agency relationship, even if he wrongfully terminated it.

Revocation by the principal must be clear and unequivocally expressed before the agent can pursue legal remedies. Expressions of the principal's dissatisfaction with the performance of the agent do not amount to revocation of the agent's authority. Conduct that clearly indicates an intent to revoke may constitute revocation, for example, the principal takes back property entrusted to the agent for the purpose of the agency or retains another agent to do what the original agent was authorized to do.

If the agency is not created for a specified time period, then it exists at will, and the principal can discharge the agent without liability. Similarly the principal can without liability discharge the agent when the latter is guilty of misconduct.

As a general rule agencies are not irrevocable because of the power, as opposed to the right, of a principal to revoke an agent's authority. There is one instance, however, when even the power of a principal to revoke an agency does not exist and the authority of the agent is irrevocable by the principal and that is when the principal has created an *agency coupled with an interest*. An agency coupled with an interest occurs when the agent has an *interest in the authority* or an *interest in the subject* matter.

An agency coupled with an interest exists when the agent has an interest in the authority as a result of giving or paying consideration for the right to exercise the authority of an agent. In simpler terms, the agent is more than an employee and usually is in a creditor relationship with the principal in order to make sure he (the agent) gets paid. For example, a bank, in return for a loan, is given as security the authority to collect rents due the borrower and apply the rents to the payment of the debt. The bank in effect becomes the borrower's agent with an interest in the authority given to collect rents.

An agent has an interest in the subject matter when he pays consideration for an interest in the property with which he (the agent) is dealing. For instance, an agent has an interest in the subject matter when he is authorized to sell property for the principal and is given a lien on the property as security for a debt that the principal owes the agent. The irrevocable agency, that is, an agency coupled with an interest, is not terminated by the death, insanity, or bankruptcy of the principal even though these are all events which by operation of law normally terminate an agency.

Renunciation by the Agent

Like principal, the agent has the power, but may not have the right, to terminate an agency. When the agent withdraws from or abandons the agency, he is essentially renouncing his authority to act for the principal. If the agency agreement is to continue for a specific term or until a specified event, the agent has no right to renounce or abandon the agency unless the principal is guilty of some wrong concerning the agency relationship. If the agent improperly renounces the agency, that is a breach of the contract with the principal, and the principal is entitled to recover damages he sustains from the agent. The principal is not entitled to specific performance of the agency agreement to force the agent to continue his work. When the agency is at will or gratuitous or the principal violates the agency agreement, the agent has the right, as well as the power, to renounce the agency.

Termination by Operation of Law

Death

The death of either the principal or agent ordinarily ends the authority of the agent, even if the death if unknown to the other. Thus, if an agent, not knowing the principal has died, enters into an agreement with a third party on behalf of the deceased principal, the agreement is void. This rule can cause hardship to either the agent or third party. The agent, because he lacks authority due to the death of the principal, may be liable to the third party for breach of warranty of authority. The third party cannot hold the estate of the principal liable to enforce the agreement, and the agent cannot be forced to perform the contract for the deceased principal.

Some states provide that the death of the principal does not result in revocation until the agent has received notice and does not affect third parties who deal with the agent in good faith and are unaware of the death. These statutes are generally limited to principals who are members of the armed forces. Some state statutes provide the agency may continue after the death or total incapacity of the principal provided the statutory language is used in a power of attorney creating the agent's authority.

The death of the principal does not automatically terminate an agency coupled with an interest. The banking section of the UCC also provides that the bank (the agent) can continue to exercise certain types of authority given by a customer (the principal) after the customer's death, and this includes paying and collecting checks, drafts, and notes. This particular exception only applies if the bank has no knowledge of the death of the customer. Even if a bank does know of a customer death, however, it has authority for ten days after the death to pay checks drawn by the customer unless it received a stop payment order from a party claiming an interest in the account, such as an heir of the deceased customer.

Insanity or Incompetency

The insanity of the principal or agent normally terminates the agency. If the insanity of the principal is temporary, the agent's authority may be merely suspended rather than permanently terminated. In some states the principal's incompetency, but not adjudicated incompetency, does not revoke the agent's authority to bind the principal to a third party when the third party has no knowledge of the incompetency and if an injustice can be prevented by sustaining the transaction. In some states the agency may continue after the incompetency of the principal provided that the statutory language is used in a written power of attorney. Finally, the insanity of the principal will not terminate an agency coupled with an interest.

Bankruptcy

Bankruptcy is a proceeding in federal court providing relief to financially distressed debtors. The filing of a petition in bankruptcy initiates the proceedings. The filing of bankruptcy by a principal normally terminates the agency. However, the bankruptcy of the principal will not terminate an agency coupled with an interest. The filing of bankruptcy by the agent will not terminate the agent's authority unless it impairs the agent's ability to act for the principal. For example, if the credit standing of the agent is important to the agency relationship, the bankruptcy of the agent will terminate the relationship.

Insolvency of either the principal or agent does not usually terminate the agency.

Impossibility of Performance

The loss or destruction of the specific subject matter upon which the agency depends terminates the agency as a legal entity. For instance, if the principal gives authority to the agent to sell his car and the car is destroyed, the performance of the agency is made impossible. Impossibility of performance does not include the principal breaching the exclusive authority of an agent to perform an act that the principal instead performs. For instance, the principal gives the agent exclusive authority to sell his car but then sells it himself. The agent's authority in this case is not terminated, but breached.

Loss of Qualifications

This loss involves the failure of the agent or principal to acquire or maintain a license from a governmental agency that is necessary for the conduct of the business related to the performance of the agency. For instance, if the principal hires an attorney to represent him and the attorney is disbarred, the disbarment terminates the lawyer's authority to represent the principal. In the revocation of a liquor store license, the authority of the salespersons to sell liquor at the store is terminated.

Subsequent Illegality

A change of law subsequent to the employment of the agent, which makes the agent's actions for the principal illegal or criminal, also terminates the agency relationship. For instance, the principal directs his agent to drive to Canada and purchase a truckload of apples. Soon afterward, in order to control a pest associated with the Canadian apples, the U.S. government quarantines their importation. As a result, the agency is terminated. An agency coupled with an interest is terminated by subsequent illegality.

Disloyalty of the Agent

A breach of the agency relationship occurs when the agent violates the duty of loyalty he owes the principal. The duty of loyalty is transgressed whenever the agent acquires or asserts any interest that is adverse to the principal.

Unusual Changes in Business Conditions

The agent's authority terminates when there is any change in business conditions or events that would lead a reasonable person to realize the principal would not wish the agent to act under those circumstances. The changes that occur must be unusual and must not have been contemplated by the parties when the agency was created. Such changes include changes in the affairs of the principal, in the subject matter of the agency, or in external events. For example, the principal may direct his agent to sell land at a specified price. If gold is discovered on the land, which greatly increases its value, the agent should realize the principal would not want him to go ahead and sell at the previously authorized price. A sudden change in economic and political conditions may terminate the agency, such as an outbreak of war that leads to a drastic change in the market value of the subject matter of the agency; for example, the war may place the principal and agent in the position of enemies if they are citizens of the warring countries.

Notice of Termination

In order to be relieved of liability from the acts of an agent, the principal must notify third persons with whom the agent might deal of the agency's termination if the termination is due to the acts of either the principal or agent. The principal is not liable and need not give notice to third parties when the agency is terminated by operation of law (e.g., death, insanity, or bankruptcy).

Failure of the principal to give third parties notice of termination of the agency may result in creation of an apparent authority that allows the third party to hold the principal liable for the acts of the agent. The rule applies regardless of whether termination was by the agent or the principal or whether the termination was rightful or wrongful. The principal must give *actual notice* to all creditors and customers who have actually dealt with the agent (a telephone call, a personal visit, or a letter). Actual notice is not required if the third party has learned from someone else that the agency has ended. Actual notice is effective at the time it is received.

The principal must give a lesser form of notice, called *constructive notice*, to the parties who might have known about the agency but who have not previously done business with the agent. Constructive notice is some kind of public notice, usually a newspaper announcement in the legal classified section of a newspaper circulated in the community where the agency was generally known or in an appropriate trade journal. Constructive notice is effective at the time it is properly published even though it may never be read.

If the principal does not give proper notice, he is liable on any contract the former agent makes with a third party. Where notice is actually received, the power of the agent is ended without regard to whether the proper form of notice has been given. Consequently, if proper notice is given, it is immaterial that it does not actually come to the attention of the persons to whom it is directed.

Selected Bibliography

Anderson, O. J. *Outline of Business Law: Comprehensive Volume.* rev. ed., Totowa, N.J.: Littlefield, 1975.

Brennan, Bartley A. and Kubasek, Nancy. *The Legal Environment of Business.* New York: Macmillan, 1988.

Brody, David E. *Business and its Legal Environment.* Lexington, Ma: Heath Publishing, 1986.

Catanzano, Henry R. and Whitman, Douglas. *Modern Business Law.* New York: Random House, 1984.

Christiansen, Larry A. *Business Law: A Study Outline.* Dubuque, Ia: Kendall-Hunt, 1981.

Clark, L. S. and Kinder, P. D. *Law and Business.* 2d ed., New York: McGraw-Hill, 1987.

Corley, Robert N. and Reed, O. Lee. *Fundamentals of the Legal Environment of Business.* New York: McGraw-Hill, 1986.

Delaney, Patrick R. and Gleim, Irwin N. *CPA Examination Review: Business Law.* New York: Wiley, 1986.

Fass, Peter M. and Gerrard, Barbara S. *The S Corporation Handbook.* New York: Clark Boardman, 1987.

Fisher, Bruce D. and Jennings, Marianne M. *Law for Business.* West Publishing, 1986.

Francisco, Albert K. and Smith, Albert A. *A CPA Review of Business Law: 1983–1984.* Reading, Ma: Addison-Wesley, 1984.

Getz, George. *Business Law.* 5th ed., Mission Hills, Ca: Glencoe Press, 1977.

Griffith, John R. *Legal Environment of Business.* New York: Wiley, 1984.

Henszey, Benjamin N. and Myers, Barry Lee. *Introduction to Basic Legal Principles.* 4th ed., Dubuque, Ia: Kendall-Hunt, 1986.

Lieberman, Jethro K. *Business Law and the Legal Environment.* 2d ed., San Diego, Ca: Harcourt Brace Jovanovich Inc., 1988.

Lyden, Donald P. and Reitzel, D. *Business and the Law.* New York: Wiley, 1985.

Meiners, Roger E. and Ringleb, Al H. *The Legal Environment of Business.* 2d ed., St. Paul, Mn: West Publishing, 1985.

Miller, Roger L. and Jentz, Gaylord A. *Business Law Today.* St. Paul, Mn: West Publishing, 1988.

Minars, David A. *Business Law: A Comprehensive CPA Law Review*. Dubuque, Ia: Kendall-Hunt, 1984.

Reams, Bernard D. *Law for the Businessman*. Dobbs Ferry, N.Y.: Oceana, 1974.

Rosenberg, R. Robert. *Schaum's Outline of College Business Law*. New York: McGraw-Hill, 1977.

Ross, Martin J. and Ross, Jeffrey S. *New Encyclopedia Dictionary of Business Law: With Forms*. 2d ed., Englewood Cliffs, N.J.: Prentice-Hall, 1981.

Schantz, William T. *Commercial Law for Business and Accounting Students: A Complete Business Law Text and CPA Law Review*. St. Paul, Mn: West Publishing, 1980.

Teich, Albert. *Business Law: Problems and Solutions*. Dubuque, Ia: Kendall-Hunt, 1981.

Wiesner, Donald A. and Glaskowsky, Nicholas A. *Schaum's Outline of Theory & Problems of Advanced Business Law*. New York: McGraw-Hill, 1985.

Index

About the Author

SIDNEY M. WOLF is an attorney and environmental consultant in Stowe, Vermont. He has taught on the college level, has worked as a Washington lobbyist for environmental groups, and has been a guest on PBS's McNeil/Lehrer Report and Good Morning America. His first Quorum book was *Pollution Law Handbook: A Guide to Federal Environmental Laws*.